Stonewall Jim

Also by Willie Walker Caldwell

Donald McElroy, Scotch Irishman

The Tie That Binds

STONEWALL JIM

*A Biography
of
General James A. Walker, C.S.A.*

By His Daughter

Willie Walker Caldwell

Northcross House, Publishers
Elliston • Virginia

Library of Congress Cataloging-in-Publication Data

Caldwell, Willie Walker, 1860-1946.
    Stonewall Jim : a biography of General James A. Walker,
C.S.A. / by Willie Walker Caldwell.
    p.   cm.
    Includes bibliographical references and index.
    ISBN 0-9617256-4-8 (alk. paper) — ISBN 0-9617256-5-6 (pbk. :
alk. paper)
    1. Walker, James A. (James Alexander), 1832-1901. 2.
Generals—Southern States—Biography. 3. Generals—Confederate
States of America—Biography. 4. Confederate States of America.
Army—Biography. I. Title.
E467.1.W16C34 1990
973.7'5'092—dc20
[B]   90-36114
                                                               CIP

Cover by Robert Turner, Jr.

The portrait of James A. Walker featured in the front jacket
illustration was produced from Nineteenth Century photographs.

This book is printed on alkaline paper for durability
Manufactured in the United States of America

Table of Contents

Introduction

By M. Caldwell Butler

My grandmother, Willie Brown Walker Caldwell, the author of this book, died in 1946 at the age of eighty-six. I was twenty at the time and had the opportunity to know her well and appreciate her. Born in 1860, an infant in the Civil War, a child of Reconstruction and a young lady in the time when Virginia began to find itself again, she was an interesting and intelligent person. Her legacies were many, but the greatest was this biography.

The subject is her father, James Alexander Walker, Brigadier General, Army of the Confederate States of America. Although the manuscript is more than fifty years old and has been made available to numerous historians, it is now published for the first time. It is a fascinating, well-told story. I recently read it for the third and fourth time, and each time I enjoy it more.

General Walker was a tall, large person, physically impressive, frequently described as a superior horsemen. All reports we have indicate that he was genial and outgoing and I suspect quite charming. He had a reputation as quite a disciplinarian on the job but quite friendly when not on the job. My mother, who was about eight years old when he died, remembered him for his many playful times with her and the other grandchildren on the lawn in Wytheville, Virginia.

Few on either side saw more combat in the Civil War than Walker. He was a Confederate officer of the story-book tradition: bold, reckless, romantic, idealistic, emotional, at times foolhardy. He fought from the war's early battles around Harpers Ferry to the surrender at Appomattox, and he was in the thick of most of it. After the war, he served in the Virginia House of Delegates in 1871 and 1872 and was elected Lieutenant Governor of Virginia in 1877 as a Democrat. He was active as a Funder in the famous debate between the Funders and the Readjusters. He was elected to the United States Congress as a Republican from 1895 to 1899, two terms. And he died in 1901, still a Republican.

He had a sharp tongue and a short fuse (traits which, fortunately, have been bred out of succeeding generations). Dr. James I. Robertson in his history of the Fourth Virginia Infantry reports that when the Fourth Virginia was making its way back across the Potomac in August of 1862 they encountered General Walker drunk in the road.

If he had been a private, he would have him put in the guardhouse, so the report goes.

And further, Dr. Robertson says:

Walker may have had an overfondness for whiskey but he also went to extraordinary lengths to see to the welfare of his men. One rainy evening during the long encampment in Central Virginia, Walker received orders to bivouac his men in the open. The Brigadier saw no reason to subject his troops to the hardships and dangers of the elements; therefore he sent an order to the Quartermaster of the Wagons who was a mile away with directions to obtain sufficient tents and rations. His well-fed men slept in comfort that night. The next morning Walker doused himself with water, appeared before his superior and moaned, "Well, General, we had a rough time in the rain last night."

Another person reported that when he encountered General Walker in his post-war period of success, he enjoyed a mint julep before breakfast. This gives us some insight into the man: he lived life to the fullest, and he enjoyed it.

Willie Brown Walker Caldwell was an adoring daughter writing of a man who was not only her father but also her hero and her best friend. She makes free use of the license granted to one in that position. Yet in some respects she does not do him justice: later historians have revealed General Walker as perhaps more valiant, more colorful—although no more important—than she knew. She relates much, but by no means all, of his military career. There are gaps in her story which, if filled in, would add to Walker's stature.

Yet her story is at times charming, perceptive, original. Walker's description of First Manassas in a speech made many years later, which she quotes verbatim, is both informative and moving. It is informative because he tells of the disorganization in both armies, the difficulty he had in finding his own general, and the confusion that must be characteristic of all new armies. And it is moving as he tells of finding the battlefield where the Stonewall Brigade had earned its name the day before and viewing the bodies of so many of his former comrades in the Pulaski Guards which he had organized and trained a short time before.

She covers great battles with particular attention to her father's involvement, such as Chancellorsville where, in my grandmother's phrase "the true and tender Jackson" on his death bed said "Give the Stonewall to James A. Walker." She cites official recommendations for his promotion to Brigadier General. But her quoting his speech at the time was most revealing to me in showing the eloquence with which Walker addressed his former command, the Thirteenth Virginia Regiment, when it became clear that he was to be promoted to command the Brigade. She quotes in full his impressive description of the Bloody Angle in the Wilderness Campaign, when he received his only wound in the war, a wound that removed him from battle for several months, and when the Stonewall Brigade was virtually annihilated.

She also tells of Walker's life after Appomattox, where, at the age of thirty-two, with one good arm, a good riding horse, a team of mules, a wagon, and an old nag he was able to trade for all the tobacco he could load in the wagon, he set out for his home in Newbern, Virginia. Thus begins an entirely different kind of story, but one no less interesting.

My grandmother, then a child, describes the resumption of his law practice, which flourished; his nomination for Lieutenant Governor in 1870 (he withdrew); his association with General William Mahone in developing the Atlantic, Mississippi and Ohio Railroad (which eventually became the Norfolk and Western/Norfolk Southern); his commitment to the education of his children; and his involvement in the big political issue of the day between the Readjusters and the Funders over the payment of Virginia's forty-five million dollar debt. General Walker was aligned with the Funders because, we are told, that he felt an honest debt must be paid; but the Readjusters eventually won for which I think we must be grateful.

She describes the election of 1877 when her father was elected Lieutenant Governor. She reports that in 1881 he declined the nomination for Governor with the understanding that he would be nominated for Attorney General. When a coalition of opponents thwarted that nomination, it marked the beginning of his disillusionment with party politics and the Democratic party.

She describes family life in Wytheville, Virginia, where the Walkers moved in 1879, in a large house that is still there. She tells how three of her four brothers came down with typhoid, and two died of it, in a three month period. With difficulty, she tells how General Walker had a fist fight in the courtroom at Newbern with a younger lawyer, not a very wise endeavor for a man with only one good arm, and suffered blows that adversely affected his health from then on.

After 1881, it was Walker's view that the future of Virginia lay in industrial development and in correcting the state's backwardness along educational, civic and cultural lines. He also felt that the Democratic party which now controlled the state was clearly going in the opposite direction, and they were getting progressively stronger. When Cleveland was elected President for the first time, Virginia sent a solid Democratic delegation to the Congress as usual and that was followed by pretty much the demise of the Republican Party. By the middle of the 1880's it was really just a one-party system in Virginia, which dominated politics and enacted legislation largely controlling the electoral process.

The Readjuster Party, with which Walker had aligned himself, eventually became the Republican Party in Virginia. This Party nominated him for Congress in 1894, and, in a shocking surprise to the Democrats, he won election. He won again in 1896, but the Democratic candidate defeated him in 1898. It was the feeling of the Republicans that there were glaring frauds in the election, and Walker chose to contest it. In the taking of depositions, Walker was involved in a gunfight in which he was shot in the chest. Although he survived, for all practical purposes the injury led to his death.

In his history titled *The Stonewall Brigade,* Dr. Robertson reported that, by the end of the first month after Walker assumed command of that famous unit, the men of the Brigade affectionately called him "Stonewall Jim." Dr. Robertson, himself, refers to "Stonewall Jim" on more than one occasion in his fine volume. We have used that term in the name of this book, not only because it connotes the command he always cherished more than any other, but also because it calls attention to the fascinating relationship between Walker and Jackson, so well described in this book, from

Walker's student days at VMI until Jackson's death, and even afterward.

Moreover, it is interesting to note that the designation "Stonewall Brigade" was not given to that body of men until after Chancellorsville in May, 1863, when General Walker took over. Prior to that, it had always been known as the brigade of the general who commanded it. Thus, for a very short time, it was known as Walker's Brigade. But when the Secretary of War designated it the Stonewall Brigade, General Walker was its commander. So if you want to be accurate about this thing, General Walker was not only the last commander of the Stonewall Brigade, he was the only commander of the brigade officially called Stonewall Brigade. All the more reason to name this book *Stonewall Jim*.

The title my grandmother gave the book was *More Than Conquerors*, certainly a fitting theme which she develops in her own Introductory.

My grandmother relates her father's story in language that I consider charming, a style that, in itself, helps to reflect how she and her generation and her father's generation thought and lived. Her book is not a comprehensive description of the events in which her father played such an important part, nor even the definitive biography of her father. Historians will note that her attention to bibliographic attribution of the sources she has used leaves something to be desired. But her qualifications to write this book, beyond the fact that my grandmother was an excellent writer and a successful author and novelist, lie in the fact that, above all else, she had a profound love and knowledge, built over her entire lifetime, of her subject.

(Caldwell Butler is a former member of the U.S. House of Representatives.)

Author's Introductory

During the last ten years of his life General Walker planned to write his memoirs of the Civil War in order to pay tribute to the gallantry of the two famous units he commanded. To this end he made notes on the page margins of the many volumes of Civil War history he collected and read, and also accumulated some original material. After his death I added to this manuscript accounts of campaigns and battles, letters and stories of old comrades, including newspaper clippings, my own collection of his speeches, and information concerning his youth, his legal business, his political and his military career.

While waiting for a favorable opportunity to put this material together, World War I overtook us, and there was no interest to spare for past events while history was making itself so stupendously before our eyes.

The recent revival of interest in biography, the broader understanding in both the South and the North, of the causes and results of the War between the States, have led me to think that the time has come for the story I have wished to write, based on the material we have pieced together.

Especially have I felt that this sketch should be written because of the confirmation by recent political events of those convictions which molded the last decade of my subject's life and for which it was a sacrifice.

James Alexander Walker qualifies as a worthy subject for biography by sixty years of undaunted struggle for the things he believed in and for his gallant revolt against the things he could not endorse. His whole life was a struggle, a continuous fight against odds. And though in every *great* fight of his life, he lost, he never recognized defeat nor knew malice, and always he bore about him the manner of a conqueror—of one who has and will yet again overcome.

His first revolt was against the tyrannical authority of the old fashioned school teacher, whose methods Dickens has made familiar to us; his second was against what he regarded as an imputation of his honor and an injustice in the classroom by a stern professor; his third was with his state, in support of the theory of secession, and afterward against the policy of reprisal adopted by her conquerors. He took issue with the growing sentiment against forcible readjustment of his state's debt and the subsequent surrender and compromise which it caused. Finally, he had the supreme courage to espouse the policies of the Republican Party in a partisan, solid South, because he had come to believe in those policies which were devised for the best interests of an industrially developing section. It was to his political convictions that the charmed life he bore through four years of the bloodiest war in the history of the United States paid forfeit.

James Alexander Walker led a seemingly charmed life on the battlefield. He was in the thick of the conflict from Harpers Ferry, in May, 1861, to Appomattox in April, 1865. As an officer in the Army of Northern Virginia, which never stopped fighting for four years—save for brief intervals when weather compelled its inaction—he was the leader of two of the hardest fighting units: the Thirteenth Virginia Regiment and the Stonewall Brigade. My research leads me to believe that probably, with the single exception of Longstreet, he took part in more battles and skirmishes than any other officer in Lee's army.

He was in the front line when Jackson flashed his sword at Falling Waters, and he was still fighting at Sayler's Creek protecting the retreating army when the flag of surrender was raised by Lee's order at Appomattox. He led troops in the fierce battles of Front Royal, Winchester, Kernstown, Cross Keys, Port Republic, Gaines Mill, Malvern Hill, First Cold Harbor, Cedar Run, Second Bull Run, Slaughter's Mountain, Ox Hill, Harpers Ferry, Antietam, Fredericksburg, Second Winchester, Gettysburg, Payne's Farm, Mine Run, Wilderness, Spottsylvania Court House, Petersburg, Fort Stedman and Sayler's Creek. Hardly any of these meant a single engagement, for they usually covered from two to ten days fighting with several skirmishes leading up to a final battle, with others following it, either in pursuit or in retreat. General Walker was once asked if he could count up the number of more or less bloody encounters with the enemy he could recall during his four years of war. He took a pencil and a piece of paper and announced the total as fifty-six. "There are doubtless others I can't recall just now," he added.

He was wounded only once with a shattered elbow joint, which kept him out of active service during a part of the summer of '64. Until then he had seemed to be bullet proof, and his men declared among themselves that the bullet had not been molded which could harm "Big Jim Walker."

It is not primarily because of his honorable war record, however, that his story seems worth the telling. In no sense have I attempted to write a history of the Civil War, nor even an account of the campaigns of the Army of Northern Virginia. Rather, I wish to preserve his story because I believe the history of our country would be poorer did not some one preserve the spirit of such a man and the atmosphere of the times which produced him. For General Walker's character was outstanding in its qualities of honesty, courage, and loyalty to conviction. Circumstances were never adverse enough to daunt him, nor were all the machinations of his enemies able to conquer his spirit.

The men of his period, especially in the South, were a rare breed, compounded of pioneer traits and colonial tradition, who blended democratic principles with aristocratic tastes into a mixture of easy social standards with high principles and an exaggerated sense of honor. In politics their loyalty was first to their states, and second to the United States. They persuaded themselves that it was possible to have an effective federal union while yet reserving to the states all rights of state government and state contracts, including the right to secede.

It is with the hope of preserving the characteristics which marked the southern men of this time—men different, delightful, forever gone—that I set myself the task of compiling a biography of one who I believe was a fair example of the best type of his age. This lawyer, soldier, statesman, gentleman; this virile, magnetic personality who worked, fought, loved and laughed so spontaneously during this period was the idol of my childhood, the hero of my girlhood, the pride and inspiration of my young womanhood. He was the most courageous, the keenest minded, the most magnetic person I have known.

Of all the characteristics of this man, courage was, I think, the most dominant, the one which had most to do with shaping his life. His was not ordinary physical courage or mere bravery, but rather that rarer quality which combined mental, moral and physical courage, which does not stop to count the cost of following convictions and which lives without acknowledgement of fear. I have often thought that my father was born without the sense of fear, that he never knew it, hence was courageous with that same spontaneity which one recognized in all he did.

James Alexander Walker, Brigadier General, C.S.A., died unconquered and undismayed, leaving a memory which is yet green in the hearts of many who knew him in their childhood or youth, and who still speak of him as one who won them by his personality and inspired them by his ideals.

He was the product of an age which has passed, an age in many respects as striking in its characteristics as he was. If this introduction to the life story of General Walker should induce some to read further to become acquainted with the man and his times, and through that acquaintance be led to a better understanding of those events which finally cemented this Union of States and made possible our present nation, I shall feel that I have done well to complete a long deferred task.

ONE

The Math Professor

There was little love lost between the stern professor of higher mathematics and the proud, sensitive cadet at the Virginia Military Institute.

James A. Walker, the cadet, a tall, erect, graceful youth, six feet in his stockings—proud of the fact that he could span his waist with his two hands when buttoned up in his military jacket—was high spirited, quick tempered. He evinced already an almost super-sensitive notion of honor and an inability to reckon consequences when he felt that honor impeached. It was a trait which now, on a fine spring day of 1852, and more than once afterwards, led him into the commission of acts which might have been called foolhardy.

The professor was Major T. J. Jackson, who had come to the Institute two years earlier to fill the chairs of Mathematics, Experimental Philosophy and Artillery Tactics.

Walker, a senior, standing well in his classes and an officer in his company, had been a cadet of the Second Class when Jackson had reported for duty. "Vividly do I recall his personal appearance at that time," Walker said in later years. "There was nothing of the 'preux chevalier' in his address, his manner or his bearing." He described Jackson as "tall, ungainly, with large feet thrust into heavy boots, too large by two sizes; solemn visaged, taciturn, matter of fact, dyspeptic, irritable, with marked peculiarities of voice, of gait and of manner."

Jackson had graduated at West Point in 1846, just in time to see service in the war with Mexico. As a lieutenant of artillery, he won commendation for gallant conduct at Carubusco and for his bravery at Chapultepec received the brevet rank of Major.

His students asked about it: "Why didn't you run, Major, when your command was so badly cut to pieces at Chapultepec?"

Jackson's answer gave the key to his character: "I was not ordered to do so," he said. "If I had been ordered to run, I should have done so."

Thus does Walker record the impression the new professor made upon the cadet corps, their attitude toward him, and Jackson's way of meeting that attitude. Other accounts of Jackson as a professor at V.M.I. confirm it. For this military genius, this man of stainless character and exalted Christian faith, was not a success as a teacher of youths.

The Virginia Military Institute, then less than fifteen years old, had proved a useful agency in developing a vigorous type of young manhood in the South. No school had finer traditions of honor and courage and few have excelled it in thoroughness of instruction in the courses given. The curriculum, though strictly limited, was thorough in the rudiments of English, Latin and mathematics. Discipline was unsurpassed, and in military training it ranked next to West Point. Duty was held paramount, and the unquestioned obedience of youth to authority was inculcated as a basic principle of life.

Nor did the cadets spare each other. Severe demands were made by third and fourth classmen on the fortitude of the "plebes," it being the privilege of each third classman to inflict on each plebe, if he chose, the rite of military hazing known as "buckin'". In addition, the unfortunate plebes were expected to be the humble, swift "fags" of the two upper classes. The West Point plan prevailed, of only one furlough during the four years, coming at the end of the second year. The other two summers were spent in camp.

When James A. Walker went to the Institute, the second class, after returning from their furlough, passed it around among themselves that it was well to let Plebe Walker alone. Perhaps it was gratitude for his own escape which prompted Walker's merciful course toward future plebes, involving him in many a fisticuff in their defense against such bullies as were inclined to undue harshness.

When Jackson came to the institute, Walker later told about the new professor from his student vantage point:

Jackson's peculiarities were seized upon by the rollicking cadets whom he was to instruct and command, and, like boys the world over, they at once proceeded to guy and torment the new teacher in every way in their power and to make him the

subject of innumerable practical jokes. In his absence, carica-
tures of him were drawn upon the blackboards of the classroom, in which his body was swallowed up in his boots or in a
stiff military collar and stock. From behind buildings and
around corners he was saluted with cries and cat-calls and
student wit, which he never deigned to notice by so much as
even raising his eyes from the ground whereon they were kept
at the regulation distance of fifteen paces in front, or by changing his gait as he marched on with the unfaltering step of a
soldier on dress parade.

Finding that taunts could not move him or cause him to
turn aside, his tormentors resorted to more active measures
and from the tall towers of the Academy dropped stones and
brickbats in his pathway, one coming so near as to barely miss
his head. Even this could not startle him or so much as cause
him to raise his eyes or change his step. After a time the cadets
came to understand him and to appreciate his character for
courage and justice, and to respect and love him for his kindly
heart and noble soul.

Such was the situation when the incident occurred which
deprived the youth of his diploma and planted a lasting regret, as
was afterwards shown, in the mind of the older man.

A class in trigonometry was on. It was a subject Walker liked,
in which he stood high, and prided himself on his proficiency.
Jackson sent Walker to the board and gave him a difficult problem
from the review lesson to demonstrate. The cadet was jubilant, for
it happened to be a problem he had struggled with and solved in
preparing his lesson. With something of a flourish, Walker stated
and quickly solved it.

Professor Jackson dictated another problem or so to the other
members of the class, then turned back to Walker, glanced at the
board and said: "Correct, sir. Rub it out."

Walker complied.

As he was about to take his seat, Major Jackson commanded,
"Captain Walker, I wish you to restate that problem and demonstrate it again."

"May I ask why, sir? I understood you to say it was correct."

"I did, Captain Walker, but I wish you to do it again," with
increasing sternness from the professor.

"Not until you tell me why, sir," came Walker's hot response.

"Consider yourself under arrest," said Major Jackson. Stepping to the door, he called the officer of the day and ordered him to march Captain Walker to the guard house.

There, Walker fumed and stormed, insisting that he had been grossly insulted before the class and that he meant to have satisfaction. At once he wrote a challenge to Major Jackson demanding "the satisfaction due a gentleman for an unprovoked insult." He contrived through a friendly guard to have it put into Jackson's hands.

The only reply the rash cadet received was an order of expulsion, the only satisfaction a premature journey home, where his father's disappointment first made him regret his conduct.

Years later, when Jackson had left immortal fame on earth to enter, as he confidently believed, upon immortal joys in Heaven, and when the foolhardy cadet had won renown as soldier and officer, fellow professors of Jackson told Walker that his challenge had by no means been received with the scorn and contempt he supposed. Instead, Major Jackson had at first insisted upon accepting it.

"If the young man feels that I insulted him, gentlemen," said Jackson earnestly, "he has a right to demand satisfaction, and I do not see how I can refuse it to him."

With considerable difficulty they persuaded him that it would never do to establish such a precedent, and gained his reluctant consent to the decree of expulsion.

A few weeks later, Walker would have graduated third in his class. It is characteristic that he did not feel himself disgraced. Instead, a few weeks after his return home, he got together a party of young people—among them the girl he later married—and conducted them to "the Finals." Received warmly by the corps as something of a hero, he danced gaily at the ball in his new suit of "cits," disgruntled but undismayed by the loss of his diploma.

Years later, the diploma was sent him by gracious act of the board, at Jackson's request, during the Valley Campaign. Walker recognized the deed as a tribute to his military record and not as an acknowledgment that he had been in the right or that his punishment had been unduly severe. For by that time he had come to realize that discipline is the foundation of accomplishment and that in military matters any act of disobedience is insubordination.

TWO

Growing Up

Born August 21, 1832, on his father's farm in Augusta County, Virginia, near the post office of Mt. Meridian, James Walker played, tramped to school and hunted as a boy over the expanding meadows bordering the middle branch of the Shenandoah River. It was where later he marched and fought as Colonel of the Thirteenth Virginia Infantry in Stonewall Jackson's brilliant Valley Campaign.

Among the earliest of the Scotch-Irish migrating to the Valley of Virginia had come Walker's pioneer ancestor, John Walker of Wigton, Scotland. The Walkers had gone, with others, first to Londonderry, Ireland, at the earnest solicitation of King James of England "to help establish a law abiding Protestant colony in the heart of brawling Ireland." But like others of their blood, they found neither the people nor the country to their liking. To them, the Irish seemed shiftless, idolatrous, and hardened to insurrection and pillage. Nor did England's policy toward her Protestant colony in Ireland please them any better. English laws discriminated against Irish manufacture and trade, her people looked down on their neighbors across the channel and denied them civil liberty. Moreover, Presbyterian dissenters were treated with a degree of harshness only less severe than the cruel statutes England enforced against Roman Catholics.

Thus in 1730 this sturdy Wigtonite John Walker brought his wife and seven children to free America with its large frontiers and limitless possibilities. They probably landed at Philadelphia. Most of the Scotch who came to America by way of Ireland were graziers and farmers by inheritance and preference. These immigrants who formed communities and became a unique people with characteristics all their own were called Scotch-Irish.

Reports of rich valleys, yet unclaimed by settlers farther south in the more genial climate of Virginia, wooed John to further

journeying. With family and household goods and the nucleus for
future flocks and herds, he made a patriarchal march up the Valley
of the Shenandoah, pitching his tent near a creek in a wooded vale
in what is now Rockbridge County, Virginia, and was then Augusta
County. He and his neighbors jocularly called their community "the
Creek Nation." The settlements, and the stream along which they
settled, took the name of "Walker's Creek."

John of Wigton had grandchildren by the score, most of whom
went west from time to time to take up lands in Kentucky,
Tennessee, Missouri, Indiana or Michigan. From one of those who
remained in Virginia descended the subject of this biography.
Poorly kept family records, together with the loss of an old family
Bible, carried west, make it impossible to trace now the exact
number or names of the grandsons of the first John, or to say
whether the John born August 31, 1769, was a grandson or a great
grandson of John the first. Legend has it that the father of this
second John was named James, son of John of Wigton, and that
James claimed twenty-one sons and daughters.

At any rate, the second John settled in Augusta County,
married Sarah Connely in 1791 and had eleven sons and daughters.
Second among the eleven was Alexander Walker, born October 30,
1793. Alexander married Hannah Hinton, and they had seven
children. James Alexander Walker, later General James A. Walker,
was the fifth of those seven.

Presbyterian in creed, the "Creek Nation" was composed of God-
fearing folk of thrifty habits and simple tastes. Inured to the
dangers of the pioneers of the border lands, they cleared and tilled
their fields industriously, and bent all their spare energies to the
building up of school and church. They trained their sons and
daughters to revere both, and to measure life by the claims of duty
rather than by the impulses of nature. Further migrations for their
children were recognized as destiny. Indian massacre was a daily
menace. Yet they allowed no fears to deter them from whatever risk
the call of the hour imposed. Neither did they sit down to useless
repining after a blow which might have terrified the strongest. By
habit, they "trusted God and took courage."

The Walkers and their neighbors attended the "Old Stone
Church," which they completed about the year 1748. Men, women
and children labored at constructing it, transporting sand, timber
and stone from Middle River on horseback, building it to serve the
double purpose of church and fortress in time of Indian raid. It was

a labor of love as well as of necessity; to this day its walls bear testimony to the thoroughness of its framers.

The first pastor of the Old Stone Church was the Reverend John Craig, typically Scotch-Irish, pioneer and Presbyterian pastor of unique personality and great force. He did valiant service, not alone as preacher but as Indian fighter and defender of the church fort. As late as the childhood of James A. Walker the Stone Church congregation retained pioneer characteristics. It assembled its congregation from a radius of fifteen miles, four fifths of it on horseback. Mothers carried infants on their laps, sometimes with another child on a pannier behind. Even grown daughters often rode on panniers behind their parents, or wives behind their husbands. Youths on curvetting colts, hardly more than bridle wise, helped to break them in to saddle and bridle. The ride to and from church seemed to the youngsters the redeeming feature of the long day.

I have heard my father tell with evident pleasure of the boys hurrying on in front of their elders, pretending to be unable to hold in their colts, and running a succession of glorious neck and neck races all the way home. When these boys were somewhat older the day's excitement came in a scramble to the stiles after service in pursuit of the most popular girls—followed by a race after some coquettish one, "riding off" from her would-be-escort.

The tedium of an all-day service for restless children made a lasting impression on the boy. General Walker in later years said that he got such an overdose of church-going in childhood as never to have relished that form of spiritual nourishment in maturer years. Yet he spoke of the Sabbath of his childhood with tender humor, for the remembrance of the old church and his pious parents was dear to him. He also revered deeply the religious faith of his forefathers. The family, he related, rose by sun-up on Sunday mornings, ate a simple breakfast, and, while the men saw that the stock was fed and watered and the horses saddled, the women set the house in order and packed the lunch, which they had prepared on Saturday. They then locked up the house, admonished the slaves to remember the Sabbath, mounted the waiting animals and set off for Sunday School.

They recited catechism, repeated memorized psalms, listened to long prayers and joined in solemn hymns of nine and ten verses. Then came a brief recess, when younger members of the congregation were allowed to walk about in the church grove for a quarter of an hour. The boys might hide behind a big tree to have a game of marbles or swap jack knives. The girls, careful of their Sunday clothes, strolled demurely, gossiping in imitation of their elders and giggling about everything and nothing as girls of all the ages have done.

When the deep bell tone rang out, the congregation reassembled for the morning service, with a sermon that frequently ascended in close logical sequence to its "sixteenthly" conclusion. Again, a recess followed, for an hour this time, with luncheon under the trees, or in bad weather in the "session house," where fretful babies were taken by their mothers and bad boys might be led for summary chastisement.

By two o'clock all assembled again in the church to hear the afternoon sermon, not so long as the morning version. The sun was low in the western sky when they finally reached home, having spent the entire day "in prayer and praise, in hearing and reading God's word," as the shorter catechism commanded.

Next to the influence of the church in the homes of the Scotch-Irish pioneers was the influence of the school. Piety and learning first, thrift and the joy of life after them; this was their creed and practice. If anything must be left out, it was "the joy of life," for the first two were indispensable. If one served his God and did his duty to his generation he could manage to dispense with early happiness and look to the joys of Heaven for his reward. Thinking thus, and living up to their belief as faithfully as mortal nature permits, the Scotch-Irish became a serious minded, almost stern people. They were the Puritans of the middle and southern states.

They relied on the "old field school" for the learning they considered so essential for their girls and boys, especially for their boys. Even for those youths who might later go on to colleges and academies, "the old field school" must lay the foundation. Pioneer schools kept alive the traditions of learning and gave the youth of the Valley of Virginia a fair groundwork of education. Still, they were poor substitutes for good schools. Often, they were under the sole dominance of a master, who not infrequently was a petty tyrant. Teaching was "out of the book;" the method: memorizing and reciting by rote, with frequent birchings to assist the process. The Scotch schoolmaster of the period was often a good match for his English counterpart, immortalized to lasting dishonor by such Dickens' characters as Squeers in *Nicholas Nickleby*.

School lasted ten full months a year, and each daily session was nine hours long, with an hour allowed for recess. The children sat on hard benches, too high for the younger children to rest their feet on the floor, and learned by heart long "rules" they could not understand from such involved grammars as "Murray's" and complicated arithmetics as "Greenleaf's." Each time the schoolmaster spoke, they looked up in fear of sharp reprimand or birching, hardly daring to steal a glimpse of waving trees and blue sky through the small high windows or open door.

Walker disliked one of the teacher-tyrants so much that he took a solemn oath that as soon as he was big enough he would repay with interest at least one of the beatings he endured. He later declared it was a source of lasting regret that he was unable to keep that vow because the teacher died before Walker was big enough to execute it.

Older boys often played truant, and for "Jimmie," as he was known then, it was the defiant practice. On the way to school, a walk of two or three miles, he gave the other children of the household the slip and made a bee line for the forest. There he found freedom, peace, delight; instead of close air were sweet woodland odors; instead of the schoolmaster's harsh tones were carolling of birds and chattering of squirrels. In late summer he found berries and nuts. In spring he found May apples, honeysuckle balls and strawberries; even in winter he found hidden stores of nuts.

His habit of truancy offended his teachers. If he did it too often, some one was sent back home to inform on the deserter. Then his father looked stern, called the slave Adam from the quarters, and commanded him to find Jimmie and bring him home. The superannuated slave whistled "Old Digger," a toothless, ancient hound, to his side and put him on the scent. All day Digger might be heard yelping wheezily on his track, the cracked voice of Adam urging him on. At the sound, the fleet-footed Jimmie would break into a run, distance his pursuers, turn on his tracks to baffle them, then go to playing till the scent was hot again. Toward evening, the fugitive would be caught, and the three would go home wearily and peacefully together. Although he might get a whipping, it was so much milder than the several he likely would have gotten that day at school that always he counted himself the gainer by the day's adventure.

THREE

Newbern

Walker was twenty years old when the quarrel with Jackson brought his education at the Virginia Military Institute to an end. Home again in Augusta County, having received all the educational advantages his father felt able to give him, he found it incumbent to devise some means of earning a livelihood.

The first thing which presented itself was a vacancy for a teacher in the neighborhood "pay school." Walker canvassed the community, secured between twenty and thirty pupils, and "took up" school in the fall of 1852.

Among his pupils were two or three young women of eighteen or nineteen and several young men as old as he was and larger physically. Now realizing the necessity for strict discipline, Walker emulated his former professor of mathematics. And just as it had done for Jackson, strictness brought on rebellion against the teacher from one student; when Walker chastised the pupil a fight occurred, with victory for the teacher and complete submission of the pupil. After that, things went smoothly.

Before the session closed, however, Walker had decided that he did not wish to make teaching his profession.

That summer, he joined an engineering corps going out from the valley to locate the Covington and Ohio, later the Chesapeake and Ohio, Railroad. He spent about eighteen months in the wilderness of what is now West Virginia and Kentucky along the Big Sandy River, in the rough, monotonous life of an engineer's camp. The experience was sufficient to eliminate another calling from his list, even though he made good at it. Those months of open air and active life, however, completed the building up of a vigorous physical manhood, with great powers of endurance. It also confirmed the habit of doing his immediate task to the best of his ability—however little to his liking it might be.

Walker returned home when the corps was disbanded, its work finished, with his mind made up to study law.

He obtained permission to read in the office of John B. Baldwin (afterwards Judge Baldwin) of Staunton, applying himself diligently for more than a year, with a weekly quiz under Mr. Baldwin. In the fall of 1855 he matriculated in the law class at the University of Virginia, having the special advantage of the instruction of the learned jurist John B. Minor. During the single session he spent there, he enjoyed the study of law as much as he later enjoyed the practice of law, and he realized joyfully that at last he had found his true vocation.

He was duly licensed to practice in the summer of 1856. That fall he settled in Newbern, the county seat of Pulaski County. It was a section that many confidently believed would become the richest and most populous part of the Old Dominion. A railroad was being built through this fertile blue grass region of the state, developing a new potential for the territory and its resources. No one foresaw the cataclysm of Civil War which would set back the clock of progress many years and turn the tide of prosperity in other directions.

Newbern was a village of about two hundred inhabitants, situated two and a half miles from the railway station at Dublin. The old macadam road that traversed the state from east to west was its main street. In later years, it was to become almost a deserted village. In 1893, the court house burned. The citizens of the county voted to build the new court house at the growing town of Pulaski, more conveniently located on the railway. Later the highway was routed through Pulaski. Many of Newbern's citizens followed the paths of progress leading away from the old town. Its streets have now disappeared; other fires have wrought further destruction. No ambitious young lawyer of later years would think of settling in the village of Newbern, but in 1856 it seemed a place of promise, a town with a future, and young Walker began his career there with high hopes.

Genial in temperament, of strong social proclivities, adaptable, witty, eloquent, young Walker made his way rapidly in the confidence and affection of the community and in his profession. He soon knew everybody in the village. He became, too, a favorite with the substantial farmers from the Hiwassi, Back Creek, Possum Hollow and Drapers Valley neighborhoods, who did their trading and "lawing" in Newbern.

At the end of two years, Walker felt he could afford to marry the girl to whom he had been engaged since the V.M.I. finals—when he had danced with her in "cits" rather than a first classman's resplendent uniform with a captain's stripes. In November of 1858 he was married to Sarah Ann Poage, youngest child of Major William Poage of Augusta County and his second wife Margaret Allen. They were married in the Old Stone Church in which both had often attended all day services, when young Walker admitted he used to divert himself from the tedium of the sermon by admiring the soft, rounded neck and pretty ears of Sarah Ann Poage.

FOUR

Civil War

Clouds of civil war, charged with sectional misunderstanding and shot with the forked lightning of mutual recrimination, hung over the United States during the summer and fall of 1860. So vociferous were the fanatic and the agitator that the warnings of wise men were unheard amid the clamor; until even those, like Abraham Lincoln and Robert E. Lee, who would have given an arm to preserve the union, came to realize that war was inevitable; that the sword alone could settle the point at issue and clear away all obstacles to a completed union—if indeed union were possible among so many states with such divergent views and interests.

Walker welcomed war as far as personal inclination went. But in wife and baby—for he and Sarah had become parents—he had given hostages to peace. He had just been elected Commonwealth's Attorney for Pulaski County. Moreover, his reading in his favorite subject, history, led him to know that civil wars are always the bitterest, the most stubbornly fought, and the most disastrous. He faced the future with serious apprehension.

Though his ancestors were Federalists and Whigs, he had been educated politically in the school of Jeffersonian democracy and was therefore strongly imbued with the doctrine of states' rights. He saw that Virginia would feel in honor bound to follow her sister states of the South should they secede from the Union. It was apparent that South Carolina and Georgia were determined on that course. War must come. It was the part of common sense to be prepared.

More assiduously than ever he began to train the militia company of which he was captain. He had organized it some months previous; it had selected the name "Pulaski Guards," elected Walker its captain and been duly commissioned by Governor

Letcher. Regularly each week the company practiced drill by the strict code and rules of the Virginia Military Institute.

In a few months the company presented a soldierly appearance and could execute a few simple maneuvers. There was no toleration shown the shirk; no slouching was permitted; these volunteers were made to understand that they were organized on military principles, for the purpose of learning to be soldiers. No act of mildest insubordination was overlooked.

One volunteer who attempted a minor act of insubordination was so severely reprimanded that the incident rankled. Next day he met Walker when both were off duty and expressed his opinion of his captain's supposed harshness in insulting terms. Captain Walker's answer was uncompromising: he declared his determination to have discipline in his company while a man belonged to it. The offended private grew still angrier and challenged Walker to a fight. Walker announced himself ready then and there, chose fists for weapons and flung off his coat. The encounter was fierce and somewhat prolonged, but Walker emerged victor, with many bruises and a black eye, his antagonist being even worse disfigured. When the challenger declared himself satisfied, Captain Walker offered to shake hands, the offer was accepted, and one trained soldier was ready to lay the foundation of the later efficiency and loyalty of the Pulaski Guards.

Immediately on the passage of the Act of Secession by the Virginia Assembly in April of 1861, Governor Letcher called for troops. The Pulaski Guards was one of the first companies to respond. With his recruits at his back, Captain Walker hastened to Richmond, was put into quarters at the old fair grounds, and assigned to the Fourth Virginia Infantry under Major James T. L. Preston [brother-in-law of T. J. Jackson]. Here he drilled his men still more indefatigably. He was called on to whip other companies into shape, his military training making him especially serviceable in mobilizing raw recruits.

The Virginia troops, including the Pulaski Guards, were soon ordered to Harpers Ferry to check the anticipated Federal advance from that direction and to destroy such stores of ammunition and guns as were there. At Harpers Ferry, Walker found that his former mathematics professor, T. J. Jackson, early in May had been made colonel and put in command of the post. General Joseph E. Johnston joined them the latter part of the month with additional troops and took command. Having destroyed the bridge, the guns and the machinery for making them, Johnston abandoned Harpers Ferry on June 15 and moved toward Winchester to concentrate his troops.

The army was now divided into brigades, the Virginia troops forming one under Jackson's command. Jackson's promotion to the rank of brigadier did not reach him, however, until after he had won his spurs in the first encounter on Virginia soil between Federals and Confederates in the skirmish at Falling Waters. This encounter was between the advance guard of General Robert Patterson's army, which after waiting a while on the north bank of the Potomac had finally crossed near Williamsport, and the skirmish line of Jackson's brigade. In this minor engagement, Jackson wrote his wife that his men acquitted themselves well. It would not find a place in this narrative at all except that Captain Walker and the Pulaski Guards were among those troops who won Jackson's commendation. Jackson immediately recommended Walker for promotion "for gallantry on the field of action at Falling Waters."

With his notice of promotion, Walker received an order to report at once to General Jackson. Embarrassed at the prospect of presenting himself before his austere ex-professor, Walker called on a friend, who was also a friend of General Jackson's, Captain William McLaughlin of the Rockbridge Battery, to tell him of his awkward situation and ask his advice. McLaughlin later told the story, which was published in a newspaper article some years after the war:

> Walker was a horsemen of the rarest type, tall, square built, with military bearing. Eyes bold, features strong, with a look almost severe except when a twinkle of humor or a friendly smile softened it.
>
> "McLaughlin," said Walker, as soon as they had exchanged greetings, "I am in a hell of a fix. I've been promoted and ordered to report to old Jack. I have not seen him since our unfortunate difficulty in your town, while I was at the Institute. Captain, how do you think General Jackson will receive me, or will he receive me at all?"
>
> McLaughlin told him he felt sure that General Jackson would receive him as if the incident had never occurred and that he, McLaughlin, would go with him to Jackson's headquarters.

The general was sitting at the door of his tent completely absorbed in writing—sitting bolt upright and looking as solemn and impassive as a grave stone. He did not seem to observe the two young officers approaching till they were directly in front of him. Then he rose, greeting McLaughlin cordially, but did not seem to notice Walker.

Expecting a rebuff, Walker stood very erect, his head thrown back, whereupon General Jackson extended his hand and greeted Walker in a most friendly way. Walker responded cordially, then stated he had received notice of promotion and had been directed to report to General Jackson for assignment.

Thus did the stern ex-professor testify to his restored confidence in the pupil whose acts of disobedience and insubordination he had rebuked not more severely, Walker now realized, than they had deserved.

Walker's immediate association with the Pulaski Guards now ceased and was never renewed. Assigned as lieutenant colonel of the Thirteenth Regiment, he soon made his reputation as one of the most dashing and capable of the younger leaders of the Confederacy. He was not yet thirty years old.

Walker, joining the Thirteenth in its bivouac at Winchester's fairgrounds, regarded the unit as the most gallant band of fighters in Lee's army and the fittest body of men he ever knew. Whenever there was occasion to mention this company to the day of his death, his face glowed, his eyes kindled, and his voice rang with pride, as he paid them some tribute.

"There were never soldiers like the gallant Thirteenth before or since," was a typical comment of his about that regiment. "Every one of them was worthy to have been an officer. They knew as well as I or anyone what their duty was, and if there was any blundering in orders their good sense and soldierly instinct righted the mistake. As to fighting, they never hesitated, never wavered; the only trouble was to make them quit. I could lead them anywhere. With the Thirteenth behind me I dared undertake anything. They were pretty nearly annihilated more than once, but never whipped—not a single time."

Then his voice would break, the tears would fill his eyes, as he would add, "They were good fellows, gentlemen in the best sense of the word."

After a movement toward Martinsburg to stop an expected attack from Patterson, the Thirteenth retired to Winchester. There Jackson joined General Johnston in watching lest Patterson might again essay to cross the Virginia line, while awaiting orders from Beauregard and Longstreet at Manassas Junction.

The orders came on July 18, and they were urgent. Beauregard was under attack. He needed Johnston and his men immediately.

That evening, the Thirteenth, like the rest of Johnston's troops, moved out in a forced march. Walker was at its head, as the regiment's new band played "The Girl I Left Behind Me." They forded the Shenandoah next morning and crossed the Blue Ridge at Ashby's Gap. The real war had started.

FIVE

Manassas

General Walker gave an excellent description of his involvement in the First Battle of Manassas in the following address delivered on July 21, 1892, before the James A. Walker Camp of Confederate Veterans at Pulaski, Virginia:

Thirty-one years ago this day was fought the first battle of Manassas. A lonely railroad station in Virginia surrounded by pine forests and broom sedge fields became a historic spot, and its name will be preserved in history and romance to the "last syllable of recorded time."

It was the beginning of the fierce struggle which for four years deluged the land with blood, and filled the country with mourning and with ruin. The first battle of Manassas will occupy a place in history of more importance than it deserves from a military point of view, either on account of the numbers engaged, the generalship displayed by the commanders on opposing sides, the casualties of the fight, or the results achieved.

The numbers engaged were not one-third those employed on many subsequent occasions—as Second Manassas, Gettysburg, Wilderness, Fredericksburg, and other battles. The whole force of the Federal army on that day did not exceed forty thousand, while the Confederate forces under Johnston and Beauregard did not exceed thirty-five thousand. Of those, not more than thirty thousand Federals and twenty-five thousand Confederates were actually under fire.

Compared to the *great* battles of the war between the states, the engagement was but a skirmish; although to the volunteer militia, who had never before smelled powder, heard the music of the guns, or felt the thrill of joyous battle, it was

as great a day as Waterloo. But it was the first clash of re-
sounding arms between Northern and Southern soldiers de-
serving the name of a battle, and the hopes and fears of both
sides were centered on the result. The authorities, both Federal
and Confederate, were ignorantly deluded into the belief that
one pitched battle would end in the triumph or the overthrow
of the Confederate government. The victory remained with the
Southern troops, but the victors were nearly as much demoralized by success as the vanquished by defeat. In order to illustrate this I trust I will be pardoned for recounting my own
personal observations and experience on that day.

As is well known to the survivors of the Old Pulaski
Guards, whose first Captain I had the honor to be, I was promoted to the rank of lieutenant colonel and assigned to the
Thirteenth Virginia Regiment, then commanded by A. P. Hill, a
short while before the battle of Manassas. I thereby resigned to
our gallant comrade Colonel R. D. Gardner the glory of commanding the company on this occasion, when by their unflinching courage and cool bravery they contributed their full share
to that baptism of fire and blood which gave to General Jackson and the brigade he then commanded the soubriquet of
"Stonewall" which it bore to the close of the war, and which is
one of the "few immortal names that were not born to die." My
regiment was with Kirby Smith and was one of the very last to
arrive at Manassas Junction. It marched from the Valley across
the Blue Ridge to a station on the Manassas Gap Railroad
called Piedmont about thirty miles from Manassas. It reached
this station on the afternoon of July 20th from whence it was
to be transported by rail.

By bad management, the two trains which were to bring up
this rear guard were delayed, and it was eight or nine o'clock
on the morning of the 21st before the troops were embarked.
The first six companies of Hill's regiment were placed on the
foremost train of the two, but for want of room on that one,
four companies under my command were placed on the last
train. After much delay this train pulled out and crept with
snail-like pace on its journey. No officer on board seemed to
know anything about what was to be done, or to have command
of the train or the troops on it. After frequent and unwarrant-
able stops it came to a permanent standstill, in hearing of the
battle which had commenced and which was much nearer to

the railroad at that point than at the junction. After a long stop it was ascertained that the engineer and part of the crew had deserted the train and fled, and it was said that they were Union men and went to the enemy. But a soldier was found upon the train who knew how to run a locomotive, and we were landed safely at Manassas Junction five miles from the battlefield sometime in the afternoon.

Just here by way of digression, I would remark that a year later Jackson's foot cavalry would never have taken up valuable time fooling with railroad transportation. They would have just marched on all night, and by early dawn they would have bivouacked within rifle shot of the enemy's picket line.

I got my little command off the cars, but could hear nothing of Colonel Hill or the other companies of his regiment, and no one appeared to give orders or take command. A number of citizens and men in uniforms were moving about and standing in groups talking excitedly about the battle and circulating the wildest rumors as to how the fight was progressing. The prevailing idea seemed to be that the Confederates were beaten and in full retreat upon the fortifications around the station. It was difficult to get any information from these people, but after some inquiry I learned that Colonel Rhett of General Johnston's staff was at the station, and when I found him he ordered me to report to General Johnston at the "McLean house" and to move as rapidly as possible because our troops were being sorely pressed.

Accompanied by a guide, I made the best time the hot weather and dusty roads would permit. As soon as we began the march stragglers were met coming in, first singly, then in twos and threes, and then in squads, and all had the same tale of defeat and retreat of the Confederates to tell. Presently others passed who had been in the fight, some slightly wounded accompanied by one or more comrades to take care of them. Then soldiers bearing rudely constructed litters on which were stretched dead or severely wounded officers and soldiers, and from them we got the first encouraging accounts of the progress of the battle.

They told us that our troops were driving the enemy and would urge us to hurry up. Even the wounded would wave their dying hands aloft and with their expiring breath give a feeble cheer. As we moved on the sound of the firing grew

fainter and fainter and receded from us, showing that the
enemy was being driven back. The road and adjoining fields
became thick with officers and soldiers, mixed up pell mell,
without sign of organization or of command, hurrying towards
Manassas. All were full of excitement and enthusiasm but none
seemed to think there was further use for discipline or further
work to be done.

The McLean house, to which I had been directed and where
I found General Johnston, surrounded by a large staff and a
number of other officers, was situated on an eminence overlook-
ing the battlefield and Bull Run, towards Sudley's Ford and
Stone Bridge, in the direction in which the enemy were retreating. I could see the very last of the retreating Federals scurry-
ing along the other side of the Stone Bridge in the direction of
Washington, while a few disorganized and scattered Confederates who had followed them down to the bridge were keeping
up a desultory fire at long range, and one or two pieces of
Confederate artillery were slowly firing at the rapidly vanishing foe.

When I reported to General Johnston, he seemed to take no
notice of me for a while, but afterwards turned to me and,
expressing some surprise at my late arrival, ordered me to join
Colonel Hill and the rest of the regiment. This order was more
difficult to obey than it seems, for no one knew or could tell me
where Hill was, and it was like looking for a needle in a hay-
stack to find anything in that army.

It was then very late in the afternoon, so I stacked arms
near the McLean house and strolled over the battlefield. My
men followed my bad example. In my ramble I first struck the
battlefield where Jackson's brigade had lain under the heavy
fire of Rickett's battery before they were ordered into the
charge. I knew this by the uniforms of the dead, for there was
nothing living left on the ground. The battlefield was deserted,
and not a living being save myself was in sight. The stillness of
death reigned around the Henry house where only a few hours
before the fierce battle had raged and the thunder of guns and
roar of musketry had mingled with the rush of armed foes, the
shouts of battle, and the groans of the wounded.

Among the first dead I came across was a group of five laid
side by side, and on their caps I saw the letters "F.L.V." which
I knew stood for Fort Lewis Volunteers, a company from Mont-

gomery and Roanoke Counties which belonged to the same
regiment with the Pulaski Guards. A little farther on I saw
another group of dead, side by side covered with their blankets,
and by the letters "P.G." on their caps I knew that they belonged to my old company, the Pulaski Guards. Reverently and
slowly I lifted the rough blankets which covered their faces,
almost afraid to learn which of my friends had been slain, and
looked upon John Woolwine, John Honaker, and James Crow-
ell, three of the best soldiers in the company. The setting sun
lit up their dead faces and gilded the tears which a soldier shed
for them.

I wandered over the plateau around the Henry house and
down the slope towards the turnpike where the fight had raged
most fiercely, and I saw dead men and dead horses, dismounted guns, muskets, knapsacks, and blankets strewn over the
ground, but not a single organized body of troops of any description. The survivors of the two armies had disappeared, as
completely as if the earth had swallowed them.

My little command bivouacked in the open field near the
McLean house, and no sound of war or of marching columns
disturbed the repose of the men that night. It commenced to
rain in the night and rained all next day. I spent the morning
trying to find A. P. Hill but could obtain no tidings of his
whereabouts. In my travels I could find here and there a bivouac where fragments of companies and regiments had collected, but no organized commands ready for fresh service.

At the [Manassas] junction there were a few regiments on
duty with some show of discipline, while thousands of officers
and soldiers were moving around or standing in groups discuss-
ing the battle. Each seemed to think the war was over and they
would be sent home as soon as the railroad could furnish
transportation.

Here I saw the first Federal prisoners, several hundred in
number, huddled together and guarded by Confederate soldiers.
They seemed to be the chief object of attention and curiosity,
and citizens and soldiers crowded around with jeers, jibes and
threats. It was a new experience to the prisoners, and as they
stood shivering in the rain, waiting for they knew not what,
they were as miserable looking a lot of human beings as I ever
saw. Another object of curiosity was a "Long Tom," a rifled

cannon, which had been captured, and which they said would throw a ball three miles.

In the afternoon I heard that A. P. Hill was at Fairfax Station on the railroad, some ten or twelve miles east of Manassas. I gathered my men together and marched in that direction, bivouacking that night in the rain by the road side. The next morning we reached our destination to find the men and officers dejected because the war was over and they had not been allowed to participate in the fight.

In all this time, from the evening of the twenty-first to the morning of the twenty-third, I found, outside of a few troops guarding prisoners and on duty around the stations, not a single body of troops fit for active service except one small company of cavalry doing picket duty at least fifteen miles from the nearest hostile troops. This detail will show how utterly the Confederate army was demoralized by its victory, and how utterly impracticable it would have been to follow up the enemy by a vigorous pursuit on the day or the battle or the next day. One or two brigades that had been guarding the fords on the right about Union Mills and were not engaged were in marching order, but with these exceptions there was not a company which had officers to command it, or an officer who had a company to command.

As for the Federals, they were utterly routed, horse, foot, and dragoons. When Kirby Smith's division arrived upon the field and took positions on the Confederate left, the Federals lost heart and fled as for their lives, abandoning their cannons and their trains, throwing away their muskets, their knapsacks, their cartridge boxes, and everything which might impede their flight, even to their coats, and ran as fast and as far as their legs would carry them. Thousands of them poured over the Long Bridge into Washington City next day, believing the rebels with long Bowie knives were close at their heels. The only Federal troops not routed and disorganized was a division of infantry held in reserve about Centreville which was not brought into action, and which formed a sort of rear guard to the fugitives, and kept up the appearance of orderly retreat; but they were ready to follow the example of their fellow comrades on the first appearance of a Confederate force in pursuit.

This battle began the war in Virginia, and closed the campaign of 1861. The rest of the year was spent in masterly inactivity by the armies; but in terrible activity by both governments, preparing for greater battles to come. Both sides had believed that sixty days would end the war. Mr. Lincoln and Mr. Seward, his Secretary of State, expected that a single battle would give them possession of Richmond and decide the fate of the Confederacy.

Nor were they unreasonable in their expectations of victory. The objective point of the campaign was Richmond, and four district armies numbering in all one hundred thousand men threatened that city, while the Confederate forces opposed to their armies did not exceed fifty thousand. First, there was General McClellan in West Virginia with ten thousand men, confronted by General Garnett with not more than thirty-five hundred. Second, there was General Patterson in the Valley of Virginia around Winchester with thirty thousand, confronted by General Johnston with fifteen thousand. Third, there was General McDowell opposite Washington City in Virginia with fifty thousand, confronted by General Beauregard with twenty thousand. Fourth, an army at Yorktown of ten thousand was confronted by Huger and Magruder with three thousand.

The real advance was to be made by McDowell and the other three armies were to threaten their adversaries and prevent them from reinforcing Beauregard when attacked. The plans were well laid and easy to be carried out, since the Confederates were outnumbered two to one at every point.

On July 11, just as McDowell was ready to move, General McClellan advanced in West Virginia, attacked and defeated General Garnett, scattering his command so as to render it unable to help or assist in further defending Richmond.

About the same time General Patterson advanced threatening General Johnston with an attack. But General Johnston, as early as the tenth of July, had been advised from Richmond that McDowell was about to advance with thirty-five thousand men against Beauregard. He was ordered to abandon the Valley, evade Patterson and bring his troops to the aid of Beauregard when necessary. General Patterson had strict orders not to let Johnston escape. With thirty thousand men against fifteen thousand, the odds would seem to make a failure on his part impossible. But after parading his troops in front of Johnston until the eighteenth, and believing that was enough to keep his adversary in place, Patterson fell back to

Charlestown. Johnston, in turn, leaving a small force to follow Patterson and keep him amused with the idea that the entire army was in his front, slipped away on the evening of the nineteenth and was leading his troops into action on the twenty-first before Patterson missed him.

It was well planned and splendidly executed, and General Johnston was, of all the Confederate leaders except Jackson, the best fitted to execute such a maneuver. To accomplish this required consummate skill and ability. He was required to avoid an engagement with a force twice his own, and yet not retreat or seem to avoid a battle. Had he moved a day too soon he would have been missed, followed, and forced to face about and give battle. Had he moved a day too late he would have been unable to render the required assistance to General Beauregard.

The authorities at Washington required General McDowell to leave fifteen thousand of his fifty thousand in the fortifications around Washington City when he advanced to fight Beauregard and capture Richmond. Thus it happened that he carried only thirty-five thousand men into the battle to fight about an equal force, while thirty-five thousand men at Charlestown under Patterson and fifteen thousand around Washington City were within hearing of the guns, where they were of no possible use while their comrades were being defeated and routed. The army of McDowell was equal to that of his adversaries, but it had the regulars of the old army as a nucleus, was better armed and equipped, was better handled on the field, had the best of the battle at the beginning, and would have won, had it not been for the superiority of the rank and file of the Southern troops. The Confederates were flanked, outnumbered three to one on the left, driven back in confusion, but they never ran and continued to rally, to fall back and reform, until reinforcements came up. When the Federal troops were outflanked by Kirby Smith's troops, and forced to retreat, their retreat became a rout, which could not be stopped or controlled.

The battle was won in spite of the blunders of the Confederate commanders by the superiority of the rank and file of the Southern army over the men of McDowell's army. The Confederates were whipped but they did not know it. They were flanked, the left driven back nearly two miles. Confronted at every point with superior numbers, Generals Barnard Bee and Francis Bartow killed, Major C. R. Wheat and other officers wounded and carried off the field, yet they rallied at every available point and renewed the unequal combat. Their conduct is unequaled in the history of raw militia who had never before been under fire. Although driven from position after position, and pressed back by overwhelming numbers, they retreated sullenly, fighting every inch of ground, and never for one moment gave way to fear, or were stricken with the slightest panic. Had they given way in flight or in panic all would have been over before the reinforcements could have arrived. They were utterly undisciplined and without experience, but they were brave, determined and possessed of that individuality which is characteristic of volunteer troops and was especially so of Southern volunteers.

The Federal troops on the contrary, when flanked by Kirby Smith and driven back, were seized with panic and fled incontinently, refusing to rally or even to look behind. I know it is popular to boast of the valor of the Confederate troops, but I am not here to speak more favorably of them than they deserve. I have tried dispassionately to consider their merits and their achievements, and I believe history will bear me out in the statement that no better troops ever fought, or achieved more under circumstances so unfavorable.

This was especially the case with the men who composed the armies of 1861, 1862 and 1863. In 1864 and 1865 the morale of the troops was not so good. The majority of the volunteers of 1861 and 1862 who went to the war as volunteers and who fought from principle had been killed, wounded, or were in northern prisons, and their places were supplied by conscripts and men forced against their will to do battle for their country. The majority of these had no stomach for the fight, and most of them were opposed to the war on principle. Many of them were good soldiers and obeyed their officers, but they lacked the spirit which actuated the boys who rushed to the front at the first call to arms, ready to die in defense of the Southland. History at last is beginning to do them justice, and the world will one day value them at their true worth.

SIX

Thirteenth Regiment

A few days after First Manassas, General Arnold Elzey's brigade, to which the Thirteenth Regiment and James A. Walker belonged, was sent to Fairfax Station to protect railroad communications. The men of the Thirteenth operated in sight of Federal outposts and, at times, could see the unfinished capitol dome in Washington. Late in August, they skirmished with Federals, and Private Marcellus Robinson of Company A was killed, the regiment's first casualty of the war. Later, after cheering President Davis on a visit to the front, they moved on October 16 to Centreville to join the rest of the army in winter quarters.

Winter camp life was not without its compensations. War, so far, seemed to the boys in gray less grim than it had been painted. The men were not only willing but enthusiastic and full of assurance of victory, to be followed by glory for themselves and independence for the southern states. Commissary supplies were ample, uniforms new, buttons shiny, tents and blankets whole, rations plentiful and boxes from home frequent. The life was a jolly one at times. There was fiddling, singing and yarn spinning around camp fires, and now and then impromptu theatricals.

General good fellowship prevailed, and among the officers there was frequent exchange of courtesies. No one of them was more hospitable nor more delightful in the role of host than Colonel Ambrose Powell Hill, Walker's commanding officer. Trained at West Point, an officer in the "old army" as the Confederates phrased it, Hill was fond of entertaining his brother officers with all the state and elegance circumstances permitted.

One evening, by the light of pine torches, a number of them met around Hill's mess table to enjoy with much relish a new dish he had promised them, one he had eaten when on duty in Texas. The dish was barbecued ox-head, and it was to be the *piece de resistance*

of a feast. Walker, one of the half score guests present, later
delighted in telling of it.

Urbane, charming, pleased as usual to be host, Hill was
confident of a gastronomic triumph. When the first course was
removed, two servants were dispatched for the ox-head, and the
guests eagerly awaited the promised treat. Considerable delay
ensued, but Hill concealed his growing nervousness by keeping up
an animated conversation. Presently, an amazing odor floated
under the tent flap—a combination of burnt flesh, singed hair and
scorched horn—as the servants approached, bearing between them,
on a huge platter, the much vaunted dish; their mouths were
spread in an irrepressible grin, their noses elevated and their heads
turned away from their burden, though each had an eye cocked
across it in the direction of the waiting host.

With a comprehensive glance at the object, Colonel Hill waved
his hand in the direction from which it had come, and in thunder-
ing tones he ordered, "Take that thing away and bury it!" Then he
added: "That fool cook pretended he had barbecued an ox-head
before and knew just how it was done. I failed to remind him that
it had to be dehorned, skinned and dressed before roasting. Bring
on the ham!"

The guests ached to laugh, but their host's manner forbade the
liberty. Lively talk went around the table. Someone told a funny
story, and the peals of laughter which followed were not solely in
tribute to its wit.

In December, the Thirteenth moved again, to a new campsite
one and a half miles from Manassas along the railroad, a camp they
named Camp Walker after their lieutenant colonel. There, they
spent Christmas, eating fried beef, bread, butter and coffee, and
looking to a new year. By the end of January, they had built log
huts for all, living in them eight to a hut.

Winter ended, and in the spring of 1862 the reorganization of
the army took place. Major M. S. Stringfellow writes of it thus in
his manuscript sketch of the Thirteenth Virginia Regiment:

The Maryland boys were detached and put in a Maryland
regiment, much to our regret. From that time we had only nine
companies. Our army moved back to the Rapidan on its way to
Richmond. Our regiment suffered a severe loss at this time.
Colonel Hill was promoted and taken from us. Whilst we never
fought a battle under him, his discipline, judicious management

and consideration for his men had endeared him to them. He
was succeeded by Colonel James A. Walker of Pulaski County.
By nature and education a soldier, he at once won the regard of
his men and during their whole connection their relations were
of the most friendly character. The men were fond of him and
he of them. Hill laid the foundation of reliability, but it was
under Walker that the Thirteenth rose to its highest excellence.

I cannot forbear quoting further from a letter of Captain
Samuel D. Buck of Winchester and later of Baltimore to illustrate
the feeling which existed between Walker and his men:

Gen'l Walker was my Colonel, he was my friend—as he was
to every soldier who did his duty. To all such the tenderest care
of his big heart was vouchsafed. When a man failed in his
duty—he felt the heavy hand of discipline and his officers'
displeasure. We have been in some trying places side by side.
His cool courage was of itself an assurance of success. At
Sharpsburg he commanded our brigade and it was through him
I was promoted to first lieutenant for meritorious conduct in
the Maryland campaign. And as a matter of course he won my
confidence and love. An amusing instance comes to mind just
here and may interest you. It will bring to your mind his loyalty to those who stood firm to duty.

After we had crossed the Potomac River we were in camp
near White Post. A friend and I left camp and called to see
some ladies nearby and get dinner. We had left camp without
leave. My friend was in the Quartermaster department and a
private in my company. We were sitting in the parlor having a
charming time, the anticipation of a good dinner giving zest to
the conversation, when I looked out of the window to see, to my
dismay, Colonel Walker and staff riding up to the gate. My first
impulse was to retreat by the rear door, but those lovely girls,
old friends of mine, and the anticipation of a real feast out-
weighed my dread of the colonel's displeasure, so I stood my
ground.

When the colonel entered I met him as a friend of the host
and family. His greeting was as genial as a prince's, and I saw
in his eye all was well with me. Soon after dinner was announced and when we stood back of our chairs, to my surprise,
General Walker's voice was heard. "Ladies, before we partake

of this delightful dinner, I desire the pleasure of introducing my new lieutenant who won his promotion on the field of Sharpsburg. It is a pleasure to introduce so meritorious an officer as Lieutenant Buck!" Then, turning the sublime to the ridiculous he said to my companion: "Well, B-, why don't you do as Buck did?"

It rather cut my friend, and he said, "Well, Colonel. is it any disgrace to be a private?"

"No, B-, but it is darned inconvenient to carry a musket." All enjoyed the speech, but none so much as the boy to whom it was addressed.

Colonel Walker, who took command of the Thirteenth on February 26, on duty was very strict, and nobody ever presumed or thought of taking any liberties. Off duty, however, the colonel was very approachable, and his boys, as he called them sometimes, presumed to take some liberties with him. On one occasion, I think it was in winter quarters near Hamilton's Crossing four miles from Fredericksburg, some of the boys had been snow balling. The notion struck them that they would attack headquarters, so over they went and surprised the colonel washing his face for breakfast. They made their attack, routing the colonel and his staff. For once he showed his heels, but not a temper.

SEVEN

Crazy Jackson

Stonewall Jackson's Valley Campaign is now recorded in military annals as a masterpiece of strategy possible of execution only by a born military genius: an Alexander, a Caesar, a Frederick the Great, or a Jackson. It is studied in military schools as a series of masterly movements hardly equaled in history, by which one small army neutralized three armies of the enemy, each more than its equivalent in numbers. General Walker, an active participant in the campaign, summed up its achievements in these words from a speech before the Westminster Club of Boston:

On the first day of May, 1862, Jackson left his camp at Swift Run Gap and began his march in the celebrated Valley Campaign which, on the eighth of June following, was terminated by the Battle of Port Republic, only eight miles from the spot whence he had started just six weeks before. In this brief space he had marched four hundred miles, fought five battles and engaged in almost daily skirmishes, had defeated three armies under Banks, Fremont and Shields, captured four thousand prisoners, twenty pieces of artillery, ten thousand small arms, a vast quantity of commissary and quartermaster stores, with a total loss on the Confederate side of one thousand killed, wounded and missing.

The results of this campaign were of incalculable service to the Confederate armies in Virginia. With less than twenty thousand men he kept at bay one hundred thousand, drawing them from the support of McClellan's army at Richmond to defend the national capital. It left a part of Jackson's army free to reinforce General Lee in front of Richmond and weakened General McClellan by calling General McDowell's troops from his command, to assist in protecting Washington City...

If we seek the secret of Stonewall Jackson's success as a
military leader we can only find it in the fact that he was by
nature a military genius which is not governed by rules or
controlled by precedents; and we look in vain for reasons on
which to rest its action. Genius is higher than reason and
works not by rules. It is guided by intuition which seldom, if
ever, errs. As the homing pigeon returns to its cote through the
tractless wastes of ether, without guide or compass and with an
unfaltering wing, so military genius reaches its conclusions
without the aid of reason or the help of precedents. This great
soldier seemed to possess the power, the instinct, to divine the
condition, purposes and movements of the enemy at all times.
There are many instances in his career to prove this.

In his Valley campaign, after he had crossed the mountains
which bound the Valley on the west and attacked and driven back
Fremont's advance guard under Milroy, Jackson's plan of campaign
was to recross this mountain, unite again with Ewell's division near
Swift Run Gap, and attack Banks before Fremont could join forces
with him. Jackson was three marches from Banks by any route
open to him. Fremont was only one march from Banks. To strike
Banks before Fremont reunited with him was the military problem
that presented itself to Jackson.

Major Jedediah Hotchkiss, of Jackson's staff, relates that
Jackson asked him to ride, and taking him a distance from camp by
an obscure road, he suddenly drew rein and turning to his staff
officer, said:

"General Fremont is at Franklin. Banks is at Harrisonburg. It
is only thirty miles by a good turnpike road between the two
armies. Fremont will try to join Banks, and it is of the greatest
importance that he should be delayed. There is a company of
Confederate cavalry camping at the foot of the North Mountain on
the turnpike between Harrisonburg and Franklin. Take twelve
cavalrymen and proceed at once as rapidly as possible to the camp
of that company, take command of it and with the aid of the
citizens of the neighborhood blockade the turnpike so as to render
it impassable to troops. Impress horses along the way if necessary,
but you *must* reach there early tomorrow morning. Send one of your
men back every hour to report progress."

The major obeyed orders and riding all night with the greatest
speed possible reached his destination at sunrise next morning. and

before night had destroyed the bridges and completely obstructed the road. In Fremont's report of that campaign, he says he was prevented from joining Banks at Harrisonburg because the rebels had rendered the road impassable to his troops.

To illustrate the dispatch and secrecy with which General Jackson conducted his movements, General Walker told of this anecdote about Jackson's Valley Campaign.

Many men of great genius have borne the reputation of being crazy, and Stonewall Jackson was, at the beginning of the war, no exception to the rule. In March of 1862 General Johnston's army withdrew from Manassas Junction to confront McClellan on the Peninsula, leaving General Ewell's division on the Rappahannock River, in Culpeper County, to watch the enemy in that quarter. General Jackson was then in the Valley, and after the affair of Kernstown had retired up the Valley and placed his back against the Blue Ridge at Swift Run Gap. There he was in position to menace the enemy's flank and rear should he attempt to march on to Staunton, or to cross the mountain and join his forces with those of Ewell and retard the movement, should General Banks attempt to reinforce McClellan in front of Richmond.

But General Banks remained inactive while General Jackson conceived and planned the brilliant campaign which ended in the defeat of four armies, in the brief space of forty days. His first move was to call General Ewell's division quietly and suddenly from Culpeper to the Valley at Swift Run Gap.

General Jackson's army occupied the south side of the Shenandoah, and General Banks the north side, the center being about what was then Conrad's Store but is now Elkton on the Shenandoah Valley Railroad. The Confederate cavalry, vedettes and pickets were posted along the southern bank of the stream while the infantry was encamped two or three miles in the rear, right in the gorge of the mountain along the Swift Run Gap turnpike. When Ewell's division marched down the western slope of the mountain on April 30, they came upon the old camp of Jackson's infantry, with the fires still smoking, but not a man was left to tell what had become of them. They left no sign, not even an old musket or knapsack as a souvenir. The cavalry still remained and stood sentinel on the banks of the river, acting as a curtain to screen from the eyes of the enemy in front the scene shifting going on behind the drop.

General Walker's regiment, the Thirteenth Virginia Infantry, was placed in an old filthy camp. He asked permission to move it to a cleaner ground, but was told to remain where he was and to require his men to build and keep up fires on the same spots they had been kindled in before. This hint was enough to prove that Jackson had gone prowling off somewhere, and was trying to fool the enemy into the belief that he was still there, that behind the cavalry there was nobody but Jackson. Ewell's division settled down quietly in Jackson's old camps and for two weeks were busy drilling, organizing and equipping the raw recruits which were drafted from the militia at home to reinforce the volunteers. During this time General Banks remained in blissful ignorance of Jackson's movements, but not more so than were Ewell and his men.

As for Walker, in his subordinate position, he had no right to concern himself with Jackson's whereabouts or anything else except his own regiment and duties.

After the troops had been at Swift Run for ten days, Walker went to division headquarters which were established in a little brick farm house on the side of the main road from one to two miles in his front. Arriving at the house, he found General Ewell's favorite horse saddled and tied in front of the gate, while three or four couriers with their horses were ready to accompany their chief.

When he entered the room used as an office, Walker found General Ewell stalking up and down the floor, booted and spurred, ready for a ride, with his cap drawn down low upon his forehead, but in a very bad humor, blowing up at his staff in unmeasured terms. He scarcely noticed Walker's presence, and Walker did not deem it a propitious time to make a request for the favor he desired and so remained silent.

Ewell left the house and went out the front gate, much to the relief of his staff. Walker followed to return to his camp, but found the general, his long regular cavalry sabre buckled around him, striding up and down the road, evidently in no better humor than when he came out. As Walker passed him he gave the usual military salute which Ewell returned without speaking.

When Walker was about to mount his horse, the general turned back to meet him and called out abruptly, "Colonel Walker!"

As soon as they came within a step or two of each other, Ewell stopped suddenly, looked his colonel in the face for a few seconds, and then astounded him by this question: "Did you ever hear anyone say Jackson is crazy?"

To this, Walker replied cautiously that he had heard a few persons suggest the idea that he was partially deranged or a "little cracked."

Then Ewell put this poser: "What do you think of him? Do you think he is a sane man?"

Walker parried the thrust by replying that he had formed no opinion on the subject, but that "General Jackson certainly had some marked peculiarities."

With that, Ewell broke out into a white heat. "I tell you, sir, Jackson is crazy," he said. "He is a crazy man if there ever was one. What do you think? He has left me here with one little division of infantry and two small regiments of cavalry, confronted by General Bank's whole army, and the enemy can surround and capture my command any day. He has been gone ten days, and I am as ignorant of his plans or his movements or whereabouts as you are, or as any private soldier in my command."

The statement astonished Walker, and he said so. A moment's silence followed, and then the general said, "I have a strong notion to take my company across the mountain, march to Richmond and report to General Lee. What do you think of that?"

Walker modestly ventured to ask what Ewell's last orders from General Jackson were.

"I have no orders," Ewell replied. "When Jackson left here, he told me to remain until I received further orders from him, but it has been ten days since that, and if I do not hear from him in a day or two I will fall back across the Blue Ridge."

Then mounting his beautiful thoroughbred mare, Maggie, that he prized above all other horses (she was killed under him at Gaines Mill), he started at a run down the dusty road towards the river. He was a splendid horseman, loved to ride at a dashing gait, and was soon far ahead of his couriers, who trailed behind him.

Walker rode slowly towards his camp reflecting on the odd predicament General Ewell was placed in, by being under the command of a general who left him in utter ignorance of his plans and movements and without orders, and was almost persuaded that General Ewell was right and that Jackson was crazy.

As Walker came near his headquarters he saw a man in citizen's dress running at full speed, followed at a distance by an officer with a pistol in his hand, firing at the fugitive. To his surprise, he saw that the officer was his brigade commander, General Arnold Elzey, a West Point graduate, and a man who had

spent his whole life in military service. Elzey had very rigid notions
of military etiquette and military subordination and could not
understand the difference between the volunteer troops he then
commanded and the regular enlisted soldiers of the Old Army.

When Walker came up, General Elzey commanded him to come
to him.

Walker followed Elzey to his tent, where the senior officer
greeted him with the searching inquiry, "What sort of damned men
have you got in your regiment? That fellow you saw me after is a
private in your regiment, and don't you think sir! he walked into
my quarters and thrust a paper in my face, which he said was an
order authorizing his discharge from military service, and threatened me with a suit for false imprisonment if I refused?"

Colonel Walker told him the man was one of the levies of
Virginia militia who had been ordered out by the governor of the
state, temporarily to assist the volunteers in preventing the enemy
from marching further up the valley, and that he was some country
gentleman who believed that the civil law was above the military.
Walker said it was a man who still believed in the supreme efficacy
of the writ of habeas corpus and thought that the threat of a suit
for false imprisonment in a Virginia court, before a Virginia judge
and a Virginia jury, would cause the bravest son of Mars to quake
in his boots.

Like all hot tempered men, Elzey soon cooled down, and he
laughed heartily at the occurrence, expressing his gratification at
his bad marksmanship and that he had not hit his human target.
Then the conversation turned to some orders recently issued from
division headquarters which were very distasteful to General Elzey,
and which he grew excited over. After expressing his opinion about
them very freely, he turned his attention to General Ewell,
declaring that General Ewell was crazy, and added, "They called
him Crazy Dick in the old army."

That was too much. Walker smiled as he related what Ewell
had just said about Jackson. He wound up by saying he was in a
bad box, since the army was commanded by a lunatic, the division
by a crazy man, and from the scene with the militia man just
witnessed there was great room to doubt the sanity of his brigade
commander. This again put the general in a good humor, and he
asked Walker to take a drink. This order was obeyed with alacrity,
and the general was told that his last well-timed movement had

removed all doubts from his subordinate's mind that there was no questions of his sanity.

Walker finished the story this way:

Two days after these occurrences, a rumor came to my camp that Jackson had fought a battle somewhere and had defeated somebody; but this was all that could be learned. Hastening to division headquarters, I found General Ewell and his staff in great good humor; General Ewell turned to me as soon as I entered the room and said, "I have heard from Jackson at last." He then produced a fragment of paper on which was written these words:

McDowell, May 8th, 1862

General Ewell:

BY THE GRACE OF GOD WE DEFEATED MILROY HERE TO DAY

Yours,

T. J. Jackson.

General Ewell read the dispatch and said, "I told you he was crazy. No one but a crazy man would have written such a paper as that!"

Then he read it over and said, "'By the grace of God.' Now what has the grace of God got to do with the whipping of Milroy, or with fighting anyway?"

I ventured to inquire where Jackson was then, and what his next movement would be, but General Ewell declared that he had no hint of what he was going to do next, and that the dispatch which was sent by a special courier direct from the battlefield of McDowell contained all he knew.

In a day or two afterwards, the crazy Jackson and the crazy Ewell had joined their forces near Harrisonburg, General Banks had fallen back to Strasburg, and in four weeks they had defeated three armies commanded by Banks, Fremont and Shields—each larger than the little army of Confederates commanded by crazy generals. No more was heard of any of them being crazy after the Valley Campaign.

EIGHT

Cross Keys and Port Republic

Several more days elapsed before Ewell received orders to join his forces, including Walker and his Thirteenth Regiment, with Jackson's at New Market. Part of Ewell's command did so, and the rest joined Jackson at the junction of the Mt. Sidney and Keezleton roads.

With Ewell in advance, Jackson marched rapidly down the Luray Valley to Strasburg, arriving just ahead of the enemy. Ewell deployed Walker's Thirteenth Regiment to check Fremont, who was advancing on the road between Front Royal and Winchester, and the deployment worked.

Next day, May 25, the Battle of Winchester was fought. Elzey's brigade, by Jackson's orders, followed the Valley Turnpike through the town as the enemy gave way on either side. The men of the Thirteenth Regiment pressed on with their usual eagerness, leading the first unit, Walker at their head.

The citizens of Winchester remaining in the town, mostly children, women and old men, rushed into the streets to greet the boys in gray with demonstrations of joy. General Walker told of "lovely young ladies and fair proud matrons pressing to the edge of the sidewalks to speak through glistening tears, impulsive words of heartfelt thanks to their deliverers. The sight of the hated bluecoats fleeing before the Virginia boys had so filled their hearts with joy and exultation that customary reticence and ceremony was cast to the winds."

Some of the ladies kissed the powder stained hands of the soldiers, while others called God's blessing down upon them and still others offered lunches or trays of fruit. It made the soldiers' hearts burn with pride and zeal and sent them on, determined to win greater victories.

Two days later Banks' entire force had been driven across the
Potomac, immense military stores had been captured and between
two and three thousand prisoners sent to the rear. Total Federal
losses were 3,050; Jackson's entire losses were four hundred, of
which sixty-eight had been killed.

Military analysts and learned historians have told in detail over
and over again of Jackson's threatened movement on Harpers
Ferry, of the paralysis of McClellan's plans, of the Federal reinforcements hurried to the Valley, of Jackson's surpassing strategy
by which he saved his captured stores, threw the North into a
panic, and then backed in fighting array to the pass near Strasburg, ready to confuse, mystify and overwhelm in turn the armies
of Fremont and McDowell. This narrative is concerned with only
those movements and battles in which General Walker participated,
and to relate incidents of campaigns and marches not heretofore
published, illustrative of the spirit of the Confederate troops.

By burning bridges, blocking roads, and a series of rapid
movements, Jackson prevented the junction of the two Federal
armies descending upon him from opposite directions. He then sent
prisoners down the main valley to Staunton, paused a few days at
Harrisonburg, and took position at Port Republic, near Brown's
Gap, on the shortest line of communication with the army of
General Lee.

His army enjoyed a well earned and much needed rest on June
6 and 7 in the green pastures and open forests along the road
between Cross Keys, where Ewell held the rear, and the north bank
of the river at Port Republic where the advance encamped. A small
cavalry force scouted down the river, watching Shield's toilsome
progress along the muddy roads over which Jackson had recently
struggled for nearly three days. Fremont, finding that the rear of
Jackson's army was in position near Cross Keys, about six miles
from Harrisonburg on the road to Port Republic, concentrated his
army and gave orders to advance on Sunday morning, June 8th, for
an attack on the Confederates.

Ewell had posted his division on opposite sides of the road on
rising ground behind a creek that ran along his front, with his
flanks extending into forests on either side. He placed batteries in
the road in his center which swept the open country between him
and the Keezleton Road, running nearly parallel to his line of
battle. Fremont deployed his five brigades of infantry, a regiment

of cavalry and several batteries along the Keezleton Road. His entire fighting force was about 11,500 men.

To resist these, Ewell had Isaac R. Trimble's, Elzey's (including Walker and the Thirteenth) and Richard Taylor's regiments and a Louisiana battalion, besides five companies of artillery, in all about five thousand men. Ewell's first position, according to Hotchkiss, was nearly at right angles to Fremont's; his right rested on the road to Port Republic about a mile from Cross Keys, whence his line extended nearly parallel to the Port Republic Road to within a half mile of Cross Keys, with his left retired.

Fremont advanced his left, turning on his right, and brought his whole line into position, parallel to Ewell's on the hills northeast of Mill Creek, protecting his right with batteries and a detached brigade. This movement, boldly and skillfully executed, brought his whole line into a dangerous position, which he apparently did not comprehend in his ignorance of the topographic conditions of the field; it gave Ewell an opportunity to detach Trimble's brigade from his right, move it through a forest, and reform it opposite Fremont's left.

Colonel Walker, with two Virginia regiments, the Thirteenth and Twenty-fifth, moved in on Trimble's right as reinforcements in an effort to turn the Federal flank. Moving too far to the right, his troops were staggered momentarily by musketry and canister, but Walker pressed on desperately. After a short struggle, his troops, along with Ewell's full force, pressed forward, and together they drove Blenker from his position on Fremont's left and forced him into full retreat to the Keezleton Road.

The Battle of Port Republic was fought next day, June 9, and though Jackson's brilliant plan was somewhat marred by defective construction of a bridge, it was also successful in scattering the army of Shields just as the Battle of Cross Keys had demoralized that of Fremont. Walker's Thirteenth Regiment was deployed but not engaged in the Battle of Port Republic.

A typical incident of the experiences of Jackson's foot cavalry at Port Republic is told by the manuscript historian of the Thirteenth Regiment, Major M. S. Stringfellow:

Owing to rapid movements we had no rations, and Cross Keys was fought on an empty stomach. That night our wagons came into camp about three o'clock in the morning, and our boys commenced getting out cooking utensils when General

Ewell rode up and said: "Boys, I'm sorry for you, but you must put your utensils back as we have to march at once."

We now marched to Port Republic. Here the Thirteenth was detached, and ordered to make a detour around the side of the mountain to flank a battery which Shields had posted just below Lewiston—he having marched up the Luray Valley. The route selected for us was an exceedingly difficult one owing to the dense growth of mountain laurel. In many places the men had to crawl on their hands and knees. We finally reached the battery but only in time to see the Louisiana boys capture it. Though we had had a hard time we did not fire a shot.

We now followed Shields' army which was in full retreat as far as Conrad's Store, thirteen miles from Port Republic. We marched back the same evening, and never stopped until we reached the top of the Blue Ridge at Brown's Gap, making a distance of thirty miles and no rations. Two whole days and two nights without food, during which time we had fought two battles and marched thirty miles.

There was a Frenchman in Company A, who had been under Magruder on the Peninsula; Old Pete, as he was called, had contended that Magruder was a better general than Jackson. When we reached the top of the mountain, one of the men asked Peter which he thought the better general now.

"Magruder no march man up a tree," he answered angrily.

Finding that Fremont had fallen back to Harrisonburg, and that Shields would trouble him no further, Jackson moved his army to the pleasant meadows near Weyers Cave and rested them three days. The men lay down to sleep, rose up to eat and continued to repeat the program until June 17th. Colonel Walker was within three miles of the home where he was born, the fertile gently rolling wheat lands where he so happily had spent his childhood and youth. His parents and sisters had heard in an agony of trembling apprehension the guns of Cross Keys and Port Republic. For the better part of two days, his younger sister had walked up and down the road leading across fields to the main pike, longing for tidings yet dreading to receive them. Walker had no time to visit his home, however. Jackson's discipline was strict. Walker was now a loyal subordinate and faithful officer. At any moment orders might be given to resume the march or to repulse a surprise attack.

During the three days of rest, the officers maintained a ceaseless vigilance.

On June 17th, the army broke camp and turned its face toward Richmond, though they were given no hint of their final destination. The Valley Campaign was but a training for the great struggle which was to be fought out around the Confederate capital. The rapid marches and vigorous campaign had culled out the weak and faint hearted, so that the men composing Jackson's corps, as it filed through the pass of the Blue Ridge on its way to Richmond, were the bone and sinew of his army. General Jackson's reputation as a master strategist and an invincible leader had been fully established. He was likewise secure in the confidence and affection of his men and had become the hope and an idol of the Confederacy. But his quiet, self-contained manner, his modesty, and his humble reliance on Divine power, had not been changed by his brilliant success.

General Walker later related an experience he had with Jackson during that period:

At the Battle of Port Republic, I was in command of Elzey's brigade and was ordered by my division commander to report to General Jackson. The battle had already commenced, and riding rapidly ahead of my men I found General Jackson entirely alone, dismounted, standing quietly by the roadside holding his horse by the bridle. Dismounting I approached him and, announcing my command, told him that I had been ordered by General Ewell to report to him.

The Confederate troops which had been engaged were falling back, being pressed by Shields' advancing troops, but old Stonewall seemed to pay no heed to what was going on, although the road where we stood was being shelled by a battery planted on a little eminence about a half mile in front and which commanded the road on which our troops were approaching. He began to give many instructions, but before he had finished a shell struck the old Virginia "worm fence" within twenty feet of us and sent the rails, in splinters, flying in every direction. Jackson and his horse stood as immovable as if cut out of marble and paid no more attention to the cannon ball than if it had been a firecracker.

For myself and my own horse, we were both dodging and jumping around so that I lost the thread of the general's dis-

course and was compelled to ask him to repeat, which he
started to do without the slightest change of countenance or
position. Before he had gotten through with this second attempt, another shell fell just behind us in a pond of water and
exploded, throwing water all around us and spattering us with
mud. Myself and horse again repeated our disgraceful perfor-
mance while Jackson and his horse remained as before unmoved. I had the mortification of again asking the general to
repeat his order, which he did at last successfully. Then mounting his horse he turned his face towards the river in rear of his
retreating men and rode quietly across the low ground at a
slow walk with his head cast down, seemingly paying no attention to the battle which was going on and in which his troops
were getting badly worsted. As I watched him he seemed to me
more like some old Scotch Covenanter on his way to the meeting house on a quiet Sunday morning than like the commander
of an army engaged in battle.

NINE

Seven Days

Jackson's corps, already dubbed "Jackson's foot cavalry," soon found itself on the march again. Orders as usual were to cook three days' rations and be ready to march at dawn. Walker, in a sketch of "Stonewall," tells of these cavalry-like infantry advances:

When making one of his rapid marches Jackson gave his troops but little rest by day or by night. His standing order was to march at early dawn and woe to the subordinate officer whose column was not on march before sunrise. It was often late in the night before the march was ended and the column was allowed to rest for a few short hours before resuming the swinging gait peculiar to the foot cavalry. On these forced marches Jackson's staff knew absolutely nothing of his intended movement, not even his division commanders. He took no counsel save that of his own familiar spirit—the genius of war—and with the God of battles. It was said that he held only one council of war during his career and that failing to approve his plans, he declared "That is the last council of war I will ever hold." And he kept his word.

By the time of the advance toward Richmond, Jackson's men had begun to develop, however, a sort of sixth or military sense, which enabled them to guess the answer to the question, "Wonder who old Jack's after now?"

When they had reached Charlottesville, they pretty well knew that he "was after" McClellan this time and that they were bound for Richmond. They were being hurried forward by a method more or less peculiar to Jackson, by what the men called "ride and tie." Their route was planned to parallel the Virginia Central Railway; a train of passenger coaches would pick up the stragglers and rear troops, carry them forward

several miles and dump them. Rested, they would lead the
march, while the train backed to the rear of the column to
repeat the process.

By Saturday, June 21st, the corps reached Frederick's Hall
in Louisa County, about fifty miles from Richmond. There
Jackson allowed both his men and himself a Sabbath day's
rest. But at 1 A.M. Monday he set out for Richmond and, using
a relay of horses, reached the city at 1 P.M.

Meanwhile, the army also moved forward toward Ashland.
It was an intensely hot and dusty day, and the men's canteens
were soon empty. With no chance to refill them on the march,
the corps reached Ashland late in the afternoon choking from
dust and exhausted from the march under a broiling sun.

McClellan, apparently confused about Jackson's whereabouts, inquired of the Federal secretary of war, Edwin Staunton. Meanwhile, Banks and Fremont were planning an attack
in the lower valley. But McClellan was not so badly deceived,
for on the twenty-fifth he telegraphed Washington: "I am
inclined to think that Jackson will attack my right rear."

Major Stringfellow will continue the narrative for us:

We reached Ashland on the twenty-fifth. The next morning
we struck across the country to come in on McClellan's flank.
That night we went into camp at Hundley's Corner. The enemy
moved a force in our direction which was met by the First
Maryland, Sixth Louisiana and Thirteenth Virginia, before
which they retired. Next morning, we commenced our advance
in the direction of the firing which now indicated a general
engagement. The Thirteenth was deployed in front as skirmishers. We passed over a considerable extent of country, and it
was about 3 o'clock in the evening when we approached the
battlefield of Cold Harbor. General Ewell met us, and ordered
Colonel Walker to close up, and move to a point where our line
had given way. The point indicated was a wooded knoll.

We moved forward under a heavy artillery fire, marching
into the breach. Instantly we were engaged in a deadly contest
at close range, some times almost together and at no time over
fifty yards apart. The smoke became so dense that the men
could only locate the enemy by the flash of their guns. The
carnage was fearful on both sides. The volleys of musketry

were so loud we could not distinguish the report of the cannon. But we could see the effect of the shot and shell as they cut down the trees around us. Just before dark, [General John B.] Hood's Texans and [General E. M.] Law's Mississippians charged and swept the enemy from our front. Two thirds of the Thirteenth had been killed and wounded, but it had not lost a foot of ground.

It was a glorious victory at a frightful cost. We had in our four years experience many sad days, but this was the saddest of all. Our loss was not mere fighting material, but old school mates, friends of our youth, messmates endeared to us by the intimacy of over a year. In Company A there were five brothers; three were killed, one badly wounded, and one slightly wounded. When we formed next morning to follow McClellan the Thirteenth could muster only seventy-five men.

We took part in the Battle of Malvern Hill. Here, Early took command of our brigade, Elzey having been wounded. Also, we had a skirmish at Harrison's Landing which closed the Seven Days fight. Jackson's corps soon returned to the vicinity of Gordonsville, from which point he moved toward Culpeper Court House, crossing the Rapidan into Madison.

General Walker later told his more personal reminiscences of the "Seven Days" battles around Richmond that summer of 1862:

On the twenty-seventh of June, as the Thirteenth Virginia Infantry was going into battle at Gaines Mill, the color sergeant, Fendall Chiles of Louisa County, was severely wounded by a shell fragment and was borne from the field. As the colors fell from his hands, one of the color guard, a youth named Cheshire from Hampshire County, Virginia [now West Virginia], seized them, exclaiming as he did, "They are mine now! Colonel Walker promised them to me if anything happened to Sergeant Chiles."

An hour later when the regiment was engaged in the hottest and most prolonged infantry fight I ever knew, as I passed along the line I saw the brave little color-bearer standing bolt upright in an exposed position, holding the colors aloft, unmindful of the Minie balls that were whistling thick around. Going up to and touching him, I pointed to a tree nearby and made a sign to him to get behind it. In a short time I returned

down the line and saw the colors still in the same position I
had left them, the color-bearer having declined to take advantage of my permission to seek shelter. Before I reached him,
the colors went down, and the color bearer pitched forward on
them as if still guarding them in death, for he was shot
through the heart and died instantly, saturating the bunting
with his life's blood.

I beckoned one of his comrades to me, and we lifted his
body and picked up the flag, wet and dripping with his blood. I
handed it to another brave man.

The flag carried by the regiment that day was a Virginia
state flag which had been presented to the regiment by Governor Letcher. It went into the fight scatheless, but it came out
literally shot to pieces. The bunting was riddled, and the staff
in three places was nearly severed in twain, so that it was too
weak to be borne with the regiment. We carried it around in
the regimental headquarters wagon until after the Seven Days
fighting around Richmond was over. We then sent it back to
Governor Letcher, who had it placed in the State Library,
where it remained until Richmond was evacuated and then fell
into the hands of the enemy.

The gallant boy who so nobly died on it was buried in a
soldier's grave on the field of battle with nothing to mark his
last resting place. But I have cherished his memory as one of
the bravest of the brave and can yet in my mind's eye call up
his form and his face as he stood unflinching and unmoved in
that storm of war, setting a noble example for his comrades.

His home was in the enemy's lines, and I heard nothing
from his friends until thirty years afterwards, when I visited a
camp of Confederate veterans in Hampshire County. Inquiring
if any of the friends or family of Color Bearer Cheshire were
present, I was told that his mother was on the ground. I sought
her out, sat with her on a fallen log in the grove, and told her
of the circumstances of her brave boy's death. She had never
heard them before and only knew that he was killed in battle;
but even after thirty years it seemed to be a comfort to her to
know that her boy had died the death of a hero.

Another incident of this same battlefield is to me personally
one of the most tender and touching in all history. There was
in my regiment a young man named William B. Mansfield, the
son of a minister in Orange County, Virginia. Private Mansfield

was detailed as clerk at regimental headquarters. His position excused him from drill and guard duty, but on the march and in battle he took his place in the ranks.

A very short time after the brave little color bearer was killed, I saw Mansfield lying behind the root of a tree where he had been placed by his comrades. He was mortally wounded and suffering great pain, but as I passed he beckoned me to come to him.

I knelt beside him and put my ear to his lips, asking if he wanted to say anything. He whispered, "Lie down beside me," at the same time putting his arm around my neck and trying to draw me down.

I said, "I cannot lie down. I must be at my post."

His life was fast ebbing away, and he knew it, but he still tried with his feeble strength to draw me down. "Just lie down here beside me a few moments until the hottest of this fire is over," he said. "You will be killed if you don't."

Gently withdrawing his arm, I left him and never saw him again, but a nobler, more unselfish spirit never died for his country.

The ground on which we fought that day was a plateau thinly wooded, sloping down from our rear and towards the enemy. Over this plateau the fight raged hotly and incessantly for four hours. Reinforcements were brought up by either side four or five times, and the last party reinforced would press the other back so that the same ground was fought over several times. On the Confederate side at one time, the remnants of three brigades were all mixed up and were being slowly pressed back by the enemy. The plateau was covered with dead and wounded, and it seemed as if we would be driven off the field. At this juncture of affairs two incidents occurred that were strikingly characteristic of two well known Confederate officers.

When we were barely able to hold our ground, Major Wheat of the Louisiana Tigers rode up and asked how we were getting along. I told him we were hard pressed and could not hold our position much longer unless we were reinforced. He replied, "Why don't you charge them?"

I said, "We are not strong enough."

The major, who was always ready to charge against every odds, replied, "My brigade is coming up, and I intend to charge them."

I assented to his plan and told him my men would go as far as his. Just then his little brigade, not over two hundred men strong, came up in line, marching rapidly, and eager for the fray.

Major Wheat was a large man, weighing about 240 pounds, looking every inch a soldier. He wore on that day a red sash around his waist and was mounted on a very large clay bank horse which made him a conspicuous mark. When he men came up, he rode in front of his men, sword in hand, and waving it over his head commanded, "Charge!" His men followed him at quick step, but he had gone a very short distance when he was mortally wounded and falling from his horse said to his men, "Bury me on the field boys," and died. Wheat was a born soldier. He had fought in foreign lands. He too died the death of a brave soldier.

The other incident is connected with General Ewell. When our troops were most sorely pressed and their ranks had been badly thinned, when their ammunition was exhausted and they were being supplied from the cartridge boxes from the dead and wounded, when their own officers could no longer inspire them to make another forward movement, they suddenly set up a wild cheer and with one impulse rushed towards the enemy, driving them back and re-taking the plateau.

The movement was sudden and unexpected, and I was at a loss to account for it, until I saw General Ewell in front of the line, sitting quietly on his favorite mare "Maggie" with one leg thrown over the pommel of his saddle, looking as cool and pleasant as if on dress parade. General Ewell was at that time the idol of his troops, and his presence did more to inspire his men than that of any other commander I ever saw on the field with the exception of Stonewall Jackson. He had ridden up in front of the line and quietly shown himself to the men, and his presence at that critical moment so cool and self confident, with the light of victory in his face, was to them assurance that all was going well and that the day was ours.

General Ewell beckoned me to him and said, "General Elzey is wounded. Take command of the brigade and tell the men to hold their ground a few moments longer. Hood's Texans are coming up to their support."

In a few moments the famous Texas brigade came on in splendid array. They had not been in the fight that day and were fresh and strong. They scarcely checked their gait as they met the enemy, but swept them off the field like chaff before the wind. The remnant of the Virginia troops who had held the ground for hours fell in with them and joined in the pursuit of Fitz John Porter's vanquished corps.

That night the headquarters of the brigade was established some two miles in the rear of the battlefield, and scattered men were collected there. By eight o'clock next morning the survivors of the battle were all in line, ammunition and rations were distributed, and details made to bury the dead. By ten o'clock the brigade was on the march in the direction the enemy had retreated. We passed right over the battlefield of the evening before where all was still and quiet, but the ground gave painful evidence of the fierce struggle. Hundreds of dead lay unburied, while dead horses, deserted guns, abandoned wagons, muskets and all sorts of military stores covered the ground and obstructed the road.

One more illustration of the spirit of the Confederate soldier I must give.

At the battle of Gaines Mill, of which I have been writing, the surgeon of the Thirteenth Regiment, Dr. W. S. Grimes of Gordonsville, Virginia, one of the best men in the army and a most faithful, efficient and tender surgeon, had established his field hospital at a small church a mile or two in the rear of the battlefield, and there all the wounded who could walk had gone and those who could not had been carried. The regiment had lost, in killed and wounded, about fifty per cent. The church could not hold them all, and many lay on the ground outside. It was a sorrowful sight. Some had died during the night and were lying covered with their blankets, awaiting a soldier's rude burial. Many were mortally wounded and were quietly awaiting the end; many were moving about with all sorts of wounds, heads and limbs bandaged.

In company with the surgeon, I visited the wounded men, and I do not remember hearing one complaint, and hardly a groan escaped their lips. There seemed to be one common feeling of exultation over the victory and of pride in the conduct

of the regiment to which they belonged. Even the dying men as
they held my hand would say, "Colonel, how did the regiment
behave? Did we do our duty?" There was not one unmanly word
uttered by all these suffering and dying soldiers, not one tear
was shed, nor was an expression of regret uttered by them.
They had fought like brave men; they suffered and died like
heroes.

One of the most serious obstacles to McClellan's advance on
Richmond via the Peninsula was the swampy character of the
ground. It was little less of a hindrance to the city's defenders.
More than once it has been said that it was not so much the
gallantry of the Army of Northern Virginia as Virginia mud which
defeated McClellan. The only advantage of the mud to the Confederates lay in the fact that McClellan could not bring up the heavier
guns from his boats on the river, making the combat of the
Confederates, who had no such guns, against superior numbers a
little less unequal.

The experience of Colonel Walker and his company at the Battle
of Malvern Hill [July 1, 1862] before Richmond illustrates the point.
Toward the close of the battle, Walker with his regiment and one
other of the Fourth Brigade, Ewell's division, was sent to reinforce
a part of the Confederate line which was hard pressed. It was
almost sundown. The Fourth Brigade had been lying in reserve,
and except for an occasional shell from the enemy's gunboats it had
not been under fire that day.

In order to reach the battlefield they had to cross an area of flat
land which was completely commanded by the numerous guns of
the enemy. The only way to cross this space with any hope of
surviving was to go two or three at a time at full speed. This
consumed a good deal of time, and it was almost dark when Walker
reformed his line under shelter of a heavy growth of pines on the
opposite side of the flag.

Advancing through these pines, the men came out into a broom-
sedge field across which the shells from the enemy's guns were
skimming the ground in quick succession. Advancing in line of
battle they crossed the field, on the opposite side of which they
encountered a very serious obstacle in the form of an extensive
marsh. Without stopping to ascertain whether it could be crossed
or not, Walker plunged in, the men following him. It was quite dark
as they floundered through the muck and mire, which was over

their knees from the start and in some places deeper. The suction of the mud pulled off one of Colonel Walker's cavalry boots. With that tucked under his left arm and sword in his right hand, he waded on, calling to his men to follow.

After great difficulty some of the men succeeded in crossing. An order to reform found more than half missing. Colonel Walker determined however to move forward with what troops he had. They climbed a steep hill and found themselves on the edge of an opening in which they could see the blazing guns of a heavy line of battle not more than two hundred yards in their front. Under cover of darkness they approached within twenty steps of the left of this line. There, Walker halted, uncertain as to who these men were. As he waited, trying to satisfy himself, four men were seen dragging out a wounded man. Captain Buck approached and examined them closely to find they were the enemy. He at once reported that fact to Colonel Walker.

Just then, a man from the firing line came back, discovered the Confederates, and fired at one of the Thirteenth. He was instantly killed by a bayonet thrust. The colonel, thinking his force too small to have any effect upon such a heavy line, determined to withdraw quietly. This he did, returning the way he came. His second crossing of the swamp completely broke up his command.

Captain Buck and a few others, finding themselves separated from their command and not knowing which way to go, lay down where they were and waited for daylight. When light came they went in search of Colonel Walker to find him with six men seated on a gun carriage. Walker always said he never knew what command or position of the enemy they had stumbled upon, nor just how his company got to where they finally found themselves. But he was sure that the enemy, except the one who shot at them and was killed, never guessed their presence in front of the Federal guns. Walker and his command literally had been lost on the field of battle at Malvern Hill.

TEN

Cedar Mountain

McClellan had failed to take Richmond and was now ordered back to the line of the Potomac in front of Washington. The corps of Fremont, Banks and Shields, fresh after a period of rest in the Valley, were formed into a new Army of Virginia; General Pope was put in command, and a new "On-to-Richmond" movement was planned by way of Gordonsville. The intent was to break Lee's line of communication with his base of supplies in the Valley, and, by detaching his troops to join the new Federal offensive, enable McClellan to escape unmolested from outside Richmond to move to Washington.

But Lee foresaw the move and on July 13, while Pope consolidated his new army, sent Jackson to Gordonsville with twelve thousand veterans. On July 27, another twelve thousand under A. P. Hill were added to Jackson's command. At that same time, Pope's orders fell into Lee's hands and were made public: the Federal war office had instructed Pope to require every man, woman and child in the area to take the oath of allegiance to the Federal government. The order roused much indignation in the Confederate ranks and stirred fresh bitterness throughout Virginia.

Jackson's advance reached Gordonsville on July 19. From the "little mountains of Orange," he watched his adversary, rested his men, and with his topographical engineers made an intensive study of the country. He found his opportunity on August 7. On that day, Pope moved forward to Culpeper Court House, sent a portion of his command on the road leading to Orange Court House, and left men strung all along the way to the foot of the Blue Ridge.

Jackson moved his men by concealed roads on August 7 to the vicinity of the Rapidan River. Next morning he drove in the Federal cavalry and took a favorable position on the low watershed between the Rapidan and Cedar Run, posting his guns on the slope and crest of Cedar Mountain. The force in front of him consisted of about eight thousand men under Banks.

Early in the fighting, Walker and his Thirteenth Virginia, serving as skirmishers along part of the line, advanced a little way into a woods. General Early watched the movement from a nearby position. According to J. William Jones' reminiscences of the battle, after the Thirteenth had advanced several minutes into the woods, Colonel Walker called back in his ringing voice: "General Early, are you ready?"

"Yes; go on," Early replied.

Soon, there was sharp skirmishing, followed by the roar of battle. Walker was in the midst of it again.

Banks attacked about 5 P.M., although there had been a sharp artillery duel lasting about two hours in the morning. Major Stringfellow now picks up the story of the battle, in which Federal casualties numbered 2,400 and Confederates 1,300:

> The enemy now opened on us with two batteries. But owing to the judicious manner in which General Early had posted us, the danger was slight. We suffered intensely for water as we lay in the broiling noon-day sun from 12 o'clock until about 5 o'clock in the evening.
>
> Just east of our position there was a cornfield, the corn in the roasting ear state. Suddenly, a loud cheer was heard in the direction of this cornfield. Looking, we saw a line [of Federal troops] had risen from the corn and was advancing toward us. General Early called us to attention and moved forward to meet them. The field in which we were and the field the enemy occupied both sloped gradually toward a small stream, about equal distances from the two lines and bordered on each side by a narrow strip of bottom. When within three hundred yards of each other, the lines opened battle. A section of a battery was sent to us, and the battle was now begun along Early's whole front, with no apparent advantage to either side.
>
> Whilst this was going on, W.B. Taliaferro's [Confederate] brigade advanced into a piece of timber just north of the Orange Road and immediately opposite to our left. For some cause this brigade broke and came out of the woods in great confusion, followed closely by the enemy. Taliaferro's men and the pursuing enemy crossed to the south side of the county road to our left and rear, not more than two hundred yards

from us. At this juncture of affairs the section of artillery which had been sent to help limbered and galloped to the rear. Our regiment was now ordered back to escape capture.

A scene of wild confusion followed. It seemed as though history was about to record a defeat for Stonewall Jackson. Only an act of heroic self devotion could avert it, and the Thirteenth was there to perform it.

Hardly waiting for the command of Colonel Walker, and as if by common consent, the men halted and, instead of continuing to retreat, wheeled to face the enemy. The [Federal] line in our front, having noted the confusion, had rushed forward with loud cheers, confident of victory. One company of the enemy had reached the position just left by the Thirteenth, and their whole line was not over one hundred yards from us. Our regiment was now surrounded by the enemy on three sides: front, left and rear. Paying no attention to what was on its left and rear, it steadily delivered a direct volley which caused the Federal line in our front to pause. Our men kept perfectly cool and again fired deliberately, having stepped forward as they loaded.

The enemy began slowly to give back, contesting every foot of ground. Gradually, the Thirteenth gained ground until they reached the position they had left. Step by step they then continued to force the Federals toward the stream, and then across it to the foot of the rise in the cornfield, the distance between the two lines steadily diminishing as the Thirteenth closed on them. The Thirteenth now reached the stream, pouring a deadly hail into the enemy's line which began to waver and in a few moments broke in wild confusion. Instantly the Thirteenth charged.

The enemy's line of retreat was toward Culpeper and somewhat diagonal with the county road. As the Thirteenth approached a knoll over which the county road passes, a column of the enemy's cavalry charged them, coming at full speed down the road with drawn sabers. On an occasion like this the military books say you must form a square. There was no time for it. All that could be done was for every man to square himself, which the boys did.

Just as the head of the column of Federal cavalry reached the foot of the knoll referred to, our boys delivered a volley and as quick as thought the head of that column went down. Those

in the rear were carried by the impetus of the charge into the
mass of dead men and horses. It was a wild scene and beggars
description. Into the charging mass, the bullets flew thick and
fast. Of those who came to this point very few escaped. Those
who were not unhorsed turned at right angles to their line of
charge and rode off across the stubble field just across the road
from the corn field. Here they encountered the fire of one of A.
P. Hill's brigades which had emerged from the woods from
which Taliaferro had been driven. Scarcely any escaped.

The rest of this column now came to the knoll. Seeing the
fate of those in front, they drew rein, turned and galloped to
their rear. Captain Zeby Ross of Company B was on the mountain, acting as guide for General Ewell. He told me that they
witnessed this chase and that General Ewell remarked, "That
is something I never saw before—the rear of a column break
first in battle."

This ninth day of August, 1862, was a glorious day for the
Thirteenth, and the boys were just where they wanted to
be—in front.

J. William Jones' story of the battle states that when Taliaferro's brigade and half of Early's brigade were driven back in
confusion and "a great disaster seemed inevitable," the artillery
stood fast to their guns with grape and canister, while:

Colonel J. A. Walker and his famous old Thirteenth Virginia stood firm as a rock...Jackson himself dashed upon the field,
the very personification of the genius of battle, and rallied his
broken legions with magic words and heroic examples...His
presence acted like a charm; his officers caught the inspiration;
the fugitives rallied at once around the heroic nucleus formed
by Colonel Walker with the Thirteenth Virginia, the "Stonewall" brigade came forward in gallant style...the enemy was
repulsed, and the disaster turned into victory. Just at this
point in the battle, I witnessed the charge of a magnificent
column of Federal cavalry, who came forward...Walker threw
the Thirteenth Virginia behind a fence and delivered, as they
galloped back, a withering fire at very short range, which
emptied many a saddle.

Dabney's *Life of Jackson*, too, gives the Thirteenth the credit for saving the day—saying it was around this heroic nucleus, the Thirteenth Virginia, that the remnant of Early's brigade formed.

A more personal touch is given the gallant conduct of the Thirteenth Regiment at Cedar Mountain by this extract from Dr. Abner C. Hopkins' manuscript narrative:

At the Battle of Slaughter's Mountain [more accurately known as Cedar Mountain], whilst Early's brigade was engaged with the enemy's center, our troops to our left gave way, allowing the enemy to pass to our left and rear. General Early commanded his brigade to retire to prevent capture. It did so except the Thirteenth. That being the left regiment positively refused to obey. It was their first and only act of disobedience in the whole war. Our boys, many of whom were standing upon their "native heath," could not entertain the idea of falling back. Stories of how Pope had been treating our friends had come through the lines, and we longed for a chance to engage him. Paying no attention to what was on our left and rear, the boys went straight for the enemy's center, solitary and alone, drove it back and routed it. Whilst in pursuit of it a column of cavalry charged hoping to check our advance. They too were almost annihilated. We pursued the retreating foe until darkness stopped us.

Colonel Walker now rode back to know what had become of the balance of the brigade. He met General Early, who addressed him in language more forcible than polite:

"Colonel Walker, what in the hell has become of the Thirteenth? I have sent back to Orange Court House and can hear nothing of it."

The colonel replied, "At the front, sir, where the balance ought to be."

I may add "Old Jube" didn't punish us for disobedience.

ELEVEN

Almost Captured

In his later years, General Walker gave an account of a little-known episode of Jackson's campaign in August of 1862 around Orange and Culpeper Court House, in which Walker and his entire Thirteenth Regiment came very nearly being captured.

The Thirteenth had been busy immediately after the Battle of Cedar Mountain. On the day following the battle, August 10, General Ewell made a particular request that the Thirteenth should go to the front as skirmishers. which they did. On the eleventh, Company A was detailed to keep order on the field while the enemy, under flag of truce, buried their dead. Jackson meanwhile moved back to Orange awaiting the arrival of Lee.

Then the whole army advanced into Culpeper again. Informed by General J. E. B. Stuart of numerous reinforcements which had already joined or were marching to aid Pope, Jackson gave up the idea of again engaging the enemy, and on the night of August 11 slipped away to his old position along the hills of Orange. Pope had planned to attack Jackson on the morning of the twelfth. Lee with fifty thousand men now joined Jackson, anxious to defeat Pope before McClellan could join him, and began a series of strategic movements to storm Pope's left and put the Army of Northern Virginia between Pope and his base of supplies at Washington.

It was during the early days of Jackson's march up the Rappahannock prior to the Battle of Second Manassas when Walker and the Thirteenth had their narrow escape. Walker recounted it this way:

In August, 1862, when Stonewall Jackson began his famous march to the rear of Pope's army, he marched up the right bank of the Rappahannock River and on Friday afternoon reached Warrenton Springs. As the enemy had no troops on the

opposite bank, it was decided [that Early's brigade would] cross
the shallow stream. That night, the troops bivouacked on the
left [north] bank of the river, the only Confederate troops on
that side of the river.

During the night it rained in torrents, and by daylight the
little river was an angry stream, past fording for man or horses. The enemy had notice of the fact that Jackson had begun to
cross the evening before, and early Saturday morning began
moving large bodies of troops up the river to confront his adversary. This single Confederate brigade thus cut off from all
hope of retreat or reinforcement seemed certain of capture
before noon of Saturday.

But a small creek which united its waters with the river
just below Early's position, and between his troops and the
advancing columns of Pope, was also swollen by the rain and
rendered impassable for infantry, and this delayed the enemy's
advance all the forenoon. In the afternoon, they crossed the
creek and advanced in heavy force and ought to have captured
the little force in their front with ease, if they had attacked at
once and in force.

Fortunately, General Pope had been led to believe that the
whole of Jackson's corps was across the river and immediately
in his front; and the Confederate troops, by presenting a bold
front and showing themselves at as many points as possible,
kept up the deception. The afternoon of Saturday was consumed by the Federal commander in bringing up reinforcements and preparing for an advance in heavy force on Sunday
morning. All day and night Saturday the Confederate engineers
were straining every nerve to throw a temporary bridge across
the river, and by daylight Sunday it was complete.

Just as the rising sun began to gild the hill tops the imperiled brigade crossed over the river to join the rest of the corps,
which occupied the hills on the southern side of the river. They
had not a moment to spare for the enemy followed close on
their rear, lining the hills commanding the stream and the low
grounds on the south bank with infantry and artillery. As the
little brigade marched across the plain in full view of both
armies their friends rent the air with cheers and the enemy's
artillery opened fire on them. To this fire the Confederate
artillery replied from the opposite heights.

The enemy's shot and shell ricocheted around the retiring column, and the Confederate missiles went screeching over their heads, but the brave boys, glad to get back safe to Dixie and relieved from fear of northern prisons, forgot their exhaustion and danger and, as they marched, struck up the popular war song, "Stonewall Jackson's Way:"

> *Let 'em bum, let 'em bum,*
> *The way is always clear,*
> *And while they are a bumming*
> *We'll strike 'em in the rear.*

When they reached the wooded hills out of range of the enemy's guns, as was supposed, they stacked their arms and, spreading their wet blankets on the wet ground, lay down to sleep after the severe strain of the last thirty-six hours.

At this time the Reverend J. William Jones, a faithful and devoted Christian, later to become well known to all Southern people, was chaplain of the Thirteenth Virginia Regiment of Early's brigade. He was always at the post of duty, always ready to march, to fight, to preach, or to minister to the dying on the battlefield and in the hospital. As soon as the hour for morning services arrived, he stepped into the midst of the sleeping congregation, as they lay scattered about on the ground, drew forth his Bible and hymn book and began by lining out a hymn and raising a tune. A few of his congregation awoke at the sound and joined lazily in the song of praise.

The hymn sung, he offered a prayer, took his text and was proceeding to preach an able and earnest sermon. But before he had reached his "secondly," a shot from one of the enemy's guns across the river went whizzing high over the heads of preacher and congregation. At the familiar sound some of the recumbent figures raised on their elbows and listened, but no remarks were made, and the preacher continued his discourse.

But a second, a third and a fourth shot rapidly followed, each falling lower and lower as the Federals found the range. Still the preacher stood his ground and stuck to his text while his congregation became wide awake to the situation.

Presently a shot better aimed fell in their midst, and others fell in most uncomfortable proximity, but fortunately nobody was hurt. Then the voice of the faithful chaplain was drowned by the voice of the colonel of the regiment, commanding "Attention." The chaplain quietly closed his discourse and took his place with the staff.

The men without hurry or confusion folded their blankets, formed in line, and the regiment moved back out of reach of the artillery fire. There, they again stacked arms and lay down to rest, and to the lullaby of the artillery duel, slept as peacefully and soundly as babes.

TWELVE

Second Manassas

Jackson, with Walker and his Thirteenth Virginia among his troops, took up his march around Pope's rear at early dawn on the morning of August 25. Again it was a fearfully hot day, the roads were dusty, and thousands of Jackson's men, overcome by the heat, fell out of line and lay panting on the roadside. But as soon as they had rested, they followed on, and by daylight next morning they were nearly all with their regiment ready to resume the march. This time they did not find it so easy to guess where they were going, nor for what purpose. Sunset found them at Bristoe Station in Pope's rear, Stuart's cavalry having joined them at Thoroughfare Gap.

Despite the darkness of a moonless night, Jackson sent Trimble's brigade and a part of Stuart's cavalry four miles farther on to Manassas Junction, with orders to take the place, destroy the railroad, cut the telegraph lines and capture the army stores. These orders were promptly carried out. The vast stores of quartermasters and commissary supplies thus acquired were most welcome to the Confederates, already beginning to feel a shortage of shoes and clothes as well as a lack of variety in their rations. Pope, advised of the presence of the enemy in his rear, ordered a rapid march to be followed by an attack on Jackson at Manassas Junction. But Jackson had set fire to the stores he could not carry away and was hastening to rendezvous with Lee.

The Battle of Second Manassas was finally joined, on almost the same ground where the first battle of the war had been fought, Jackson's men being concentrated in the same strong position the Federals had occupied at the first battle of Manassas, part of it fought in the cut of an unfinished railroad between Warrenton turnpike and Sudley's Mill.

"It was a fierce struggle," Walker later said of the battle, "as the list of killed and wounded will prove. The Federal troops were outnumbered, and taken by surprise, but they fought like devils. For ten hours the battle raged on that first bloody day, leaving the Confederates victorious as darkness ended the conflict."

His troops, Walker said, "charged with Early's and drove the enemy out of the railroad cut, pursuing them for three quarters of a mile. The Thirteenth was then deployed as skirmishers in front of Early's brigade. Near the base of Slaughter's Mountain we encountered a force of cavalry. As we pressed forward this cavalry fell back along the road from Orange to Culpeper Court House. There I halted the regiment and waited for Early to come up with the balance of our brigade, which he did in short time, forming on our right."

Stringfellow sums up the part taken by the Thirteenth Regiment in the engagement:

On the twenty-fifth of August Jackson started to Manassas; we made the trip by Salem, Fauquier County, fifty miles, on one pound of fresh beef (no bread, no salt) and two roasting ears of corn. Our division remained at Bristoe Station while the balance of the corps moved toward Manassas. We received Pope's advance and had a spirited engagement. That night we too fell back to Manassas Junction where we filled our haversacks.

The next day our corps took up its position along the line of the Manassas Railroad. The morning of the twenty-ninth the Thirteenth and Thirty-first Virginia, under Colonel Walker, were sent across the Warrenton Pike about half a mile from Jackson's right, and in front of it. We were ordered to hold a high hill close to the pike. Soon after taking our position on this hill we witnessed a battle between Pope's left and Jackson's right. Pope's men formed within three hundred yards of us, seeming not to be aware of our presence, there being a scrubby growth on the hill which masked our position. After being badly used up the Federals withdrew.

We now discovered long lines of infantry marching from the direction of Warrenton in line of battle. At the distance they were from us, we could not determine whether they were friends or foe. Suddenly the head of Longstreet's artillery made its appearance on the crest of the hill which had obstructed our view, coming at full speed, Stephen D. Lee at its head. As Longstreet's men dashed past us our old hats and caps went up in the air, and we yelled ourselves hoarse. It was a grand sight and a welcome one to us. Passing us a short distance, they filed to the left and occupied the identical ground the enemy had just left. Almost before the wheels had stopped turning, the guns announced in tones of thunder their arrival to both friend and foe. Our mission was ended, and we started back to our brigade.

Our route lay through a bottom just in rear of Longstreet's artillery, which was now drawing the fire of the enemy, the curvature of the shells dropping them uncomfortably close to the road. We did not "let the grass grow under our feet."

We had just reached the brigade when it was ordered forward to recapture a part of a railroad cut just captured by the enemy, which it did in fine style. When Pope renewed his attack on Jackson's line, our men not only held their positions but drove the enemy with Longstreet's help in confusion from the whole field.

This engagement at Groveton Heights between Pope's left and Jackson's right on August 29 was one of several grouped as "Second Manassas." It was by no means bloodless. There were fierce assaults and desperate repulses, anxiously watched by Lee from a vantage point whence he continued to send urgent messages to Longstreet to hasten to the relief of Jackson's sorely pressed line.

Our account of the battle is drawn from Hotchkiss' Confederate Military History, Volume III. At 5:00 P.M., when less than two hours of the day remained, Pope massed the divisions of Kearney and Stevens for a last assault upon Jackson's left. General Gregg, meeting this attack, exhausted his ammunition and sent an urgent request for more, adding that his Carolinians would hold on with the bayonet until it came. But they were slowly forced backward, while the Georgians and North Carolinians of Branch dropped in behind them, and all, like Indian fighters, took advantage of every rock and tree as the stubborn Federals forced them back.

Jackson promptly moved the Virginians of Field and Early, including Walker's regiment, from his center and threw them into A.P. Hill's hot contest on his left, finally routing and dispersing the Federal attack.

Next morning, the sun rose bright and clear as the Confederates
cooked their frugal breakfasts and made ready for another day of
fighting. Pope massed his first attack on Jackson's corps but,
meeting a hot reception, drew back and waited until 3 P.M. before
making an assault in force. At a signal, Porter's men sprang
forward, wheeled left and struck fiercely the Stonewall Brigade and
Lawton's division. The lines almost intermingled, so close and
furious was the fray, while Confederate dead and dying lay side by
side with Federals. Porter's left, as he closed in, was soon exposed
to Stephen D. Lee's masked batteries, and at the same time
Longstreet opened with three batteries upon his left rear.

Unable to withstand this enfilading fire, Pope's men fled "in
routed masses." Jackson's old division leaped across their defenses
and followed in hot pursuit. Longstreet's trained men, with S. D.
Lee in the lead, sprang forward, pushing the advantage, and
Confederate batteries sent parting shots after the fleeing Federals.
Stuart on the old Alexandria road to the right heard the "rebel
yell," joined in the pursuit and rushed his brigades and batteries
far in advance.

Darkness put an end to Jackson's advance and gave Pope's
demoralized brigades opportunity to seek safety. The day's advance
and retreat had cost Pope twenty thousand of his brave men in
killed, wounded and missing. Since meeting Jackson at Cedar
Mountain he had lost thirty thousand men, thirty pieces of artillery
and military stores and small arms worth millions. The victory at
Groveton Heights cost Lee eight thousand men, mostly in Jackson's
command, including many of his noblest and bravest officers.

"War is terrible! War is hell!" But no one can question that war
as our fathers knew it bred men of high courage who were inspired
with a glorious thrill of patriotic devotion as they offered up their
lives willingly, almost gaily at times, for the cause they had
espoused as dearer to them than life itself. Yes, I think we must
admit that war bred heroes in days of old, and now that war,
modern war, is unthinkable as a court of last resort, I wonder
sometimes what training school will take its place to give the world
men of sacrificial courage who count not even their lives too dear
a price to pay for their convictions.

It had been a long summer of marching, fighting—marching,
fighting—in rain and dust and fierce summer heat—fighting
against superior numbers and undiminished resources, with
dwindling ranks and diminished supplies. Yet the Army of North-

ern Virginia, buoyed by a spirit of invincible courage, confident in the genius of their military leaders, were jubilant over their recent victory and eager for an advance into the enemy's country. Lee said afterwards that the Confederates never knew where they were whipped.

But for that spirit of confidence and courage, the fall of '62 would have been what we would now call the psychological time to have asked for a truce and negotiations looking toward peace. Indeed, it seems to me that the end of the war at this time might have spared the South the evil days of Reconstruction, with all the bitter fruit it planted. As relentless as the dread fates are the unrolling events of history, composed of man's weaknesses and necessities. Nor is it given to fallible mortal to weigh results and foresee consequences. He can but make mistakes, to face them later and bear and overcome their consequences with such ability and courage as he may command. This, too, is often a brave man's part and helps to make up the stuff from which heroes are molded.

THIRTEEN

Sharpsburg

Lee sensed the eagerness of his army for an offensive movement. He realized that the whole South was expecting it, and knew
that, if ever, now was the time to invade the enemy's territory. He
did not, however, deceive himself, nor the Confederate War
Department, as to the poor equipment of his army for such an
attempt. His only reliance was on the valor of his men and the
military skill of their leaders.

With every band in the army playing "Maryland, My Maryland"
while the men shouted and cheered, Jackson led the advance,
fording the Potomac at White's ford near Edwards Ferry, where the
water was broad but shallow. Here, General Anthony Wayne had
crossed in marching his Pennsylvania brigade to the field of
Yorktown in 1781, and here the Confederates under Evans had won
a victory in the previous October. Stopping near Frederick, Lee
concentrated his army and issued a proclamation to Marylanders
urging them to join in defense of the South and to strike for their
own independence.

Few responded. This section of Maryland was inhabited by
small German farmers more closely allied to Pennsylvania than to
the South, and a large majority of them were Union men. Meantime
strict orders had been given that all food and supplies must be paid
for and that no depredations on private property or discourtesy to
individuals would be tolerated. So well did the army obey these
strict orders that few complaints were heard and thrifty Germans
found a ready market for their surplus farm products, crowding into
camp with cart and basket and driving bargains with the strictly
rationed "Rebs" for such luxuries as eggs, butter, chickens, apples
and fresh cider.

It was necessary to Lee's plan of campaign that the Federal
garrison at Harper's Ferry, with outposts at Martinsburg, be

dislodged. He confided this objective to Jackson for quiet execution, and on the morning of September 10 his command was early on the march for Martinsburg to capture the Federal outpost there. Walker, now in command of Trimble's brigade, was with him.

The investment of the fort at Harpers Ferry took place without a single failure in any of the movements of the prearranged plan. Five days later, on September 15, Lee received this note from Jackson: "Through God's blessing Harper's Ferry and its garrison are to be surrendered." In less than twenty-four hours Jackson had finished his job and was on his way back to join Lee.

In those five days, Lee had been busy. He found himself confronted with the whole of McClellan's army, which had occupied Frederick and was now rapidly approaching in force on the National Road, toward D. H. Hill's position on South Mountain and Lafayette McLaws' on the Potomac north of Harpers Ferry. An official copy of Lee's order No. 191 had come into McClellan's possession September 13, giving full plans for the entire campaign. McClellan had instantly foreseen his opportunity to strike Lee's divided force and crush it in detail.

Lee ordered Hill to retrace his march across South Mountain and hold its eastern slope. McLaws was urged to finish his work on the Maryland Heights and move to Boonsboro by way of Sharpsburg. Longstreet was ordered to return from Hagerstown to Hill's aid on the morning of the fourteenth.

Hotchkiss reports: "As Lee rode forward to the South Mountain battlefield on Sunday morning, September 14th, followed by Longstreet's command, he could both see and hear that the mighty conflict for the possession of the passes of that mountain, now looming up before him, had already begun. The roar of cannon and musketry from Hill's five thousand men sang in his ears and the smoke of battle showed by its length along the mountain top how thin must be Hill's stretched out line, and how large must be the force massing against it."

Hill held on until the middle of the afternoon, when Hooker's corps fell on his left rear near Turner's Gap. Lee then sent in four thousand of Longstreet's men in light brigades, and the fight went on. When night fell, nine thousand Confederates still held the crest of the mountain against twenty-eight thousand Federals.

At eight o'clock that evening, Lee wrote to McLaws, "The day has gone against us and the army will go by Sharpsburg and cross the river. It is necessary for you to abandon your position tonight.

Your troops you must have in hand to unite with this command which will retire by Sharpsburg."

Jackson hastened to join Lee, after leaving A. P. Hill in command at Harper's Ferry with orders to parole the garrison and send them adrift toward Frederick City to impede any advance of McClellan's troops from that direction. So exhausted were his men that many fell by the wayside before bivouac was reached near Shepherdstown. At dawn on the morning of the sixteenth, Jackson saluted Lee in front of Sharpsburg and reported his men were just behind, crossing the Potomac.

Among them was Walker. "When Harpers Ferry surrendered," Walker noted later, "we were ordered to cook three days rations. but before we had gotten half through, news of Longstreet's repulse was received, and the half cooked bread was packed up and a forced night march begun for Sharpsburg."

Still in command of Trimble's brigade, Walker was stationed on the right of Ewell's division, just in front of the "Eastwoods," during the battle of Sharpsburg. They were vigorously attacked by Hooker's corps at dawn on September 17th and forced to retire.

Walker later wrote notes of Sharpsburg, describing it as "perhaps the hardest battle ever fought by General Lee's troops." It also was one that well illustrates their courage as well as that of their leader.

It was fought, Walker notes, in open ground without fortifications from dawn to evening by thirty-six thousand Confederates against eighty-five thousand Federals. The Confederates were forced back, contesting every inch of ground until night put an end to the strife. They had lost twenty-five per cent of their entire force, every regiment had been sent into the action, and not a reserve was to be had. Yet after dark, surrounded by dead and dying, they reformed, strengthened their lines and waited without fear for the renewal of the battle which they expected at dawn. The enemy had lost heavily, but they had a reserve force of seventeen thousand men who had not fired a gun, and reinforcements were on their way to join them. History affords few if any examples of more heroic courage than was shown by Lee and his men on the field.

Walker, commanding Trimble's brigade, lost three out of four regimental commanders and 228 out of his seven hundred men.

This summary is not made so much to laud Confederate valor as to illustrate the complete change in the mode of warfare between 1862 and later years. Reading accounts of the battles of the Civil

War and the memoirs of those who took part in them, one can
better understand the uplifting excitement of those battlefields, the
call to personal courage and initiative, the thrill of victory, the
pride in one's own regiment, and the sense of glory achieved when
promotion was awarded for "Signal valor on the field of battle."

Gone forever is such warfare—bands playing, drums beating,
flags flying, mounted cavalry dashing to the charge, gallant officers
leading in person their cheering troops, while booming artillery and
rattling musketry added to the excitement of the combat. Such a
life and death struggle provided far beyond the excitement of the
most closely contested game of the World Series, far beyond the
thrill of the best matched championship football contest. Bullets
were not felt, and death had no terrors while the thick of the fight
was on.

FOURTEEN

On the Rappahannock

After Sharpsburg, the fighting kept on to the very end of that year of '62. Just before the brilliant Confederate victory at Fredericksburg in December of '62, Walker was put in command of Early's brigade. Having led Trimble's brigade at Harper's Ferry and Sharpsburg, he rapidly was building leadership experience.

There was a brief respite during October of '62, when the Army of Northern Virginia and the Army of the Potomac watched each other from opposite sides of the Rappahannock River, McClellan waiting for reinforcements and Lee for his stragglers to come up, his sick and disabled to return and his exhausted army to recuperate.

It was during that winter that Lee wrote to his daughter-in-law, Charlotte Lee: "We are up to our eyes in mud now and have but little comfort. Mr. Hooker looms up very large over the river. He has two balloons up in the day and one at night...Your cousin Fitz Lee beat up his quarters the other day with about four hundred of his cavalry and advanced within four miles of Falmouth, carrying off 150 prisoners with their horses, arms, etc. The day after he recrossed the Rappahannock, they sent all their cavalry after him...But the bird had flown...I hope these young Lees will always be too smart for the enemy."

In the Confederate camp there were frequent consultations, anxious planning, much making and studying of maps of the surrounding territories, while appeal after appeal was sent to the War Department for reinforcements and supplies for the depleted, hungry and ragged Army of Northern Virginia, in preparation for an advance into Pennsylvania in the early spring.

On the Federal side of the river, there was even greater activity. Burnside was relieved for alleged inefficiency, and his second-in-command, Major General Joseph Hooker, went actively to the task for restoring the efficiency of his army, receiving reinforcements which brought his numbers up to about one hundred and thirty thousand. This seemed a sufficient force to surround and annihilate Lee's sixty-three thousand veterans, and to this end careful plans were laid.

The pickets of the opposing armies, meantime, were having fun with each other. It was during the quiet watches of the night, when brush wood fires cast lurid gleams across the chilly waters of the river, silhouetting the enemy's slowly pacing sentinels.

"Hello, Yank," an impertinent Confederate would call out. "Got any coffee or sugar over on your side? I've got some fine Virginia yellow leaf tobacco. Come across and I'll swap with you, safe conduct guaranteed, of course."

"All right, Johnnie, I'll risk you, but you'd better slow down your fire and keep a sharp lookout. If anything happens to me, General Hooker'll come across tomorrow and wipe you Rebs off the face of the earth."

"On the word of a Virginia gentleman, Yank; no harm shall come to you. That's enough, isn't it?"

A moment later the splash of oars might be heard, presently a murmured word of exchange and thanks between the enemy pickets, then the sound of oars again followed presently by the clump, clump of rag-wrapped feet along the worn path by the river on the Confederate side.

Sometimes the exchange would be in epithets and taunts rather than in luxuries.

"Hello there, Yank! I hear you've got a new general. Don't see how you keep up with 'em, you swap 'em so often. You've lost your Pope, eh!—found he wasn't infallible. Also your next bewhiskered incompetent! We'll get your new Hooker, hooked to the rest of 'em soon as spring opens."

"Never mind, Mr. Johnny Reb, you won't be poking fun much longer. We'd 've got you long ago but for this darned sticky mud your precious Virginia is made of."

And so on, with jeers and taunts and supposed witticism at each other's expense. It was one way of lessening the tedium of camp life and of asserting their confidence in their leaders.

FIFTEEN

Loss of Jackson

Finally came Chancellorsville, a battle that was to have monumental effect on the Confederacy and James A. Walker.

By a well executed strategic movement a large part of Hooker's army was by April 29th concentrated on Lee's flank. Exultingly, Hooker issued a general order April 30 in which he said in part: "Our enemy must ingloriously fly or come from behind his defenses and give us battle on our own ground, where certain destruction awaits him."

Lee made ready to meet the anticipated attack. Leaving Early with two brigades at Fredericksburg to watch Sedgwick with his forty thousand troops, he advanced the rest of his army to a position between the two Federal forces, so disposing his men as to face both armies.

Hooker had concentrated his army in a most formidable fortified position not far from Chancellorsville. His first day's advance toward Fredericksburg was repulsed by the Confederates. The second day's engagement was awaited while both armies rested, practically on the field of battle. During the night Lee's scouting parties returned to tell him that a front attack on Hooker's entrenched lines was practically impossible. "Then we must attack from our left," said Lee to Jackson.

By early dawn Jackson sent Major Hotchkiss to look for a road around Hooker's front and right to his rear, shorter than the well known one by Todd's Tavern. The sun had just risen when Jackson with his whole corps was marching southward, then southwestward, to the Brook Road, paralleling nearly the entire front of Hooker's position and turning his right.

"The dense forest that covered Hooker's eastward front," says Hotchkiss, "prevented his seeing the small force that Lee held opposed to him; while the fierce demonstration that Lee made all along this front with infantry and artillery, keeping an almost continuous fire, deceived Hooker as to his numbers and made him hesitate to advance from his entrenchments and ascertain what was really opposed to him.

"Taking counsel of his fears he allowed Lee to hold him all day in check, while Jackson was eagerly and swiftly marching around his right flank. The movement was about complete and promised to be brilliantly successful when, just at sunset, Jackson called a halt of his somewhat discouraged front line, in order to concentrate and reform them. Jackson now held possession of the field of combat to within a mile of Chancellorsville. Another turning of Hooker's right along the direction of this road would cut off his line of retreat and throw him into the arms of Lee. Jackson had urged A.P. Hill to form in line of battle and then to 'press them, cut them off from the United States. Lord, Hill! press them!'"

Accompanied by his staff and escort, Jackson rode along the turnpike through the twilight, intensified by the heavy forest on each side of the road, and up to his skirmish line to reconnoiter. The accompanying engineers even rode up to a Federal battery which had halted in the road, and one of them, Captain Howard of A.P. Hill's staff, was captured. The ringing of axes of a stalwart brigade of Federal pioneers told Jackson that Hooker was already throwing obstacles in the way of his advance, so he promptly turned back and rode in a trot toward his own command. As he approached Hill's newly formed line of battle, some one called out: "A Yankee cavalry charge!" Without orders the Eighteenth North Carolina fired a volley of ounce musket balls, one of which desperately wounded Jackson.

He was removed to a field hospital, and his arm amputated. A week later, from a complication of illness with the effect of his wound, Jackson in his own last words "crossed over the river to rest under the shade of the trees."

Chancellorsville ended in a glorious victory for Lee, but at the fearful cost of Jackson and 12,500 casualties in killed, wounded and missing of the flower of his army. Neither could be replaced, and from that hour the star of the Confederacy waned.

Says Lieutenant Colonel S. H. R. Henderson, professor of strategy in the British Staff College, writing of Jackson: "No general made fewer mistakes, no general so persistently outwitted his opponents, no general better understood the use of ground or the value of time, no general was more highly endowed with courage, both physical and moral, and none ever secured to a greater degree the trust and affection of his troops. And yet so upright was his life, so profound his faith, so exquisite his tenderness, that Jackson's many victories are almost his least claim to be numbered among the world's true heroes."

Other casualties among officers at bloody Chancellorsville were the wounding of A. P. Hill and the death of General Frank Paxton, instantly killed at the head of the Stonewall Brigade. That famous command had lost one after another of its generals: Jackson, Garnett, Winder, Grigsby, and now Paxton—the last three killed while leading the brigade.

Lying ill at Brandy Station, Jackson was told that once again his brigade, the "Stonewall," was leaderless, and he was asked whom he would like to have succeed the gallant Paxton.

"Give the Stonewall to James A. Walker," he said. "I do not know a braver officer."

Thus did the "true and tender Jackson," in probably the last command he ever issued, wipe out all possibility of any remnant of misunderstanding between him and his ex-pupil. I pay my own reverent tribute by repeating the words of Henderson: "His many victories are almost his least claim to be considered among the world's true heroes."

Walker's rank was now officially raised to that of brigadier general. He had been in command of a brigade for several months prior to his assignment to the "Stonewall." His promotion had already been slated, General Ewell having recommended it the previous March in the following letter:

Richmond, Virginia
March 15th, 1863

General S. Cooper
Headquarters
Richmond, Virginia

General:

I wrote a short time since recommending Colonel J. A. Walker 13th Va. for promotion, to Brigadier General.

The recommendation was based on what I had seen of Colonel Walker from March to September 1862. He was more particularly under my observation at Cross Keys, Cold Harbor

and Port Republic. At Cedar Run he was especially recommended by General Early and complimented in the strongest
terms—his Regiment twice repulsed at Cedar Run an attack of
the enemy and cavalry. His Regiment was on many occasions
selected for important and dangerous posts. This particularly at
Cross Keys, Cedar Run and Cold Harbor. Gen. Early on one
occasion observed that he had employed Col. Walker and his
regiment so often on such duty, that he was conscious of requiring of them more than from others.

Want of time prevents me from making extracts from these
reports but Col. Walker has been recommended by General
Jackson, General Elzey and General Early as well as myself.
Respectfully,
R. S. Ewell

In another report dated March 6, 1863, General Ewell mentioned that he had recommended the promotion and described
Walker as a "most efficient and gallant officer, who is already to
perform any duty assigned him...When Colonel Walker is in front
with his men deployed as skirmishers I feel secure against an
ambuscade. I respectfully and earnestly recommend him for
promotion..."

Walker's promotion was May 15, 1863, and he assumed
command of the Stonewall Brigade the following day.

It was with sincere regret that Walker took leave of his old
regiment, the Thirteenth, as the letter he addressed to them
warmly testifies:

May 20th 1863
Fellow Officers and Soldiers of the 13th Regiment:

Having been assigned to the command of Paxton's brigade, I
take official leave of the gallant officers and men of the 13th, whom
I have so long had the honor to command. And in doing so, I desire
to return to each and every one of you my heartfelt thanks for the
ready and cheerful obedience which you have always accorded to
my command. Coming among you by appointment of the Governor,
an entire stranger, from a different section of the State, I met with
nothing but kindness and friendship, and a cordial support in all
my efforts to discharge the duties of my office. For this I owe you
a debt of good will and gratitude, which will long be remembered.
But a higher and infinitely greater debt of gratitude is due you, not

from me alone, but from your country, for the unflinching courage, gallantry and fortitude, which you have displayed on more than a dozen battlefields, and for the patient endurance which you have exhibited, amid all the hardships and privations of an arduous campaign.

It would be idle for me to attempt to compliment the regiment which Gen. Ewell placed in his "Iron Brigade." The future historian will record your deeds and the name of the 13th Reg't will be immortal.

Fellow Officers and Soldiers, I found you a large regiment; I leave you but a handful of scarred and tried veterans. Yet formidable not in numbers but in that invincible spirit which never quails and never falters in the tried valor of your officers and in the glorious name you have won, which is a heritage of glory to you and to your children and which I know you will never lose but with your lives. Then when you look at your diminished numbers be not discouraged; but point to your scars and to your tattered colors, and to the graves of your brave companions in arms, who have fallen by your side, and say it is of these we boast and are proud.

In leaving you to take the command to which your bravery and good conduct have raised me, I feel that I am severing an old and dear tie. Wherever I may go and whatever future may await me, I will ever remember with emotions of pride and pleasure the gallant men of the 13th Virginia.

    J. A. Walker
    Brig. General

SIXTEEN

Gettysburg

Before his first month as commander of the Stonewall Brigade was ended, the newly promoted Brigadier General James A. Walker found himself marching his new command northward in the Gettysburg campaign.

During the Pennsylvania campaign, the Stonewall Brigade was a part of General Edward Johnson's Division of Ewell's Corps. As they moved north in June, Johnson, with the Stonewall Brigade, moved to Winchester, to prevent General Robert Milroy, commanding some six thousand Federal troops, from joining Hooker's army in Pennsylvania.

On June 13 and 14, General Walker led his brigade to the hills to the east and fronting Winchester. They skirmished all day on the fourteenth. That night, after dark, he learned the rest of the division was moving on Berryville and he was to follow. He gave this report on the ensuing action:

Calling in my skirmishers as quickly as possible, I moved by the Berryville pike and Jordan's Springs, and was within a mile of Stevenson Depot, at dawn, when heavy firing in that direction announced that the brigade in our front were engaging the enemy. Hurrying up the command as rapidly as possible, we reached the scene of action just as a portion of the enemy's forces were endeavoring to make their escape in the direction of Jordan's Springs. I ordered the Fourth, Twenty-seventh and Thirty-third Regiments which were in rear of the column to face to the left and advanced in line of battle in the direction of the enemy's column to cut off their retreat.

The Second and Fifth Regiments were moved forward and formed in line of battle on the right of the road, and on the right flank of General Steuart's brigade.

At this point Walker learned his command was needed on the
right, and he recalled the Fourth, Twenty-seventh and Thirty-third
Regiments and sent them, with the Second and Fifth, toward the
Berryville turnpike. Walker picks up the tale again:

Advancing at once with the Second and Fifth Regiments
through the fields in right of the woods, in which General
Steuart's brigade was posted, we crossed the railroad and
reached the turnpike without encountering the enemy.

The smoke and fog was so dense that we could only see a
few steps in front, and when, on reaching the Martinsburg
turnpike, I saw a body of men about fifty yards to the west of
that road moving by the flank in the direction of Martinsburg,
it was with difficulty I could determine whether they were
friends or foes, as they made no hostile demonstrations, and
refused to say to what brigade they belonged. Being satisfied,
at last, that it was a retreating column of the enemy, I ordered
the command to fire. The enemy gave way and retreated back
from the pike in disorder at the first fire, returning only a
straggling and inaccurate fire.

Pressing them back rapidly to the woods west of the road,
they made no stand, but hoisted a white flag and surrendered
to the two regiments before the others came up. Total number
of prisoners taken by the brigade at this point amounted to 713
non-commissioned officers and privates, and eighty-three commissioned officers, six stand of colors, and arms, accoutrements,
etc., corresponding to the number of prisoners taken...Total
casualties of the brigade on this day was three wounded.

Crossing into Pennsylvania, Ewell's corps, with Walker and his
men, encamped at Carlisle for two days, taking no part in the first
days fighting at Gettysburg but securing a carload of much needed
shoes and other supplies. Walker later reported on his brigade's
participation:

On the evening of the first of July the brigade, with the rest
of the division, arrived at Gettysburg, Pennsylvania, and after
nightfall took position on the southeast side of the town, near
the Hanover road, and on the extreme left of our line, on Culp's
farm, and throwing forward skirmishers, we remained for the
night.

At dawn the next morning the enemy's skirmishers were seen in our front, and a brisk fire was opened between them and my own, which was kept up during the day at long range with but short intervals of quiet. About 6 o'clock P.M. our line was advanced in a northerly direction and took position immediately on the north side of the Hanover road. In this position, our left flank being harassed by the enemy's sharpshooters posted in a wheat field and wood, I ordered Colonel Nadenbousch, with his regiment (the Second Virginia), to clear the field and advance into the wood and ascertain, if possible, what force the enemy had at that point, which he did at a single dash, his men advancing with great spirit, driving the enemy's skirmishers out of the cleared ground and following them into the woods.

When he had advanced some distance into the woods, the enemy opened fire on his line with two pieces of artillery, and he fell back into the cleared ground again, leaving skirmishers in the edge of the wood, and reported that the enemy had a large force of cavalry, supposed to be two brigades, two regiments of infantry and a battery of artillery.

This information I communicated through a staff officer to Major-General Johnson, and immediately thereafter received information from Major Doublas, of his staff, that the line was about to advance, with instructions from General Johnson to remain on the flank if I thought it necessary. As our flank and rear would have been entirely uncovered and unprotected in the event of my moving with the rest of the division, and as our movement must have been made in full view of the enemy, I deemed it prudent to hold my position until after dark, which I did.

After dark, I withdrew, and leaving a picket on the Hanover road, joined the rest of the division in rear of the enemy's breastworks, which they had driven them from the evening before.

At daylight next morning Steuart's brigade, which was immediately in my front, became hotly engaged, and on receiving a request from General Steuart, I moved up to his support and became warmly engaged along my whole line; and my right, extending beyond the breastwork, suffered very heavily. After five hours' incessant firing, being unable to drive the enemy from his strong position, and a brigade of Rodes' division coming to our assistance, I drew my command back under the hill out of the fire, to give them an opportunity to rest and clean their guns and fill their cartridge boxes.

In about an hour I was ordered by General Johnson to move more to the right and renew the attack, which was done with equally bad success as our former efforts, and the fire became so destructive that I suffered the brigade to fall back to a more secure position, as it was a useless sacrifice of life to keep them longer under so galling a fire.

An hour or two later, I was again ordered to advance so as to keep the enemy in check, which I did, sheltering my men and keeping up a desultory fire until dark.

About midnight we were drawn off with the rest of the division, and at daylight were again formed in line of battle on the heights south of Gettysburg, where we remained all day and until about eleven o'clock, when we marched with the division in the direction of...the Potomac.

Of 1,450 men in the Stonewall Brigade who fought at Gettysburg, thirty-five were killed, 208 were wounded and 87 were missing.

Because of the bravery and leadership he showed during this campaign and after, Walker soon gained the confidence of his new brigade. As a result, some of his men paid him the ultimate compliment: they called him affectionately "Stonewall Jim."

Years later, I accompanied my father to a Confederate reunion at Louisville, Kentucky, and was taken out at a dinner, given at the country club for ex-officers and their families, by an agreeable gentleman, introduced to me as Colonel Nichols. Presently, he said to me, "I have not had the honor or meeting your gallant father since we parted at Culp's Hill on the battlefield of Gettysburg."

"At Gettysburg?" I asked. "Were you in Ewell's corps? Where were you stationed—on my father's right, of course?"

"No," he answered with a smile. "On top of Culp's Hill, and doing my anxious best to stay there. Your father came near dislodging me. That was a desperately brave charge he made."

And then I knew that Colonel Nichols was in command of the Federal artillery posted on Culp's Hill, and that no small share of that Federal victory was due to his stubborn stand.

Colonel Nichols had moved to Kentucky after the war, had affiliated in business and social life with the natives and become practically one of them, honored and beloved by many of his old enemies. Mrs. Pickett, wife of the Confederate hero of Gettysburg, who led the famous charge at Cemetery Hill, was Colonel Nichols' house guest at this time. Being on the entertainment committee for the reunion, he gave a brilliant reception in his spacious home and was as much interested in making the occasion delightful as if the comrades and their families present had worn the blue and stood beside him in the defense of Culp's Hill.

SEVENTEEN

Mine Run

During the autumn of 1863, General Meade led the third "On to Richmond" movement. But his over-caution enabled Lee to hold him in check, despite the Confederate disaster at Bristoe Station and the capture of two of Early's brigades, during Lee's returning march to the Rappahannock. "Nothing prevented my concentrating in Meade's front," said Lee in his report, "but the destitute condition of the men, thousands of whom are barefooted, a greater number partially shoed, and nearly all without overcoats, blankets or warm clothing. I think the sublimest sight of the war was the cheerfulness and alacrity exhibited by this army in the pursuit of the enemy under all the trials and privations to which it was exposed."

Lee put his men in winter quarters on the sunny side of the hills of Orange, selecting a dense pine thicket where he fixed his headquarters for the winter. On November 26, Meade made a surprise attack, of which Lee was warned by the vigilant Stuart in time to bring Hill from his left to reinforce Ewell on his right. The two advancing eastward to meet Meade found a strong defensive line along Mine Run, a tributary of the Rapidan. In this Mine Run campaign, Johnson's division fought a hard battle at Payne's farm. The Stonewall Brigade lost heavily. The Reverend Abner C. Hopkins of Charlestown, West Virginia, then chaplain of the Stonewall Brigade, contributed this personal recollection of the battle:

The Stonewall was to have been the rear brigade on the march of our division that morning. But the Third Brigade was tardy in taking the road and was left far in the rear. Behind us and before the Third Brigade was the train of artillery and ambulances.

At a certain place where our brigade halted for the usual
rest we overheard some firing from our rear and left. Soon,
Major R. W. Hunter of General Edward Johnson's staff galloped from the rear and told us that some Yankees were in the
woods on our left and firing upon our train.

General Walker at once threw out the Second Regiment as
skirmishers to cover our brigade. Colonel Raleigh Colston commanding the regiment directed me to attend him. We advanced
to an open field and, finding no body of the enemy, Colonel
Colston, by General Walker's orders, took a few men and
moved in line to the left, where we located the enemy. For
hours our regiment skirmished. Then General Walker brought
to our support the rest of the brigade and ordered a charge
upon the enemy's strong line, which was eminently successful.

At nightfall we drew off and joined our army. During this
day General Walker was much exposed in full view of the
enemy and bore himself in the most gallant and inspiring
manner.

Just before night, as the heavy firing ceased, the general
and a number of us were standing together talking. He was
mounted on his fine bay horse, and Lieutenant Strother Barton
was stroking the horse's neck, when suddenly we heard a sharp
crack, and Lieutenant Barton began to spin around like a
partridge shot in the head. He had been hit in the leg and the
bone broken.

That night, I was at the field hospital ministering all night
to the wounded, and it was my sad office to aid the surgeons in
amputating the leg of both Colonel Colston and Lieutenant
Barton. [Colonel Colston died a few weeks later of pneumonia.]

The next day, through a cold November rain, I attended the
train of ambulances bearing our wounded to Orange Court
House. About midnight we loaded the last of them upon the
railroad train for the rear. The day following I returned to the
army. General Walker received me graciously and in a very
kind way said, "I'll recommend you for any field office you
want, Hopkins." I told him I preferred being chaplain.

Early in December, Meade withdrew across the Rapidan and
went into winter quarters in the vicinity of Brandy Station. Lee's
army was undisturbed for two months but was obliged to picket
vigilantly a line of twenty miles along the river. Major Hotchkiss

described that winter of 1863-64 when Lee's army had to contend "with foes more difficult to overcome than Federal soldiers:"

These were want of food and want of clothing...in the log cabins they constructed from the trees of the surrounding forest, and on beds of straw or pine boughs without blankets, but fortunately with abundant supplies of fuel near at hand. The rations were reduced to a minimum—a quarter of a pound of pork and a scant portion of meal or flour per day per man, and even that was sometimes wanting. A depreciated currency added an enormous value in paper dollars to all the necessities of life. And the high tide of starvation prices prevailed everywhere, especially in the army, where the pay of even officers of the highest grade was scarcely sufficient to meet the most common wants. Cornmeal was $50 a bushel, beans $60, bacon $8 a pound and sugar $20.

The redeeming features of these days of gloom and suffering were the bright shining of the heroic virtues, not only of the men, but of the women and children of the Confederacy...

The cheerful endurance of the Army of Northern Virginia was made possible by their sublime faith. A marked spirit of devotion characterized every portion of it. From nearly every cabin could be heard the voice of prayer and the singing of hymns of devotion. Spacious though crude log chapels were constructed by willing hands for religious services, and the country churches within and near the camps were utilized for like purposes. Not only army chaplains but the ablest preachers of the gospel from all accessible parts of the Confederacy ministered in these crude army churches to the soul hunger of Lee's reverent, and most of them God serving, officers and men.

I have often heard my father tell of this winter of actual suffering for Lee's army, as it lay in winter quarters on the Orange side of the Rapidan. Also of the great religious revival which swept over the army and which was, as Major Hotchkiss has related, a large factor in the cheerful endurance of the men. Chaplain Hopkins made this comment:

Our brigade was quartered near Pisgah Church, Orange County. We set to work early to build a chapel. When I asked General Walker for some favors to men who would work on the building, he very cheerfully ordered that they be exempted as far as possible from daily military duties.

One day in his tent, he said to me, "I want the morale of my brigade kept up to the highest point, and I want you to remember that I hold you responsible for it. You must call on me for anything you wish me to do."

The soldiers also brightened their dreary camp life with some lighter diversions, such as crude amateur theatricals, story, joke and song fests around the camp fire, varying the singing of hymns with southern songs—Sewannee River, Juanita, Nelly Bly, Robin Adair, Ben Golt, Hazel Dell, Nellie Gray, Auld Robin Gray, and so on—frequently interspersed with Dixie. Now and then a book came to one of the officers who passed it around till it was worn out. Several copies of *Les Miserables* circulated among the men, who changed its title to "Lee's Miserables" and enjoyed what seemed to them a bright pun and a delicate bit of irony.

The snowball battle, an incident of this winter which I have heard my father and other survivors recount with particular delight, is given in the language of Dr. Hopkins:

The earth was covered several inches deep with snow. The boys began snowballing. In the afternoon a challenge was sent by our Division to Ramseur's Division, a short distance away. Ramseur's Division chose General Dole for their commander and our division chose General Walker.

The two divisions met in open field. General Walker had arranged a flank movement to surprise the Louisiana Brigade in some woods on our right front. He directed our men to make large piles of snowballs on which we should fall back at the proper time. The two lines met, and a fiercer and more determined battle has seldom been fought with muskets.

Our general was quickly surrounded, his horse seized by the reins, and a combined attack was made upon him, till he could scarcely be seen for the cloud of snow. Truth compels me to tell that the capture of our leader demoralized our division and that the victory remained with the Louisianans.

EIGHTEEN

Spotsylvania

*In a speech by General Walker, twenty years after the war, on
the Wilderness Campaign of the spring of '64, this account of the
man-to-man engagement known as the "Bloody Angle" and the
charge of Hancock's corps well illustrates the sort of warfare which
was then practiced and is now obsolete. It so forcefully gives us the
atmosphere of the time—when officers were heroes, soldiers hero
worshipers and each individual deed of valor ennobled not only the
man but his company—that I shall quote it verbatim.*

*It refutes, I think, the assertion that war is and always has been
utterly degrading, without mitigating circumstances, and that it
makes brutes of men and lets loose all the evil passions to which
they are subject. Certainly I have no brief for war. It is seldom
justified or brings other than woe in its train. But sometimes I fear
that men will grow soft in their extreme zeal to put an end to human
suffering, in the indulgence of excessive pity for those who must
endure hardness, or pay the penalty of their mistakes, even of their
wrongdoing. We no longer believe that endurance develops and
hardens the moral fibre of men or that self sacrifice is of itself
ennobling. In following General Walker's address we shall see how
different was the point of view in the Sixties. Perhaps it was this
difference which made the men of that generation a special type of
men about whose lives and achievements a glamour lingers even yet:*

A little retrospection will not be amiss before speaking of
the battle of Spotsylvania, one of the battles of that hard-
fought Wilderness campaign in May of 1864. It will be remembered that the Army of Northern Virginia, having defeated
McDowell, McClellan, Pope, Burnside and Hooker, met its first
check at the hands of General Meade at Gettysburg. The Federal government then brought General Grant from the West,

flushed with victory, to command the largest and best equipped
army ever gathered on American soil. Its appointed task was to
destroy the army of General Lee and capture the capital of the
Confederate states. To accomplish this cherished object the new
commander was promised all the men, means, and munitions
of war he should ask for.

On the fourth day of May, 1863, when General Grant
crossed the Rapidan River, his whole force amounted to one
hundred and forty thousand men, while that of General Lee
amounted to sixty-four thousand, the odds being over two and a
quarter to one. Any other commander except Robert E. Lee
would have held it prudent to retire before such odds, watch for
opportunities to strike his antagonist at exposed points, and
select and fortify a strong position near Richmond. But General
Lee was as bold and daring as he was skillful and prudent, and
he knew that the men he commanded were equal to any task
that soldiers could accomplish, and that they relied on him
with unquestioning faith. They believed that whatever "Marse
Bob" did was the very best that could be done, and they believed that whatever he set before them to do, they could and
would do. General Lee knew that with such men, the veterans
of three years experience, he could hope to calculate on defeating an army of more than two and one fourth to one.

As soon as he learned that his adversary had crossed the
river he broke up his camp around Orange Court House, advanced into The Wilderness, and on the fifth gave battle to the
enemy, as soon as he came up with him. General Grant, instead of following a retreating foe, found himself compelled to
halt, concentrate his vast army and deliver battle before he had
been across the river thirty-six hours.

After two days of hard fighting, General Grant was no
nearer Richmond than when the fight began, and he gave up
the task of driving General Lee before him, or of defeating him
in a pitched battle. The seventh of May was passed in compara-
tive quiet, the Confederates confidently awaiting the expected
attack which never came. The two armies then rested about
seventy-five miles northwest of Richmond, with the Confederate right and the Federal left flank nearest Richmond, which
lay to the southwest. It will be seen that by moving by his left
flank, General Grant could pass around General Lee's right

and place his army between his adversary and the Confederate capital.

On the afternoon and night of the seventh General Grant began his first flank movement, withdrew from the front of his adversary, and attempted by a secret and quiet movement to pass around General Lee's right flank under cover of darkness and so get between General Lee's army and Richmond. It will readily be seen that General Grant had a longer line to traverse to reach any point between his antagonist and Richmond, than General Lee had to reach the same point. In military phrase, General Lee operated on the inner and shorter line, while General Grant had the outer and longer line.

But this advantage for the Confederate commander was counterbalanced by the fact that General Grant, by covering his movement with his cavalry, and with lines of infantry pressed close to the lines of his foes, making demonstrations as if an attack was imminent, could withdraw the great bulk of his army from the front, and get several hours the start before his real designs could be fathomed.

When General Grant on the seventh of May began his flank movement his objective point was Spotsylvania Court House, which would place him in rear of Lee's right flank. General Lee on the night of the seventh discovered Grant's movement, and at once began to bring up his infantry by forced marches to support Stuart's cavalry, which was already in front of the marching columns of Blue, making, as always, a gallant fight to delay them until the infantry came up.

The division of General Anderson of Hill's corps reached the Court House on the morning of the eighth, and almost at the same moment the vanguard of the Federal army came upon the ground. The advanced guards of the two armies at once grappled, the Confederates drove back the enemy and seized upon the strategic points to hold them for the battleground. While these advance guards were thus confronting each other at Spotsylvania Court House on the morning of the eighth, the remainder of the two armies, stretched back for fifteen miles, were hurrying up as fast as forced marches could bring them, and as division after division of the Federal army arrived, it would swing round the left of their line as a pivot and form on the left of the troops already in line, while the Confederates

would swing round the right flank and form on the right of
their line.

Thus all that beautiful spring day the hostile armies were
wheeling into line, and all day fierce combats and bloody skirmishes were going on between detachments and divisions as
they struggled for coveted positions. The artillery on either side
as it came up would seize upon the heights and quickly unlim-
bering would salute the new arrivals with the thunder of guns
and the screeching, bursting sounds of shot and shell. It was a
grand game of war played by two gallant armies, led by two
great generals of consummate skill and ability.

It was later in the afternoon of the eighth when Johnson's
division of Ewell's corps arrived on the field, and the enemy
were pressing our men hotly and lapping over their right flank
as we came up.

I then had the honor to command the Stonewall Brigade of
Johnson's division, and when our corps commander, glorious
old General Ewell, rode out to meet us and commanded us to
move up at double quick, the model men of that brave brigade,
notwithstanding the forced march of sixteen or eighteen hours
had nearly exhausted their physical strength, responded with a
yell and, amid the bursting of the enemy's shell and the hurtling of the deadly Minie balls, dashed into line and checked
the advance of the enemy.

This brigade was the first of the division to get into line,
and formed immediately on the right of that splendid North
Carolinian general, Ramseur, who fell at Winchester the same
year, and whose gallant Tar Heels were as true as steel and
shed luster on the Confederate armies on many a battlefield.
The other brigades of the division came up and formed in rapid
succession under the enemy's fire in the following order: on the
right of the Stonewall Brigade was the Louisiana brigade,
commanded by General Harry Hays than whom no braver,
knightlier soldier ever drew sword. His command on the fifth
had formed two brigades, but on that day General Stafford, one
of the bravest and best men I ever knew, was killed at the head
of his men, and his brigade had been consolidated with that of
Hayes. On the right of Hays came J. M. Jones' brigade, commanded by Colonel Witcher, their brave leader having also
fallen in battle at the same time General Stafford was killed.

On the right of the Louisianans came the brigade of George H. Steuart.

The position thus taken by Johnson's division was such as the fortune of battle gave it. It was determined for us by the enemy, more than by our own choosing, and formed a sharp salient. A salient in military engineering is an angle with the point towards the enemy, and is always considered objectionable from a defensive point of view, because immediately in front of the point of the angle there is a space which is not swept by the fire of those behind the works. I have frequently heard the Confederate engineers censured for allowing this salient in the lines, but as I have shown you already, they had nothing to do with forcing the line, and as I will show you hereafter, it had nothing to do with the disaster which happened to Johnson's division on the twelfth.

Soon after the division was in line, night came on, skirmishers were thrown out, and quiet reigned, but it was the hush which precedes the tornado. Tired and worn out as the soldiers were, there was no rest for them that night. The greater part of the line of the division was along the outer edge (the edge next the enemy) of a body of fine oak timber. As soon as night put an end to combat, picks and shovels were sent for and along the whole line all through the night the men worked like beavers as the crash of falling trees, the ring of axes, and the sound of the spade and shovel were heard. Trees were felled and piled up on each other, and a ditch dug behind them with the earth out of it thrown against the logs. Every hundred yards or so, a traverse was thrown up, consisting of a short breastwork of twenty or thirty feet long at right angles to the main breastwork.

The object of this was to prevent the line of battle behind the works from being enfiladed. The limbs and tops of the trees as cut off from the trunks were used to form abatis, by placing them in front of the breastworks with the sharpened points towards the enemy. By daylight, a very formidable line of fortifications frowned upon the foe, and our troops rested quietly, confident of victory should the enemy attack them. Between the morning of the ninth and the morning of the twelfth this line of breastwork was much strengthened and became one of the very best lines of temporary field works I ever saw. It was apparently impregnable. Just behind the

entrenched line of infantry, artillery was placed at the most
eligible points to sweep the approaching enemy with shot and
shell and canister.

A description of the ground in front of the Confederate
troops at this point will serve to explain the situation more
fully. Just in front of Ramseur's position there was a cleared
and open space for two or three hundred yards; then came a
dense forest of pine timber with the limbs hanging down to the
ground, shutting off all view of the interior. The enemy's skirmishers occupied the edge of the forest, nearest Ramseur's line,
and kept up a spirited fire at short range, which compelled his
men to keep close behind their breastworks. On Ramseur's
right, in front of the Stonewall Brigade, the pine forest was
much less dense and did not approach so near our line, while
our skirmishers were pushed into the timber and the enemy's
skirmishers were kept at a safe distance. Opposite the right of
the Stonewall Brigade the timber which came up so close to
their front terminated or gave out, and in front of the Louisiana brigade and Jones' brigade there was a broad plateau—an
old field without timber or obstruction of any kind extending
for six or eight hundred yards. Then the ground descended into
a rather deep hollow or ravine covered with oak timber which
belt of timber extended much further beyond and was filled
with the enemy's troops. The skirmishers from Johnson's
division were posted on the edge of this timbered ravine one
thousand yards in front of our breastworks.

All day on the ninth we were left in quiet, and on the tenth
nothing excited suspicion until after the hour of noon, when the
enemy's skirmishers in the edge of the pine forest in front of
Ramseur became particularly active and spiteful and muffled
sounds began to issue from the unseen recesses of the wood
which were suspicious. It was believed that the enemy was
massing there for an attack.

This was reduced to a certainty later in the afternoon when
in an instant a heavy column of the enemy rushed out from
among the pines and dashed swiftly across the intervening
space between them and Ramseur. They came on in column,
having a front of about two regiments, and many lines deep,
almost filling up the open space. Ramseur's men were ready
and poured a deadly volley into them, but the Blue lines did
not falter, and before our men could reload they were on the

works. The Confederates were only one line deep, the enemy's column was not less than eight or ten lines deep. Our men used the bayonets but were driven back, and the Blue Coats with three cheers and a tiger given in regular HIP! HIP! HURRAH! style moved on in pursuit. The two regiments on the left of the Stonewall Brigade had poured an oblique fire on the foe as they advanced and after the works were carried were drawn back and formed at right angles to the breastworks, from which position they delivered a murderous fire into the flank of the enemy after they crossed the line.

The triumph of the victors was of short duration, for soon Ramseur's retiring line was reinforced and in turn the enemy was driven back pell mell at a double quick, and as they re-crossed our works and the open space to seek the friendly gloom of the pine forests which they had a few moments before left in such gallant array, they were shot down like frightened deer until the ground was covered with their dead and wounded. Ramseur's line was restored and there were no further demonstrations on the tenth or the eleventh.

The night of the eleventh was damp and misty, with a dense fog resting low on the ground. During that night it was reported to General Lee that the enemy was again withdrawing from his front and preparing to make another flank movement. To meet this the artillery was at once withdrawn from the front and placed in readiness to march at early dawn. Only two guns of Carrington's Battery were left to support Johnson's division.

Before it became light enough to distinguish objects, the rapid firing of our skirmishers in the wooded ravine in front of the center of Johnson's line gave notice that the enemy was advancing and the heavy tramp of a large body of infantry and the sharp words of command could be distinctly heard. Very soon our skirmishers came falling back, firing as they came, and announced what we already knew, that a heavy column was advancing to the attack. Our men were all up and ready for them with muskets cocked, peering through the gloom for the first glimpse of their foes. For several moments, which seemed much longer, no enemy came in sight; but the tramp of armed men drew nearer and the commands of their officers sounded more distinctly. The enemy consisting of Hancock's corps of thirty thousand men, formed in column of brigades, had emerged from the ravine and had advanced about one third of the way across the open plateau before they could be seen or could themselves see our works on account of the fog.

All at once the slowly lifting fog showed them our heavily fortified position some four or five hundred yards in their front. At this expected but unwelcome sight the advancing column paused, wavered, hesitated; for at least a moment they halted and seemed to refuse the task before them. Their mounted officers rode in front and urged them on, while many officers on foot and horseback shouted "Forward, Men! Forward!," repeating the words again and again.

The moment for the Confederate fire had come. The men rising to full height leveled their trusty muskets deliberately at the halting columns, with a practiced aim which would have carried havoc into their ranks; but the searching damp had disarmed them and instead of the leaping line of fire and the sharp crack of the muskets came the pop! pop! pop! of exploding caps as the hammers fell upon them. Their powder was damp, and with their muzzle loading muskets there was no help for them. A few, very few, pieces fired clear, but fresh caps on most of them only produced another failure. A muzzle loading musket with damp powder behind the ball is as useless to a soldier in an emergency like that as a walking stick.

As the enemy received no fire from our lines they took heart and again moved forward with rapid strides. On they came, unopposed, and in a few moments had torn our well constructed abatis away and were over our works, taking prisoners of our unarmed troops. I saw Federal officers ride up to the lines and step from their stirrups on to our breastworks without harm to themselves or their horses.

In this famous and much talked of charge of Hancock's corps, I do not believe they lost one hundred men, killed and wounded. The two guns of Carrington's battery were well handled and did some execution, and the few serviceable muskets were made to tell for the brief moments they could be used. The enemy suffered heavily after they were inside of our lines, when fresh troops were brought up on our side, but they achieved almost a bloodless victory in their famous charge. I speak advisedly when I say that if the muskets of our men had been serviceable, they would never have gotten within three hundred yards of our line. One well dressed volley, such as our

men knew so well how to give, delivered at the moment the
line wavered and halted, would have thrown them into confusion and made their future movements too slow and dispirited
to render success in such a charge possible. Such attacks must
be made with dash, rapidity and united effort to ensure success.

I had peculiar opportunities for witnessing this assault;
because the enemy on this occasion, as in their attack on
Ramseur on the tenth, did not attack the Stonewall Brigade at
all, but attacked immediately on their right, directly in front of
Jones' Virginia and Hays' Louisiana brigades so that with
perfect safety and without a shot coming in my direction, I
stood upon the breastworks in front of the right regiment of my
brigade and witnessed it all.

As soon as the enemy began to cross our works, the right
regiment of my brigade, the Fourth Virginia, then commanded
by the brave Colonel (afterwards General) William Terry, was
formed at right angles to the works so as to fire down the
inside of our line, and the traverses before mentioned were of
service to both sides. I was very soon wounded and left the
battlefield, and what happened afterwards is only known to
me, as to others, as history relates it: the dreadful carnage on
both sides in that salient which gave to it the name of the
"Bloody Angle;" the touching incident of the devotion of General
Lee's soldiers to his person; when the old hero, in the midst of
the heaviest fire and when his troops were being pressed back,
rode to the front of one of his brigades just ready to go into the
fight, and offered to lead it in the charge. How his brave boys
refused to follow him, shouting with tears in their eyes: "General Lee to the rear! General Lee to the rear! We will go forward
but General Lee must go to the rear!" Until some of the men
firmly but respectfully laid their hands upon the bridle of old
"Traveller" and turned his head to the rear. Then the old hero
raised his hat in his peculiar dignified way and rode slowly
back, while the brigade went forward with more dash and
courage than ever before, because they had commanded "Mars
Bob," and he had obeyed their command.

It was in this "Bloody Angle" that an oak tree as large
around as a man's body was cut down by Minie balls alone, and
its trunk can now be seen at the War Office at Washington
city.

I have spoken of this charge of Hancock's corps because it
has been ignorantly charged that our troops were taken by
surprise. There may have been some want of care on the part
of the troops and their officers in not keeping their powder dry.
Had it been a rainy night they would have taken greater precautions, and the disaster would never have occurred. Poor
fellows! Many of them paid the penalty of their mistake on that
fateful morning either in northern prisons or with their lives.

As an illustration of the dangers and the casualties of the
campaign of 1864, it is only necessary to take Johnson's division as a sample. That division had been recruited and reorganized during the preceding winter and went into the campaign
with a major general, four brigadier generals, and a full com-
plement of field and company officers. Its rank and file was
composed of about six thousand men. On the fifth and sixth of
May, two of its brigade commanders were killed, and about one
half of its field officers, and about one third of the men were
killed and wounded. After the sixth of May it was increased by
the addition of Hays' brigade, about eight hundred strong. On
the twelfth two more of its brigade commanders were wounded,
and the one remaining, with the division commander, was
captured. Of the rank and file nearly all in line that day were
killed, wounded or captured. The whole remnant of the six
thousand was formed into one small brigade and a colonel
promoted to command it.

A fact not generally known is that on the twelfth of May,
1864, the famous Stonewall Brigade which had won renown on
so many battlefields ceased to exist as a separate organization,
and the few remaining members, not above two hundred in all,
with the other fragments of Johnston's division, was incorporated into a single brigade, called Terry's Brigade.

The official designation of Stonewall Brigade was not given
to that body of men until after the death of General Paxton at
Chancellorsville in May, 1863. Prior to that it had been known
either by its number or the name of its commander. When
Stonewall Jackson was its commander in 1861, it was officially
designated the First Virginia Brigade. After General Jackson
was promoted to Major General in October 1861 it was commanded by General Garnett, and was called Garnett's Brigade.
General Garnett having incurred General Jackson's displeasure
at Kernstown was relieved of command, but afterwards fell at

Gettysburg leading a brigade in the charge of Pickett's Division. After Garnett, General Winder commanded the brigade for about four months until he was killed at Slaughter's Mountain. While he commanded it, it was called Winder's Brigade. When the gallant Winder fell, General Jackson had Major Paxton of his staff promoted to the rank of Brigadier General and assigned to the command of Winder's Brigade, and it was called Paxton's Brigade until he was killed at Chancellorsville in May 1863.

Then I was assigned to its command, and for a few weeks only it was known as Walker's Brigade; when by authority of the Secretary of War it received the official designation of "Stonewall Brigade," by which it had been known in the army before, and which name it had received on the plains of Manassas on the twenty-first of July, 1861, when General Bee pointed to the First Virginia Brigade, under command of General Jackson, and said to his men retiring before overwhelming odds: "There stands Jackson and his Virginians like a stone wall." The compliment was paid to the brigade for its gallant stand as much as to its commander. On the twelfth of May 1864 in the "Bloody Angle" the old Brigade was annihilated, and its name faded from the rolls of the Army of Northern Virginia, but it will ever live on the rolls of fame, and history will record its deeds of glory.

NINETEEN

Wounded

The "Bloody Angle" not only effectively spelled the end of the famous Stonewall Brigade. It took the brigade's commander, General Walker, out of action for several months.

The wound Walker had received at the "Bloody Angle" was in his left arm, the elbow bone having been completely shattered. The injury occurred early on the morning of May 12 when Hancock's corps of Grant's army overwhelmed Johnson's division, under Colonel Witcher, and then rushed down the works, first upon the Louisiana Brigade and then upon the Stonewall Brigade. Dr. Hopkins described it:

When they reached our brigade, General Walker met them at the head of his men and fought like a tiger. Soon he received a ball from a gun that was very close to him...

He was immediately carried to the hospital tent in the rear where the corps surgeon, Dr. Hunter McGuire, and Dr. Sayers, the brigade surgeon, examined his wound. Although he was unconscious from shock and loss of blood, the pain of probing for the bullet restored Walker to consciousness for a few moments, and he heard one of the surgeons say there was nothing to do but amputate the arm.

"Don't let them cut it off, McGuire," he begged. "I'd rather die than lose my arm," and he lapsed into unconsciousness as the words were spoken.

There were tears in Dr. McGuire's eyes. "I promised General Walker he shouldn't lose a limb if by any possible means it could be helped," he said later. To an orderly, he said, "Go for Dr. Galt. We'll wait till he comes."

Dr. Galt, of Baltimore, who was with a Maryland regiment, was an older and very skillful bone surgeon, bold enough to attempt a saving experiment when authorized to do so. He agreed with Dr. McGuire that there was a chance to save Walker's arm by a resection of the elbow joint, since Walker was young and vigorous. Assisted by Sayers and McGuire, Galt performed this new and somewhat delicate operation, sawing out the elbow joint, uniting the muscles and nerves of the upper and lower arm and bandaging it firmly between wooden splints. A little of the precious chloroform from the hospital supplies was spared for the actual operation, but the only disinfectant at hand was cold water.

Hopkins was present and lent what aid he could during the operation, when he said some six or eight inches of bone were removed. He recalled:

While under the influence of chloroform, the General abused the doctors and said: "I just wish I had you all at the front. I would put you where the bullets fly."

When he passed from this influence I told him how he had spoken to his doctors. He was mortified and asked me to apologize to them for the way he had spoken to them. Of course they understood it, but the general would not be satisfied until his apology was offered.

A youthful orderly had been dispatched to the Valley of Virginia as soon as General Walker was wounded, to notify his family. On the fourth day he returned with Dr. Frank Walker, older brother of the general. The next morning, the wounded officer, now burning with fever and delirious, was put, with several others, on stretchers and loaded in a jolting ambulance which was headed toward Staunton. Walker recalled the journey as a long nightmare of bad dreams and incessant thirst. He did not remember reaching his father's home on Middle River, where parents and sister received him with great anxiety, believing his days numbered.

A week later, his brother Silas, a dashing young cavalryman of Stuart's Division, was also brought home to be nursed. His wound happened to be in the side of his heel, as to which fact he was very sensitive, it being a boast of Stuart's cavalry that they never turned their backs on the enemy.

Having been informed of her husband's condition, my mother managed to reach the Middle River plantation not long after Major

Silas Walker's arrival. She had journeyed in her mother's carriage
for the first fifteen miles of the way, then by broken railway stages
to Charlottesville, and across the mountain to Staunton where the
Walker carriage met her. In her arms she carried her first-born son,
Alexander Ewell, leaving at home two little girls in the care of her
mother, who, though past seventy years of age, was remarkably
vigorous and capable.

Mrs. Walker had scarcely rested from a fatiguing journey when
the news came that General David Hunter was raiding the Valley,
with orders to burn barns and crops and do everything possible for
the devastation of that "granary of the Confederacy." The once quiet
valley plantation was no longer a safe place for two wounded
Confederate officers, and hasty arrangements were made to take
them to Pulaski County.

Father Walker provided a double buggy and team. The general's
anxious mother and sister quickly gathered together a substantial
lunch, pillows for the wounded foot and arm, and other comforts,
and an early morning start was made the day after the report of
Hunter's approaching raid reached the neighborhood.

Meanwhile, women and slaves drove horses and cattle to the
mountains, buried family silver, and hid a part of the stores of meat
and grain under floors or in attics and cellars. The slaves were just
as afraid of the Yankees as the whites and just as concerned for the
safety of their masters' families and belongings. There are but few
instances where they could even be bribed to reveal the hiding
place of family valuables or stores of food.

Major Walker's swollen and bandaged foot did not prevent him
from driving the double buggy along the valley pike toward safety,
leaving Mrs. Walker to care for the baby and, at each wayside
spring, to pour water over the burning wounds of her disabled
soldiers. General Walker was able to hold the sturdy baby in his
right arm now and then, in order to rest the weary mother, for they
drove from early morning until late evening, making only brief and
needed stops.

They found comfortable resting places each night, usually at
private homes, since taverns were few in that part of the state and
most of them were closed, war having taken their proprietors to the
front. Always the travelers were made warmly welcome by their
hosts, or more likely hostesses. The daughter of one of their
hostesses years later wrote the following letter to General Walker,
reminding him of one of those instances of tender thoughtfulness

which the women of the Confederacy were ever ready to lavish on their wounded heroes:

Johns Hopkins Hospital
June 4, 1894

Dear Sir:

While lying here in the hospital, suffering greatly from effects of a surgical operation, which, for the present, has nearly deprived me of the use of my right arm, I received a bundle of papers from my husband, Mr. Isaac Willis, Indian-town, Va.

On opening them the first I saw was the "Richmond Dispatch" and the first thing my eyes rested upon was: "A readable letter from General Walker, giving war reminiscences." My first thought was: I wonder if *he* remembers, while on his way from the battlefields around Spotsylvania Court House, stopping and spending the night at the house of a poor widow, Mrs. Ann F. Lipscomb.

I am one of that widow's daughters. It was I who helped your brother, I think Dr. Walker, dress your arm. And it was I who put the flowers between your arm and face to prevent you from smelling the wound. Well do I remember your saying, "Thank you, lady; I hope I may some day be able to render you a service."

All of this may, possibly, have passed from your mind, but it made a lasting impression on me, so I thought I would write and ask you if you remembered it. And too, I have a favor to ask of you. I would be so glad to have your photograph. Can't you send me one? I would thank you very much for it.

Within a month Major Walker was able to drive the team back to Middle River, but General Walker's recovery was not so rapid. His wound suppurated badly, and for weeks he was consumed with septic fever until he was barely able to totter about from porch to couch or from room to room, a wreck of the erect, vigorous, stentorian-voiced officer who had led the bold charge on Culp's Hill. Had he not devised his own method of at least partial prophylaxis, to the serious alarm of his more conservative wife, there is little doubt that death or invalidism would have resulted.

Each morning he had a tubful of ice brought from the ice house, at the foot of the garden under a clump of locust trees. From this tub of ice in the cellar, a wooden bucket was filled every hour or so, and General Walker would sit with his burning elbow buried in ice, while he read or wrote with his right hand, or amused himself with his three active children.

Walker had purchased his house about the time he was elected Commonwealth's Attorney of Pulaski County, only a few months before Virginia seceded. He had made a small cash payment and assumed yearly payments. Mrs. Walker, with the help of her mother's small hoard of gold and fine management, had met those payments each year as they came due, for the most part in Confederate money, so that by the summer of 1864 there was only one more payment to be made.

Inheriting the blood and tradition of housewifely ancestors, Mrs. Walker was no less a good housekeeper than a thrifty manager. The orchard, garden and poultry yard, well stocked cellar, smoke house and store room all did their part toward the amply provided table it was her pride to set. She had even managed to keep a part of her prewar stores of coffee and sugar, and these she used freely to tempt her husband's precarious appetite during the hot days of early summer, when he found keeping alive something of an effort.

The low state of General Walker's health was not helped by his state of mind. Such news as came to him at that distance from the front was not encouraging. Grant, after his repulse at Second Cold Harbor, had been content to adopt a waiting policy as he slowly forced Lee back toward Richmond. The siege of Petersburg had begun, and even to the dauntless "Rebs" it was apparent that the Confederacy could not hold out much longer unless something like a miracle should happen.

But to the solders of the Army of Northern Virginia, a miracle was by no means an impossible eventuality, as long as "Marse Bob" was alive and in command. Early had checked Hunter's raid through the Valley and beyond Lynchburg, but not before all that was left the soldiers to live upon, as well as most of the food for the women and children, had been destroyed. Horses and cattle were driven off, barns burned, homes rifled, and the beautiful Valley made a blackened waste.

Under these conditions Lee needed every man who could rally to his standard. Major Silas Walker, still limping, had already rejoined the cavalry, even though it had lost its daring Stuart at Yellow Tavern during the Wilderness battles.

General Walker wrote to Richmond late in August that he was ready for duty, though his arm was still in splints.

He was soon ordered to Clover Depot to take charge of the reserves to whom had been assigned the duty of keeping open Lee's line of communication, via the Richmond and Danville and South Side Railroads.

Mrs. Walker and the two younger children accompanied him to Clover Depot, since the wounded arm still needed daily dressings. The ladies of the neighborhood sent comfortable chairs, curtains, blankets and other accessories to make more livable the bare rooms, over a vacant store, assigned Walker as headquarters, and almost daily some addition to their limited rations was sent in by the housekeepers of the neighborhood—a pot of jam, several pounds of butter, a sack of potatoes, a few combs of honey, etc. Also, a number of social courtesies were extended them by the charming people in and around the village, and my mother used to say that despite the deepening gloom of the inevitable end, she spent a very comfortable and happy time at Clover Depot in the fall and early winter of '64.

With customary activity and vigilance, Walker repulsed one raiding party after another, restored the oft broken lines of the railways, and kept open Lee's communications with Richmond and his southern source of supplies via North Carolina, thus doing his part toward enabling the Confederate line at Petersburg to hold on. For this quiet but important service he was warmly commended by General Lee.

In January, Walker reported his arm out of splints and asked to be sent to the front. He requested that he be given Pegram's brigade, now leaderless by the loss of the brave Pegram, because his old and still much beloved regiment, the Thirteenth Virginia, was one of its units. The favor was presently granted him, and in the last offensive of the Army of Northern Virginia—the attack on Hares Hill at Petersburg—General Walker was one of the two generals who led the attack, followed by the regiment to which he always claimed he owed his military reputation.

How well they and the rest of his command acquitted themselves in this, their last valiant gesture of offense, will be told in a later chapter.

TWENTY

Petersburg

While General Walker recuperated from his wound in Pulaski County and at Clover Depot, the situation of the Army of Northern Virginia deteriorated rapidly. Having relinquished the direct southern approach to Richmond, Grant had swung his army eastward to the Rappahannock River in the hope of reaching the Confederate capital from that direction before Lee's depleted and exhausted army could be reformed and rested. Informed by his ever vigilant scouts of Grant's movements, Lee hurried Ewell's division on the inside line of march to the North Anna River between Grant and Richmond and followed with the rest of the army.

By the morning of the twenty-third of May, he had been joined by Breckenridge from the Valley and Pickett from near Richmond and had posted his whole army in a strong defensive position, directly across the roads to Richmond.

Grant's advance on the twenty-third was delayed by misleading maps and ignorance of the roads. In the early afternoon he was in front of Lee's lines on the opposite side of the river. Late in the afternoon he had succeeded in crossing the river and in driving in Lee's left. This bold and well executed movement cut Lee's line of communication westward and threatened the turning of his left.

Both armies spent the night in throwing up lines of defensive works. The next day Lee reformed his line in such a way as practically to cut Grant's army in two. After several unsuccessful efforts to break Lee's line, Grant withdrew his army from the North Anna on the night of the twenty-sixth. As soon as he heard of the movement, Lee countered by ordering Early southward to cover the roads to Richmond from the crossing of the Pamunkey.

Lee asked Richmond for reinforcements which were not available. Grant was also asking for fresh troops, and a corps from Butler's army on the south side of the James was hurried to his assistance. On June first, Grant attacked Lee's line, forcing back his front, but was repulsed by his second line. During the night Grant swung his right around to his left beyond the road leading to Cold Harbor. On June second, Hancock assailed Lee's right, captured one of Lee's salients which Breckenridge recovered by a prompt fire of artillery, under which three thousand of Hancock's men fell upon the field. Equally bold assaults on Lee's center and left met with the same fate, and, as Hotchkiss reports, "within ten minutes the whole front of Grant's line of assault was shattered and his troops fled to cover."

The attack had been made at four thirty in the morning. At nine, Grant ordered another attack, but his officers refused to give the order to their men. McMahon, chief of staff of the Sixth Federal Corps, wrote that Grant sent a second and third order to attack, and when it "came to headquarters, it was transmitted to the division headquarters and to the brigades and regiments without comment. To move that army farther except by regular approaches was a simple and absolute impossibility, known to be such by every officer and man of the three corps engaged. The order was obeyed by simply renewing the fire from the men as they lay in position."

Hotchkiss says that Lee's veterans had by this time become almost to the man skillful military engineers and of their own impulse had thrown up lines of defense, abounding in salients whence heavy guns could send forth searching crossfires at short range against every portion of an attacking enemy. The infantry were well provided with loopholes and crevices between logs from which to fire, also at short range, with deliberate aim. Hunger had made them even fiercer combatants.

Confederate rations indeed were running low. One officer stated his men had received but two issues of rations in four days, one of three army crackers and a small slice of pork, the other a single cracker. There was also scarcity of drinking water which the scorching heat of that swampy country made a special hardship.

On the night of June twelfth, Grant began another flank movement, his fifth, from Cold Harbor to the James. By the fifteenth, his whole army was safely concentrated in Butler's rear on the south side of the James.

The historian of Hancock's corps, H. A. Walker, wrote later he had to confess that the corps had lost "something of its earlier virtue...under the terrific blows that had been showered upon it. It had averaged more than four hundred casualties a day since crossing the Rapidan, and the confidence of the troops in their leaders had been severely shaken. They had almost ceased to expect victory when they went into battle.

Lee sent the rest of his army across the James to join his advance. Beauregard with ten thousand men repulsed several assaults of Grant's army at a loss to Grant of ten thousand men in four days. Grant had lost since crossing the Rapidan about sixty-five thousand troops. Thus the two armies which during three years had confronted each other in the prolonged struggle for the possession of the Confederate capital—the Army of the Potomac and the Army of Northern Virginia—again opposed each other south of the James, and the long agony of the siege of Petersburg began.

Since Hunter's raids, the Army of Northern Virginia could no longer look to the great Valley as their storehouse; hence they must march and fight on empty stomachs. Worse still, there were no Confederate reinforcements to be had. So pitiful were the letters from home received occasionally by the men that desertions became common. Usually the deserter returned after a few weeks, calmly reporting at company headquarters and stating that he had been obliged to go home to see about his wife and babies. It was well understood that no court martials could be held in such cases.

Both armies busied themselves throwing up entrenchments in front of their lines. Lee made ready for a long and vigorous siege with all the skill, courage and tenacity at his command. The Federal disaster in the Battle of the Crater greatly encouraged Lee's men. In the North, the green-back fell to $2.80 in gold, and the *New York Times* advised that an embassy be sent to the Confederate government "to see if this dreadful war cannot be ended in a mutually satisfactory treaty of peace." Lee's men felt themselves well nigh invincible under their bold, skillful leaders. But these leaders sadly realized that it would not long be possible to maintain discipline and valor with naked, starving troops who lay shivering night after night in the trenches under the cold and snow and sleet of winter.

By the end of October, 1864, the operations in front of Petersburg were confined to defense and survival of the winter. At the close of the year Lee had forty thousand men available, of his sixty thousand enrolled men, to defend forty miles of trenches from the Chickahominy to Hatcher's Run, and Grant had one hundred and ten thousand who poured an almost ceaseless fire from mortar batteries into the Confederate trenches.

It was into this kind of situation that General Walker returned.

TWENTY-ONE

Fort Stedman

When a hardly recuperated James A. Walker returned to the front, he quickly assumed responsibility as a battle-seasoned leader and soon found himself commanding a division. At Petersburg, he found Lee's men burrowed into the earth, scantily clad in rags, eating starvation rations, waiting out the winter, as mortar fire rained down on them in their trenches.

Small wonder that the men welcomed the resumption of active hostilities in the early spring, or that the war department in Richmond, and Lee himself, began to realize the inevitability of defeat and surrender. More and more hopeless grew their situation until General John B. Gordon early in March of 1865 suggested to General Lee a desperate attempt to unwind the coil of steel closing about him. The situation which justified that attempt and its bold though unsuccessful execution are better told in Walker's own words:

Fort Stedman was a Federal redoubt, and occupied a spot near what was once the residence of Mr. Otway P. Hare, known locally as Hare's Hill. I was then in command of a division in the Corps commanded by Gen. John B. Gordon of Georgia, and my division occupied that portion of the trenches around Petersburg from the Appomattox River on the left and extending to the right to a point beyond Hare's Hill.

The enemy's lines in our front extended to the Appomattox River, thence down the river on its right bank, crossing the stream several miles lower down, and stretching out to and across the James River, thus leaving the Richmond and Petersburg Railroad in possession of the Confederates. The hostile lines were very near each other at several points, but at no other place so close together as at Hare's Hill or Fort Stedman, where they were only seventy-five yards apart.

The Confederate entrenchments on that part of the field consisted of a single line of breastworks. Their location was not the result of engineering skill, or of military choice, but was fixed by the accidental position of the Confederate troops, where the advance of the Federals was checked in the summer of 1864, at the time they came so near capturing Petersburg.

The position thus established, and the works destined to be held for more than six months against every odd, had their beginning in the slight and temporary obstructions thrown up by the Confederate soldiers in a night, to enable a feeble force to resist the expected assault of a superior force the next morning. These slight obstructions were strengthened from day to day, and the advance on Petersburg degenerated into the slow and tedious process called the siege of Petersburg.

The Federal works consisted of a front line of earth redoubts or forts at short intervals connected by a chain of earthen breastworks. One of these was located on the right bank of the Appomattox River, and another between the river and the City Point Railroad, called "Fort McGilvery," one just south of that railroad, one at Hare's Hill called "Fort Stedman," one further south called "Fort Meikle;" and one opposite the crater called "Fort Morton."

These forts, or redoubts, were much stronger and more formidable than the lines of breastworks which connected them, and were so constructed as to present a hostile front on all sides. They were filled with artillery and infantry, and so arranged that the fire from the guns of one would sweep not only over the ground in its immediate front but in front of the breastworks and the neighboring forts to the right and left; so that an attacking force would have to face not only a direct fire from infantry and artillery, but a concentrated fire from the artillery of at least three forts.

In rear of this first line, on the hills beyond Harrison's Creek, they had a second line, very much like the first; and so constructed that the forts in this line commanded the forts and breastworks composing the first line. Behind this second line was a third line of forts, manned with heavy guns, which commanded both the first and second lines.

The second line was not occupied by infantry all the while, but the troops were encamped behind these lines, near enough to be thrown into them in a very short time, if occasion re-

quired. The Federal troops in the front line were relieved by
fresh troops every few days, so that they were not subjected to
the wear and tear of constant and harassing duty and danger
all the time, both night and day, as were the Confederates, who
had only enough men to thinly occupy their one line of works.

A very short distance in front of the first line of works, each
side had placed a heavy line of *chevaux de frise* with an occasional opening sufficient to permit a man to pass through. This
chevaux de frise consisted of square pieces of timber of conve-
nient length, bored through at short intervals alternately from
either side of the square, and wooden spikes eight or ten feet
long sharpened at both ends, and driven halfway through these
holes, so that when placed in position the ends of two rows of
the spikes would rest on the ground while the ends of the other
two rows presented their sharp points to the front and rear at
the height of a man's breast.

These pieces of scantling are fastened together at the ends
with short iron chains a few inches long, so that a connected
and continuous obstruction is presented along the whole line,
which cannot be crossed, and can only be passed by clearing it
away with axes.

The proximity of the hostile lines made it almost certain
death for a man to show his head above the works on the front
line, and indeed it was dangerous to expose one's person to the
view of the enemy's sharpshooters, lying secure behind their
breastworks. The only time when the works could be approached above ground from the rear was after dark. There
were a number of covered ways constructed by digging trenches
running to the rear until out of musket range, and deep enough
to conceal a man. In some instances, these trenches were
covered over with timber, overlaid with earth, so as to form a
tunnel.

As has been before said the Confederate soldiers had to
remain in the trenches all the time, without being relieved,
because thee were no reserves to relieve them with. They
hollowed out the ground just in rear of the trenches and made
cellars or caves under the earth in which they slept, ate and
lived for five months.

One-third of the men were constantly on duty standing on
guard along the breastworks day and night to give warning of
an attack in time to enable their comrades to spring to their

feet and seize their muskets. As the pickets could not look over
the works without exposing themselves to certain destruction,
small loop holes were provided at intervals of fifteen or twenty
feet, large enough to admit the barrel of a musket and enable
the owner of the weapon to see the enemy's works over its
sights. From these little openings on either side, a desultory
fire was kept up, each side firing at only vulnerable spots,
which were these loop holes. They were easily located by the
smoke from the muskets, and their exact situation became
known to all. So accurate was the marksmanship that the wood
around the openings was worn away by the bullets, and in
many places was replaced by iron rails from the railroad track.
Once in a while a man would be killed by a musket ball coming
through these openings.

To prevent surprise in the night time, a number of pits
large enough to allow a single soldier to hide in were sunk a
few yards in front of the *chevaux de frise*, and after dark pickets were sent out to occupy them and to keep watch for any
suspicious movements. To enable them to pass in and out a few
gaps were left in the *chevaux de frise*. These pickets were
relieved every four hours.

In front of Fort Stedman the hostile sentinels were not
more than fifty yards apart, but they kept a sort of truce, never
tried to harm one another, and beguiled the weary hours by
chaffing each other.

The Federal soldiers always accosted the Confederate as
"Johnny" and the Confederates the Federal as "Yank." During
the night the musketry firing ceased, and quiet reigned unless
the mortar batteries took a notion to treat us to displays of fire
works, such as can never be forgotten by those who witnessed
them. The mortars sent their shell up into the air, leaving a
trail of light behind like a rocket, and the shell descended like
the stick of the rocket. The soldiers became accustomed to this
display and would watch the descending shells, and when they
saw they were likely to fall dangerously near, dodge into their
caves and await the harmless explosion in safety.

One morning in March, 1865, General Gordon requested me
to ride with him, and we crossed the Pocahontas bridge and
rode to a point on the hills on the left bank of the Appomattox
River opposite the enemy's second line of fortifications on the
right bank of the river in front of Hare's Hill or Fort Stedman.

We spent an hour or more examining the enemy's position through our field glasses, when General Gordon turned to me and very carelessly inquired what I thought of the position occupied by my division, and whether I thought I could hold it against an assault by the enemy in force.

I replied that I did not think I could hold my position against an assault because the enemy's lines were so close that they would dash over our works any night before we were aware of their coming. I added, "I can take their front line any morning before breakfast."

General Gordon smiled and remarked, "Don't you forget what you have said. I may call upon you to make your words good." He then told me that he had suggested to General Lee the idea of making an assault upon the enemy's works in his front and would know in a few days whether it would be adopted.

A few days later Gordon sent for his three division commanders and informed us that the attack would be made. My division was to attack Fort Stedman, and the other two divisions designated points on the right of that fort.

The attacks were to be made simultaneously by each division, the signal for the assault to be three muskets or pistol shots fired in quick succession. Each division was to be preceded by a storming party consisting of fifty pickets, carrying axes to clear away the *chevaux de frise* and one hundred picked infantry men, armed with muskets, commanded by a captain and one lieutenant, on whose courage and coolness we could confidently rely. Each division was to follow closely behind the storming party, marching by the right flank.

The preparations for the movement were simple but required some little time. Rations for three days had to be issued, cooked, brought up and distributed. The cartridge boxes had to be examined and filled with cartridges; muskets had to be inspected, the sick and disabled sent to hospitals, the storming parties selected and instructed as to what was required of them. After all these things were looked after, we had to wait for night to begin the movement. The entire corps, three divisions, had to be marched out of the trenches so as to give room to form their separate columns, and then to march back to the breastworks so as to bring the head of the columns to the spots where our works were to be crossed.

This was done quietly and with the least possible noise. No commands were given, but the words were passed in low tones from man to man. About an hour before daylight, my storming party passed cautiously and silently, one by one, over the breastworks, crept close to one of our solitary pickets in his pit, and slid down on the ground.

The ground at this point was a cornfield, but the farmer who planted it had not seen fit to gather his crop, and as the storming party moved out they made more noise among the corn stalks than the "Yank" on picket was accustomed to hear. He sung out to our picket: "I say, Johnny, what are you doing in that corn?"

To which Johnny very innocently replied, "All right, Yank, I am just gathering me a little corn to parch."

Yank answered, "All right, Johnny, I won't shoot."

After a short pause, the Yank again addressed his neighbor, "I say, Johnny, isn't it almost daylight? I think it is time they were relieving us."

Johnny sung out in a cheery voice, "Keep cool, Yank; you'll be relieved in a few minutes."

It was a clear crisp March morning. The stars were shining overhead, and save for the colloquy between the two pickets, all was as quiet as the grave.

There was no evidence that within a few hundred yards of the spot where we stood, ten thousand armed men were crouching low, anxiously watching for the appointed signal which was to hurl them upon the enemy and sound the death knell of hundreds of brave men. All our movements had been conducted so quietly that not a suspicion had been aroused, not even among the enemy's pickets, some of whom were not over fifty yards distant from our men.

I had selected to lead the storming party Captain Anderson of the Forty-ninth Virginia and Lieutenant Hugh P. Powell of the Thirteenth Virginia, officers belonging to my old brigade, who were personally known to me to be the bravest of the brave, and in whom the men had confidence. The men under them were selected from a much larger number who in response to a call for volunteers promptly offered their services. When all was ready, we awaited the agreed signal in breathless suspense.

The suspense was relieved when General Gordon came down the line to where the head of my column rested. Finding my command ready to move, he stepped to one side and fired three pistol shots in rapid succession. The last report was scarcely heard before the recumbent figures sprang to their feet, and Captain Anderson commanded, "Forward double quick." His men moved off at a trail arms, and not a word was spoken or a sound heard except the regular beat of their feet as they stepped out at a double quick.

I have read many accounts, both in history and fiction, of such attacks, and my blood has been stirred in reading them, but I never read an account of one so dashing, so orderly, and so quiet as this. The cool, frosty morning made every sound distinct and clear, and the only sound heard was the tramp! tramp! of the men as they kept step as regularly as if on drill, and the cries of the Yankee picket as he ran with all his speed into the fort shouting, "The rebels are coming!! The rebels are coming!"

Our men were instructed not to try to capture or harm the Yank, but to follow the path he took, and it would carry them to the opening in the enemy's *chevaux de frise*. They also were told not to cheer until they were on the enemy's breastworks, and then to cheer as loudly as possible as a signal for the division to follow; also to fire as rapidly as they could reload in every direction through the fort, to confuse the Federals and prevent them from rallying and forming before our main body could come up.

The gallant little band came to a halt as they reached the obstructions, and a galling fire from muskets inside the fort met them at that point. A number of them were killed and wounded during the pause. The halt was a short one, for sharp axes wielded by strong arms were at work, and the heavy blows rang out on the frosty air like the blows of giants. In a few seconds the wooden obstacles gave way with a crash, and in a few seconds more the Rebel yell made the air ring, announcing to our expectant ears that Fort Stedman was carried and that our boys were inside the enemy's works.

They proceeded at once to make it lively by firing promiscuously in every direction wherever they could see a blue coat to fire at. The enemy was taken entirely by surprise, as all were

asleep except the thin line which guarded the side of the redoubt facing our lines.

In the fort there were a number of little huts, with comfortable bunks in which the officers slept, and several of them were
surprised in their pajamas and made prisoners. The officers
and men in the fort acted gallantly and tried to form and make
resistance, but to form men in the dark just out of sleep, cooped
up in a small fort, with a hundred muskets in the hands of an
organized body of trained and daring men, pouring forth their
deadly contents on every side and making a mark of every head
that showed itself is next to an impossibility.

Captain Anderson and Lieutenant Powell both fell on the
breastworks, the first mortally wounded and the latter killed
outright. The storming party was thus left without a commissioned officer, but the circumstances made but little difference
with these men, for every one of them was fit to be a captain,
and most of them to wear the uniform of much higher officers.

But to return to the division, as soon as the wild cheering
of our boys gave the signal, the head of the column was put in
motion, and crossing our breastworks moved rapidly across the
intervening space and into the captured fort.

When the head of the column reached the enemy's works,
and the first files were on them, I found that the leading files
were lying down behind the breastworks at the point where
those before them had crossed. I inquired for the officer in
command, but, getting no answer, ordered the men to move
forward, which they did.

We had just crossed over, when a soldier sprang in front
and said: "These are my men and they shall not go." I demanded who he was, and he replied that he was captain of that
company, and that his men should not be slaughtered. He was
ordered to lead his men forward, but positively refused, and
when he did so, I made a blow at his head with my sabre,
which he dodged, and then rushed at me with the point of his
infantry sword. I stepped aside, and drawing my pistol from my
belt, with the muzzle almost touching his head, pulled the
trigger. The cap did not explode, and then his men ran between
us, as I was about to make a second attempt to shoot, saying,
"Don't shoot, General! He is our captain, and a brave man."

The captain then said he was ready to go forward and tried
to excuse his conduct by pretending that he did not know me

by the starlight, and that, if he had recognized me, he would have obeyed my orders; but I refused to accept his explanation, and told him that I would have him court-martialed and shot if we both came out of the battle alive.

We double-quicked side by side to join the companies of the division already in Fort Stedman, and the whole division followed rapidly.

As to the captain, I never saw him again, as he did not return to the Confederate lines. What his fate was I do not know. He may have been killed that morning, but it is most likely that he suffered himself to be captured rather than return and be shot by a sentence of court martial.

I have always declined to give the name or regiment of this man. If he or his descendants are alive, I would not give them pain by publishing him. He had a good record as a soldier, and was unquestionably a brave man. Why he acted as he did on that occasion can be readily accounted for. He saw, as nearly all the men in the ranks saw, that the Confederate cause was hopeless, and that they were shedding their blood in vain, and that valor and patriotism must inevitably yield to the overwhelming numbers and resources...

As the head of the columns entered Fort Stedman the resistance wholly ceased, and in the dim light of the coming dawn the fleeing enemy could be seen on every side, hastening to the protection of the second line of forts. Our being in possession of Fort Stedman made the enemy's breastworks on either side and as far as the neighboring forts untenable, and they were rapidly abandoned.

A strong skirmish line of Confederates was at once thrown forward toward the second line of the enemy's works, and got within easy musket range, but though they were guarded by a small force it was too strong to be dislodged by skirmishers. It required more than an hour for the entire division to come up and form into line, and it was sunrise before we were ready to advance.

The attacks by the other two Confederate columns were either not made, or if made, were unsuccessful, for no additional troops came to my aid in the neighborhood of Fort Stedman.

By the time the sun was above the horizon the enemy, however, had poured forth from their camps in the rear and filled the forts and breastworks of the second line with troops,

both infantry and artillery. They sent out a heavy skirmish line
which engaged ours, and a brisk and angry skirmish fire was
kept up until our troops were withdrawn. Their artillery, too,
came into play as well as the guns of their forts in the second
line, on our right and left, concentrating their fire on Fort
Stedman, and such a storm of shot and shell as fell into and
around the old fort has seldom been seen. We had failed to
carry the second line by surprise; it was manned by four times
our numbers, and our task was hopeless. Nothing remained but
to withdraw to our breastworks.

General Gordon seemed loath to give up his cherished plans
and waited to communicate with General Lee, so that for an
hour or two longer we held our captured fort and breastworks.

At last the command came to fall back to our lines, and the
troops commenced the retrograde movement, which was a
thousand times more hazardous than the advance, because it
was now in the full blaze of daylight, and the seventy-five
yards that lay between Fort Stedman and our shelter was
swept by the direct and cross fire of many pieces of artillery
posted in both the first and second lines of the enemy's works.
They seemed to fall on every square yard of ground, and to
sweep over the open space like a hot wind. They screeched and
screamed like fiends, plowing up the ground on all sides, exploding with sounds like thunder claps, sending their fragments on errands of death and destruction in every direction.

When the order was given to withdraw I sent one of my
staff out to the skirmish line to tell the officer in charge that
we were retreating and to fall back slowly, skirmishing as he
retired. This order was obeyed too well, for he fell back very
slowly fighting stubbornly all the way.

I remained in Fort Stedman after the main body of the
division had left it, watching and admiring the gallant fight the
skirmish line was making, until there was no one in the fort
except an occasional Confederate passing through. Suddenly I
heard a shout. Looking in the direction of the sound I saw a
body of Federal infantry coming over the wall of the fort on the
opposite side.

A few jumps on a double quick put the wall of the fort
between the enemy and myself, and then with a few other
belated stragglers I found myself crossing the storm-swept
space between us and our works. At first I made progress at a

tolerably lively gait, but I wore heavy cavalry boots, the ground was thawing under the warm rays of the sun, and great cakes of mud stuck to my boots. My speed slackened to a slow trot, then into a slow walk, and it seemed as if I were an hour making that seventy-five yards. Not only the artillery now, but the enemy's infantry had remanned the front wall of Fort Stedman, and the deadly Minie balls were whistling and hurtling thick as hail. Every time I lifted my foot with its heavy weight of mud and boot I thought my last step was taken.

Out of the ten or dozen men who started across that field with me I saw at least half of them fall, and I do not believe more than one or two got over safely. When I reached our works and clambered up to the top, I was so exhausted that I rolled down among the men, and one of them expressed his surprise at seeing me by remarking, "Here is General Walker. I thought he was killed!"

In this affair the Confederates lost heavily in killed, wounded and prisoners. Nearly all of my gallant skirmish line was captured, for when they fell back to Fort Stedman they found it occupied by the enemy and there was no alternative left them but to surrender as prisoners of war. There are many minor incidents and details of this bold attack, which I would like to weave into this narrative, but it already has grown too long.

The reader may ask, what was the object of this rash sally, this seemingly hopeless attack on overwhelming numbers, strongly entrenched and supplied with every appliance known to warfare. I can answer the question. The situation of the Confederate army around Richmond and Petersburg was fast becoming desperate, and unless something could be done, and done quickly, the fall of Richmond was inevitable. Desperate diseases require desperate remedies.

General Gordon conceived the bold and hazardous plan of surprising the enemy, piercing their lines in front of Hare's Hill, cutting off the troops between Fort Stedman and the Appomattox River, and by getting in their rear to compel them to cross over to the left bank of that river or be captured. Thus having opened the way to City Point, the Confederate cavalry, which had been brought up and held in readiness to act, was to dash upon City Point, capture General Grant, destroy the immense supplies stored there for the use of the Federal army, and make a raid around the rear of that army. If the way was

thus opened for the cavalry, the enemy in their line between
Fort Stedman and their extreme left was to be assailed at
various points by the Confederate troops in front of them.
General Gordon was then to attack them on the exposed right
flank and rear, with the hope of compelling them to abandon
the siege of Petersburg and withdraw to the north side of
James River.

The conception was worthy of Stonewall Jackson; it reflects
the highest credit on General Gordon, and if his force had been
sufficient to carry the enemy's second line would have proved a
grand success.

This was the last charge made by Confederate soldiers on
an entrenched position of the enemy, and while the results
expected were not realized, it showed that the soldiers of the
Army of Northern Virginia still had plenty of fight in them and
could be relied on to do all that mortal men could do.

After the failure of Gordon's movement, we all felt that our
cause was hopeless, and in two or three weeks thereafter we
marched out of the earthworks we had held so long against
such overwhelming odds and, a few days after, laid down our
arms at Appomattox.

The storming of Fort Stedman was a mere episode in the
siege of Petersburg and is scarcely mentioned in history, or
only spoken of in official reports as an "unsuccessful attempt to
carry the Federal lines near Fort Stedman, which was repulsed
with great loss." It was in fact one of the boldest movements
made during the war, and for coolness and gallantry on the
part of the soldiers engaged in it was not surpassed in any
affair of the war between the States.

TWENTY-TWO

Appomattox

Though fully informed of the desperate situation of Lee's army and the impending necessity of the evacuation of Petersburg, President Davis went, as usual Sunday morning, to services at St. Paul's Church. The church was but a short distance from the War Department, and the telegram from General Lee stating that he could no longer hold his position was sent to Mr. Davis during the service. Lee recommended that the whole line of troops be withdrawn from the James River and that Richmond be evacuated. Several days earlier he had requested that food for the army be sent to Amelia Court House, in his rear, and had been informed that it would be there.

When the army reached Amelia on April 5, supplies had not arrived. The men were literally starving and unable to retreat further without food. The night of the fifth Lee marched to Farmville where he found bread and meat for his men. The next day he repulsed an attack of Crook's cavalry, and the second Federal corps. As usual, whenever there was fighting, Walker was there.

Chaplain Hopkins recalls this engagement known as "Sayler's Creek" and the part General Walker's command took in this last stand made by the Army of Northern Virginia:

We were now retreating from Petersburg to Appomattox. Gordon's corps was rear guard, protecting and covering the retreat. It was followed by Humphrey's corps of Grant's army which pursued us vigorously.

Our mode of proceeding was for each of our three divisions to take stands alternately on the best ground we could command, by hard fighting to delay the enemy and then retreat to the front of our corps. Late that evening as we were approach-

ing Sayler's Creek in Amelia Court House, it fell to Walker's
division to make the last fight of the day.

The general fought till his division was almost surrounded,
then gave the order to retire which was obeyed with alacrity.

I can in memory now see the general grimly erect on his
dark bay horse in the midst of his weary troops, retreating
sadly and sullenly.

Lee continued to attempt to reach Lynchburg, but Thurman's
cavalry and the Twenty-fourth Infantry Corps of Grant's army
secured possession of the Lynchburg highway at Appomattox, and
Lee's army was effectually trapped. The dramatic story of his
surrender, the agony and despair of his men during the surrender,
and his affectionate farewell order are part of America's history.
General Walker was in the midst of it all.

The following excerpt from a letter from Dr. H. C. Todd of
Owensboro, Kentucky, provides, in the words of one who took part
in all the events and moving scenes of those last days of the
Confederacy, a vivid idea of the feelings of the men and the
involvement of General Walker:

During the memorable week's retreat from Petersburg I
was almost constantly near your Father, and as he rode at the
head of our Division his presence was commanding and magnetic, for he was a grand horseman.

On Thursday afternoon of this week April sixth at Sayler's
Creek, General Lee made his last stand, and being entirely
surrounded by an overwhelming force his army was almost
annihilated. Everything was pell-mell, and our division scattered.

General Walker, after crossing the creek, said to the dozen
horsemen with him, the writer being one of that number: "Men,
this looks very bad, but we will fight it out."

Then he directed two pieces of artillery, standing near, to
fire and to cover our retreat. It was now dark, and General
Walker with his dozen horsemen rode seven or eight miles to
the High Bridge near Farmville, where the remnant of our
army was to make their rendezvous that night.

Just at daylight on that ever memorable Sunday morning,
the surgeons of our Division, having been up all night, were
holding their horses at a small school house near the line of

battle, with balls and shells flying around them, when suddenly General Walker rode up and announced to the group of surgeons that General Lee would surrender.

His whole bearing was that of a man struggling under a most terrible ordeal. The end had come.

It is well known how General Lee's army went quietly into camp that Sunday morning, herded by Yankee pickets, and there remained until the following Wednesday morning. The paroles were all issued Tuesday, and that afternoon our Division was assembled near the camp.

General Walker rode to the center and sitting on his horse made one of the most eloquent addresses I ever heard. His tribute to the men who had followed him for four years was evidently heartfelt.

The next morning before day, our Division was formed ready for the march, and riding at its head was General Walker, than whom no Roman Consul making his triumphal entry into Rome could have looked more proud.

We marched a short distance to the place designated for stacking our arms. As our Division stood facing the Federal column, the command was given, "Present Arms!" and then the command, "Stack Arms!" That was the end of General Lee's army, and the ex-Confederates with sad hearts returned to their homes to become peaceful citizens.

Dr. Hopkins in his manuscript memoirs describes the surrender in much the same vein:

That beautiful spring morning our troops were marched out to stack arms for the last time and to turn them over to the victorious enemy. When this last act of our soldiers was done, "the boys" called on General Gordon and then on General Walker for a speech.

I remember the ringing tones and the brave and loyal sentiments of both Gordon and Walker. The latter heaped commendation upon the men who had stood steadfast till arms were stacked.

My father described this scene to me several times, telling how the men crowded about their officers, especially about General Lee, weeping like children. How some of them kissed Lee's boots and

stirrups and the lean sides of Traveller, the horse so familiar to
them all. How speeches of farewell were made by the officers to
their men, and how the men scattered reluctantly and slowly, many
shutting themselves in their tents to weep unrestrainedly or to
engage in sad and bitter talk with mess mates.

Not even the generous rations handed out by Grant's quartermaster could console them. That afternoon it began to rain,
continuing all night as they lay on sodden ground waiting with
heavy hearts for the morning and their parting. The sentinels could
hear sobs, groans and prayers as restless men tossed on threadbare
blankets in their leaking tents.

I had not heard, however, of the impression General Walker's
speech made upon his men until on a journey with my father to the
Confederate reunion in Louisville in 1896. I was reading, my father
having gone into another coach to look for old comrades, when my
attention was arrested by hearing someone say the name of
"General James A. Walker—Big Jim, we used to call him."

Two ex-Confederates sat behind me reminiscing. One recalled
Appomattox: "I shall never forget Walker's speech," he said, "the
day of our surrender after we had stacked arms—nor how he
looked." He continued:

He was the most superb horseman I ever saw. Sat on his
horse like Paladin. I think he had two or three killed under
him. But at that time he was riding a very handsome bay
which pranced whenever the bands played and arched his neck
like a circus horse.

Walker's division called for him after Gordon had spoken.
Walker rode to the center and stopped his horse. With a pat on
the horses' neck, Walker lifted his head and squared his shoulders as if we had won instead of being whipped, then poured
out one of the most eloquent, moving, impassioned speeches I
have ever heard. His men cheered and wept by turns and
almost mobbed him when he finished. I haven't seen him from
that day to this, but I hear he will lead the Stonewall Brigade
in our parade at Louisville, and I hope to meet him.

No tribute paid my father pleased me so much, because it was
spontaneous and unconscious of other listeners than the comrade
to whom the speaker was talking.

At Appomattox, the sun shone brightly after the April rain of the previous night, and nature put on her most enticing mood to make it easier for the men to break camp. The reaction too from those last despairing days and from the starvation and weariness of hopeless campaigning induced a more cheerful mood, so that the Confederate soldiers said their goodbyes to each other, shouldered their very light knapsacks, wrapped such tattered remnants of leather and rags about their feet as they could find, and almost gaily struck out on their homeward march, in groups, by twos, or singly, as best suited the direction each must take to reach home quickest.

What awaited them at home few knew. Some had heard of barns and houses burned, of children dead, or wives ill. All knew that devastation or decay would greet them and that severest privations awaited them. But they were going home! Never again, God willing, to bear arms—certainly never again in civil conflict. The future was theirs, and they had proved their valor, their endurance, and the honesty of their convictions.

Even their foes, after four years fierce fighting, respected them and forbore to exult over their defeat. General Grant had given them such half starved horses and mules as were left, and in every way had shown himself a generous foe. President Lincoln wanted peace and a reunited country. Above all, perhaps he would see to it that Congress would help the South back into the Union without further humiliation or undue delay.

The men who had fought for the South still loved her; they would band all their strength to her rebuilding as an integral part of the Union, which perhaps she should never have left. For after all, a united country was best, and now that the war had forever settled the question of a right by a state, or a group of states, to secede, the bonds of union would gradually become stronger between all the states. As for slavery, the South was well rid of it.

At all events, this terrible war between the states was over. There would never be another. A union cemented by rivers of blood and unmeasured suffering must endure henceforth! Certainly the Confederate soldier would be the last to attempt to sever it. For though he had fought stubbornly for his convictions, he had lost and had surrendered in good faith, admitting complete defeat. It was now his part to forget, become a loyal citizen of the United States of America, and give the best that was in him to rebuild his

own section and to heal, as rapidly as possible, the devastation and
the misunderstandings left by civil war.

I am not ready to say that these or similar reflections were in
the minds of all the ex-Confederates as they made their way back
to their homes. But I can aver that these were almost the exact
thoughts of General Walker. Brave and loyal in defeat as in victory,
he never looked back but kept head and shoulders to the front,
facing the future courageously in peace as in war. In good faith he
had accepted the arbitrament of the sword, and from the day he
surrendered at Appomattox until the day of his death, no one ever
heard him speak a disloyal word against the Constitution of the
United States nor a disrespectful one of the flag he had fought
against so valiantly. They had now again become his flag and his
country's Constitution, and he was ready to swear allegiance to
them and to do his utmost to preserve them.

Yet he had no apologies to make for the cause to which he had
given so much, saying always that the question of the right of
secession was an open question until the Civil War. Nor had he any
apologies to make for the Confederate soldier. His position with
regard to the militia of the southern states I am able to give from
his own manuscript, as a legal interpretation of the law as it then
existed:

In April, 1861, the state of Virginia was a de-facto as well
as de-jure government, having all powers of a sovereign, not
expressly granted to the general government by the Constitution of the United States. The government of the United States,
its President, its Congress, its army officers, had no more
authority or power over the Virginia militia, or over its officers,
or over the individuals composing its rank and file, except
through the Governor of the state, their constitutional and
legal commander-in-chief, than the Governor of New York...
Even when called into service of the general government,
the state had the right to appoint all the officers from the
highest to the lowest. The state of Virginia in 1861 had appointed all the officers of the companies according to her laws,
from the commander-in-chief to the junior lieutenant of companies. A military command can receive orders only through its
officers: the company through its captain, and the regiment
through its colonel, and so on up to its commander-in-chief. The
Virginia militia could only receive orders from the President of

the United States *through* its commander-in-chief, the Governor. Under the Constitution, President Lincoln had no power to command the military services of Virginia troops, or of a single individual soldier of Virginia, except through their own officers. He had no power to remove their state officers and appoint others in their places. The Virginia soldier could legally and honestly obey no officers but those set over him by the state laws, and he dared not disobey his officers upon penalty of the military law, and of military trial and military punishments.

Recognizing this as well settled law, when Fort Sumter fell, Mr. Lincoln issued his famous proclamation declaring certain southern states to be in rebellion and calling on the Governor of Virginia for her quota of seventy-five thousand troops to suppress insurrection. This requisition was addressed not to the people, or to the private composing the militia, or to the captain of companies, but to their Commander-in Chief, Governor Letcher, who alone could order out the Virginia militia and turn them over to the President to be commanded by him.

Governor Letcher, in response to the call for troops, promptly replied to Mr. Lincoln that no troops would be furnished for any such purpose. The governors of the northern states complied with the requisition of the President and ordered their state militias to Washington City to assist the United States to make war upon the South. They went forth not by the order of President or Congress but by the orders of their own commanders-in-chief, the governors of their respective states. The Governor of New York ordered his soldiers to Washington City, and they obeyed orders as all soldiers must do. The Governor of Virginia ordered the Virginia volunteer companies to Harper's Ferry, and they obeyed as soldiers should do. When these companies reported at Harper's Ferry they were formed into regiments, and Virginia colonels, appointed according to Virginia law by Governor Letcher, were placed in command of the regiments.

When the militia of the North, commanded by their regularly constituted officers, invaded Virginia, Virginia troops, marching under her flag, commanded by their Virginia officers, repelled the invaders. Was this the act of rebels? Was there treason in obeying their officers set over them by the law? They had no other officers and no other orders. Hundreds of southern soldiers were opposed to the war and did not believe in the constitutional right of a state to secede from the Union, but as soldiers they could not stop to discuss political questions with their officers. When war came, discussion was out of order. No right of private judgment can be allowed to the soldier in military affairs.

And when later Virginia became a member of the Confederate States and her Governor turned her troops over to the Confederate Army, the soldiers had no choice but to obey their superiors. They were not consulted, and still obedience was an implicit duty. The southern soldier obeyed orders when he fought; the northern soldier did the same thing, and one was no more guilty of treason or rebellion than the other. Both were right in obeying the officers and the powers set over them by law, and neither could have done otherwise.

James Alexander Walker

The author at age thirteen

Walker as a young man

General A. P. Hill

General Jubal A. Early

General Richard S. Ewell

Colonel Andrew Jackson Grigsby

Comrades in Arms

Virginia State Library and Archives

General Charles S. Winder

Virginia State Library and Archives

General Arnold Elzey

Virginia State Library and Archives

The Reverend J. William Jones

Virginia State Library and Archives

Captain Jedediah Hotchkiss

Comrades in Arms

Governor F. H. Pierpont

Governor Frederick W. M. Holliday
Walker was his Lieutenant Governor

Governor Gilbert C. Walker

Governor James L. Kemper

Political Associates

General William Mahone

Judge Samuel W. Williams
of Wythe County

Additional photos of James Walker

Stonewall Jackson House, Lexington, Virginia

T. J. Jackson as he appeared when a professor at V.M.I. Insignia on shoulder
and collar were added during Civil War.

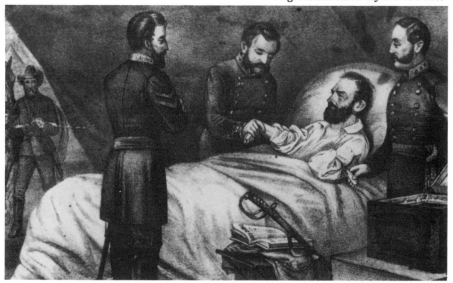

The Death of Stonewall Jackson
where he said: "Give the 'Stonewall' to James A. Walker."

Virginia Military Institute as it was when Jackson expelled Walker.

"Walker Hall" in Wytheville

The Walker Home
in Newbern

(1990 Photograph)

The Old Stone Church
in 1990. Where Gen.
Walker was married

TWENTY-THREE

Back to Newbern

General Walker's thoughts, as he rode from Appomattox to Lynchburg by greening fields, through forests budding and fragrant with spring, were divided between practical and immediate plans on the one hand and peaceful resolutions on the other.

His few Confederate dollars were worthless; he could hope for nothing from the practice of his profession until order was restored, courts reorganized and his disabilities as a late enemy of the Federal government removed. His only available assets, outside his home which was nearly paid for, were his fine riding horse, Buckeye, given him by his brother, Dr. Walker; a bony worn-out nag he had also personally owned, and a pair of mules and a covered wagon allotted him from the division of the quartermaster's stores at Appomattox and driven by his servant Joe.

Joe should have been mentioned sooner. The crowding events of campaigns, battles and marches have seemed to leave no opportunity to introduce him suitably and to commemorate his loyal and indispensable services to General Walker during his military career. A young black, inherited by Mrs. Walker from her mother, Joe had accompanied Colonel Walker to camp after his first furlough and had been with him for the last three years of the war.

Joe's endurance equalled that of Jackson's foot cavalry; his cheerfulness and resourcefulness also emulated theirs. But Joe obeyed the general's orders to stay behind with the wagons when a battle was on. No sooner did firing case, however, than Joe filled his haversack and canteen by begging from the quartermaster and filching from nearby gardens, then struck out to find "Mas Jeems." He soon acquired something of a second sense as to the disposition of the different commands and by dint of questioning could usually wend a pretty sure course for General Walker's position.

General Walker used to tell with sincere appreciation how, after many a hard fought battle, while he would be resting under some tree or in some fence corner by the roadside, he would hear Joe's booming voice calling loudly: "Where's General Walker? General Jeems Walker. Has anybody seen the General?" Soon, Joe's brown face would appear, laden haversack hanging from his broad shoulders, and presently the savory smell of bacon and onions, flap jacks and coffee, would be rising from Joe's campfire. True, the coffee didn't last after the second year of the war, but toasted wheat, or oats, or rye made a better-than-none substitute for a hot drink.

Recalling the many times Joe had ministered to his need in this way and his ever loyal and cheerful service, General Walker was troubled that there was so little he could do to help Joe get a start in the new life of freedom, for which he was entirely untrained. He found quarters and rations for Joe that first night in Lynchburg. Next morning Walker told him he was free and could go where he pleased. He presented him with the extra horse and advised him to try to sell the animal for a little gold and to look for work and wages.

"I hate to leave you, Mas Jeems," Joe said.

"I couldn't pay you, Joe, even if I had work for you," Walker said. "But you are strong and smart. You'll make your way."

"Yes, sir," Joe said. "But if you don't mind, I think I'll ride a spell before I settle down to work."

"It's natural you should want to try out your freedom, Joe," the general said, and he shook his hand. "We've been good comrades, and you can count always on my being your friend. You know where I live, and you can call on me if ever you are in trouble."

Both men wiped tears away as they turned in opposite directions. A few minutes later, Joe, smiling, mounted his nag and rode off, a new sort of Don Quixote, to seek adventures in a new world.

Joe did not forget the general's promise and often during the next twenty-five years sent him appeals for help, from his final settling place in Culpeper Court House. And during the last months of his somewhat brief life he received regular remittances from Walker, enabling him to live in greater comfort, despite the desertion of his wife.

That same morning, Walker also sold Buckeye, so named because of his satiny brown coat. The buyer was a Dr. Payne of Lynchburg, the consideration being all the fine leaf and plug tobacco Walker could load into his covered wagon. Rumors were afloat that a Federal raiding party was on its way to Lynchburg to burn the tobacco warehouses; hence all that Walker could carry away was his. Meantime, Dr. Payne could have Buckeye ridden off to the mountains to be hidden until the raiding party passed on. That left Walker free to drive the mule team homeward ahead of the raiders. Tobacco would be a salable, or least an exchangeable, commodity in Pulaski County in a section of the state where the devastation of war had not been so keenly felt as in other sections of Virginia. The mule team and wagon would be useful in many ways.

So mounting the driver's seat and touching up the rested mules, Walker struck the turnpike and headed for home.

The parting with Joe and the sale of his horse had brought fully home, for the first time, the realization that he was again a mere human cipher—no longer a general with body servants, noble steed and loyal followers at his command, but a defeated soldier, technically a rebel, with no money, no profession, no backing and no prospects, except those his own brawn and brain might be able to conceive and execute. A wife and three babies (and a fourth expected in July) awaited his return, and they had no other source of support than his exertions. Truly no time would be left to mourn a lost cause or brood over defeat.

I was but four years old in April of '65 and am told by child experts that it is hardly possible I can actually remember my father's homecoming with the vividness I think I do. Nevertheless, I shall relate the scene as I seem to recall it, though it may only be memories of what was told me later.

It was past mid-afternoon of a mild April day. We children and our nurse were playing under a big apple tree in the back yard. There were other apple trees in the yard, and they were a cloud of pink fragrance. The freshening turf was sprinkled with the fallen petals and dotted with dandelions. We were playing house, constructing "interiors" by outlining the rooms with rocks and furnishing them with colored pebbles, broken glass and bits of dishes. The real house and its grounds were very still, except for an occasional childish voice making an eager suggestion.

The sound of hoofs and a wagon clattering down the three hundred yard slope of the macadam road from the edge of the village to our gate made us lift our heads.

"It's turning in to the big gate," called the nurse shrilly, running to the plank fence and stile which separated the side of the back yard from the wood-lot. "I do believe it's Mas Jeems himself drivin' that mule team." She did not wait to confirm her belief but flew to the house calling in wild excitement: "Miss Sally! Miss Sally! Mas Jeems is coming."

We children didn't know who was meant by "Mas Jeems" and so sat still in some trepidation at seeing the mule team drive up to the stile and come to a halt. A bearded man in rusty uniform climbed out shouting, "Hello! Hello!"

By this time my mother was running across the back porch and yard to the gate where she fell crying into the arms of the big man. Her crying did not reassure us, but out of curiosity my older sister and I approached cautiously.

"It's your father, children!" called my mother hysterically. "Your father, come home from the war!"

But my father had already caught us up in either arm for a warm caress, declaring he didn't know his babies had grown up into big little girls since he had seen them. Presently my mother was in the kitchen, older children at her heels, in a flurry of eagerness to get together a sort of feast out of meager supplies.

TWENTY-FOUR

Starting Again

My one other memory of that spring of '65 seems almost as real and vivid. It is of a yard full of ragged, bearded, long-haired soldiers. Playing in the yard as usual, we had seen them march down the hill and come to a halt before our front gate. We ran panting into the sitting room where my mother was engaged in her usual occupation, of patching and darning the fast-disappearing family wardrobe. "The Yankees are coming!," we cried out. "The Yankees are coming!"

My mother dropped her sewing to meet at the front door an ex-Confederate captain. As my mother told us of it later, the captain stated that the men were what was left of a Tennessee company or two making their way home on foot, that he understood a Confederate general lived there, and they wanted permission to rest under the trees for a while, get a drink of cool water and, if the lady could possible spare it, a bite to eat, enough to give them strength to go on.

She bade the tired soldiers welcome to the grass and trees, said she would send them buckets of water from the well, and as quickly as she could would fry some meat and make some flat cakes from her limited supply of bacon sides and corn meal. She had about three middlings and a small sack of meal which had been sent her a few weeks before by some of my father's friends from Drapers Valley. She also had a few onions and potatoes from her garden stores of the fall before.

It was a day of delightful excitement for us children, for we were allowed to play with the soldiers while they were resting and waiting for their lunch to be cooked. Years afterward, I found among my souvenirs a "memory string" enriched with tarnished buttons from the worn uniforms of these returning soldiers and with tiny baskets carved from cherry stones by skillful pen-knives.

Not a few of the veterans wanted to embrace us as they told us with tear-filled eyes of their own babies waiting for them at home.

Eagerly we helped to distribute the coarse rations and sensed our mother's pride in being able to send on, refreshed and rested, this tattered, haggard remnant of the Southern army.

But the men were hardly out of sight when nurse and cook, directed by our mother, were heating water and getting out the fine combs to restore us to a sanitary condition. Head lice and body lice she expected, for even the better class of Confederate soldiers were unable to keep themselves free from these camp pests. But she was not prepared for the camp itch, which not only my sister, the nurse and I, but the baby also, developed in a few days. I am sure I remember that itch: the misery of having hands tied so that we could not relieve the terrible itching, in order to avoid breaking the tiny blisters and spreading the infection all over our bodies.

I recall too my father's vigorous doctoring. Each evening he helped to put us into tubs full of warm water before an open fire in the nursery, dried us, and then rubbed us thoroughly with a home-made salve of lard and sulphur. I think too I remember how viciously we smelled and how my mother bemoaned sulphur dyed gowns and stained sheets.

Before we were cured of our manifold sores, the only servants left on the place were the cook and her daughter, our nurse. My father had told them that they were free to go and that he was sorry he had nothing to give them. Isaac, the cook's husband, and his son, younger than the nurse girl, wandered off. But Lucy said she had nowhere to go and would stay until Isaac had been able to establish a home.

Lucy, indeed, stayed with my mother for some months until Isaac came back for her with enticing stories of what the Freedmen's Bureau would do for them if they left to do their own work.

The nurse, whose name was Judy, flew into a rage one day and slapped the baby. Her mother whipped her, and that night she ran away, never to rejoin her parents.

My father soon was able to hire a young black man to help work a tract of land he rented late in April from a friend, a Mr. Moore, a large land owner living in "Dunkard Bottom," a fertile valley on New River. His slaves gone, the land was of little service to its owner, and "Captain" Moore was glad to name a moderate rental for ten acres of his richest bottom land. The mule team, a borrowed plow and an old army tent completed the necessary equipment.

Every Monday morning, General Walker was up by daylight, and, with the hired man, loaded the plow, tent and such provisions as he could get into his wagon, and started down the pike for an eight- or nine-mile drive to Dunkard Bottom. He took turns with the young man at the plow, though his wounded left arm was no small handicap, and later the two worked side by side in the furrows, hand dropping and covering the corn.

It proved to be a fine season. Hardly was the last corn in the ground before the first stalks were shooting up, ready for the hoe. With his accustomed thoroughness and perseverance, General Walker worked that corn crop over and over again until it stood ten feet high and bore three and four full ears to the stalk.

Between times he and the hired man worked in the home garden, and thanks to the season and the good attention it got, it was a wonderful garden. My mother used to say that a kind providence saved the famished South that summer of '65 by sending the best growing season she had ever known. Cabbage heads that September would barely go into a flour barrel, and Irish potatoes were as big as a croquet ball. She shipped several barrels of each to a commission merchant in Lynchburg and got in return a barrel of flour, a little coffee and a sack of "coffee sugar," a soft, dark brown sticky mass which to the children's taste was the most delectable of sweets. An occasional lump was begged for us by an always indulgent father, from our more frugal mother.

Hard work in the cornfield still further toughened General Walker physically. He ate his coarse rations, usually of corn pone and fat meat, with relish (though reaffirming the vow made in winter quarters in '63 that were he ever again able to earn money enough he meant to live on the fat of the land for the rest of his days) and slept soundly at night under his old tent.

His wife, however, did not have his hardy temperament nor his buoyant disposition. After the birth of their fourth child and second son, Frank, in July, and the loss of the nurse girl, she suffered a complete breakdown in health and spirits. The winter before the surrender, she had been greatly distressed by the death of her mother who had lived with her for several years and who, vigorous and capable, had always saved her "baby," my mother, the youngest by eight years of a family of ten, from every hardship. Mrs. Walker's own children had come rapidly and during years of great stress and anxiety. Loss of trained service, to which she had been accustomed, and severe poverty followed, the combination proving too much for a delicately framed and tenderly nurtured woman.

But for the coming of an older sister, Mrs. Peter Woods, from Richmond, to be with my mother during her confinement, I hardly know what would have become of us children, nor of my father's corn crop. We called her "Auntie" and were devoted to her. She returned that fall to Richmond, but upon her husband's death some months after came back to Newbern to make her home with us until her death in 1874. A remarkable woman in management, tact, poise and efficiency, as well as of unusually handsome appearance, she was a godsend to us all. Even the small income saved by her from the wreck of her husband's fortune—his warehouses and their contents having been consumed in the burning of Richmond—was at my father's disposal. Between him and "Auntie" existed a warm brotherly and sisterly relationship. As she was some years older than he, General Walker always called her Mrs. Woods, treated her with ceremonious respect and asked her advice in business as well as in domestic matters. For me, she was a model in every respect, and of my position as her room-mate and favorite I was very proud. As a result of our affection, she practically adopted me.

The news emporium and loafing ground of the village was Mr. Jack Wall's store. Mr. Wall was a bachelor, bon vivant, good fellow, and something of an old dandy. He dyed his hair jet black, had a red, jolly face, and was portly, elaborately polite, and a garrulous gossip. Everybody in town and county liked "Jack" and traded at Wall's.

Here General Walker went Saturday evenings to learn such news of the outside world as came to the town by way of intermittent newspapers or an occasional traveller from "the North." The assassination of President Lincoln had brought consternation to thinking and right-minded people throughout the South. It was well known that Lincoln had no animosity toward the South or toward the Confederate soldiers. He had taken the position that the Southern states still belonged to the Union, just as a punished child is still a member of the family, and that if only they would promise to be good, by taking the oath of allegiance to the Federal government, all would be forgiven and forgotten. Time and again he had said that if only the Union could be preserved and peace restored he would be willing to yield everything else. Even the Thirteenth Amendment had his doubtful approval, as he frankly admitted to the Confederate commissioners in the Hampton Roads conference.

The excitement and recrimination, charges and threats following Lincoln's death and Jefferson Davis' arrest for complicity in the plot boded ill for the South. General Walker realized that fact, brooded over it as he followed the corn rows and went to "Walls" eagerly for news each weekend.

From Andrew Johnson, a more severe policy was expected toward the Confederate soldier, and especially their leaders, for he had said in the recent Presidential campaign that rebels should be shot as traitors, whenever caught. Though a Tennessean, he was a hater of secession and secessionists, and no one expected from him the broad policy of a Lincoln. Davis and others were arrested, charged with treason and murder, and imprisoned to await trial Some members of Johnson's cabinet counseled the continuation of Lincoln's policy.

A few weeks later on May 29th, Johnson issued his Peace proclamation by the provision of which Southerners were appointed to office in most of the Southern states, the ante bellum electorate was recognized—on condition of oaths of allegiance to the Federal government—and conventions were ordered held in the several states to frame new constitutions acceptable to the Federal government.

Application for reinstatement to citizenship was open to almost all officers and civil officials and was in no sense a dishonoring requisite. General Lee set the example by making application in June '65 to have his disabilities removed. In July, General Walker sent in his application through Governor Pierpont, as the following copy of the original shows. I found it among my father's papers and recalled the circumstances of his having secured the copy from Washington during a heated political campaign in Virginia, when he was being accused of having rushed into the arms of the late enemy of the South at the first possible opportunity:

TO HIS EXCELLENCY, ANDREW JOHNSON
PRESIDENT OF THE UNITED STATES

The petition of James A. Walker of Pulaski County, Virginia, would respectfully represent that he is a lawyer by profession, is 32 years of age, has wife and three children, that his means are very limited and his family therefore entirely dependent upon his labor in his profession for support.

At the commencement of the rebellion and for some years
prior thereto he resided and still resides in the county of
Pulaski, Va., and was captain of a volunteer company organized in the year 1859, and was, at the commencement of the
rebellion, ordered with his company into immediate service, by
the Government of Virginia. That he entered service as captain
and was regularly promoted to the position of Brigadier General, which position he held at the time of the surrender of the
Army of Northern Virginia.

Your petitioner believed in the right of secession and consequently favored and supported the cause of the South, doing
only what at the time he sincerely believed to be his duty, but
that he at all times in the discharge of the duties of his several
positions paid strict regard to the usages of civilized warfare,
protected and treated with uniform kindness all prisoners of
war, that were at any times in his hands. That he at no time
engaged in or encouraged the persecution of Union men.

Your petitioner acknowledges his error in espousing and
supporting the cause of secession, and avers his purpose in
good faith to resume and continue allegiance to the Union, to
which he has taken the oath of allegiance, as will be seen by a
copy thereof herewith exhibited and asks your Excellency to
grant him full pardon and amnesty.

> Very respectfully,
> J. A. Walker

The letter was accompanied by three endorsements. One by
Daniel H. Hoge attested to the truth of Walker's letter and added
that General Walker "was always known to be kind and courteous
to Union men and prisoners and I therefore with pleasure recommend him to the clemency of your Excellency and respectfully ask
you to grant him full amnesty, and thereby restore him to all his
rights of citizenship." Hoge, a prominent citizen of southwest
Virginia of pioneer stock noted for its intellectual ability, was
opposed to secession and had declined to take up arms against the
Stars and Stripes; yet he had not lost the respect and liking of his
friends and neighbors as was proven by his being elected to the first
Virginia Legislature after the war in the fall of 1865.

F. H. Pierpont, Governor of Virginia at that time, wrote an endorsement recommending "that this petition be placed on the most favorable footing of his class for pardon."

The third endorsement was a statement from Charles H. Simmons, a former Federal army captain and newly appointed Assistant Postmaster of Pulaski, a forerunner of those who constituted what, later on, the embittered South called the "Carpetbag Government." He wrote:

I do hereby certify that on the 3rd day of August 1865, at Newbern, Va., the oath prescribed by the President of the United States in his proclamation of May 29th 1865 was duly taken, subscribed and made matter of record by James A. Walker of Pulaski County Va.

TWENTY-FIVE

Politics

In his proclamation of April 7 announcing the end of the war and making recommendations to Congress for the reconstruction of the South, President Lincoln left Virginia out of the roll call of states which had been "in rebellion."

This was because of special circumstances in the case of Virginia, different from those in any of the other southern states. It was claimed that a "loyal government" had existed in Virginia during the entire war with its seat first at Wheeling and then at Alexandria, and that during the period from 1861 to 1865 Virginia had been represented in Congress.

In the early spring of '65 this loyal government had consented to a partition of Virginia, and Congress had recognized the new state of West Virginia. Therefore, Governor Pierpont had moved the seat of the government of Virginia to Alexandria where under the protection of Federal guns the fiction of state administration was preserved. This was recognized by President Lincoln on May 9 as the true government of Virginia and soon after this its headquarters were moved to Richmond, Pierpont occupying the historic Governor's Mansion.

Governor Pierpont now ordered that the restored state hold an election. That was done, a very limited electorate participating. The legislature so elected met in session on the 20th of June following. Mr. Pierpont recommended in his message to that body that a constitutional amendment should be drafted and proposed to the voters for ratification, to enfranchise and qualify for office a much larger proportion of the people than was the case under the revised constitution of Virginia of 1864 adopted by the "loyal convention" at Alexandria. It seemed that Mr. Lincoln's policies would be carried out by Mr. Johnson and that Virginia had only to formally adopt the Thirteenth Amendment and thus adapt herself to the new economic system as quickly as possible.

The one apparent cloud on the horizon was the Freedman's Bureau which, with probably the most charitable intent, was upholding the newly freed slaves in a state of vagrancy and idleness that was proving a menace to economic restoration. With few exceptions, they would not hire themselves to their late masters, and there was no other labor available. Naturally, as they wandered about the country in idleness, they committed depredations and were guilty of all sorts of petty offenses. Naturally too, their late masters were intolerant, suspicious, and resentful of the least gesture toward insolence. This strained situation was fanned by Federally appointed civil officers, Freedmen's Bureaus and northern school teachers whose officious friendliness toward the black was resented by the whites no less than was their attitude of scorn for the ex-slave holder.

In spite of these disturbing elements, Virginia's leaders were determined to live up to the terms of surrender and to restore orderly government to their state within the Union as soon as might be. This was the outspoken policy of General Lee, who was still Virginia's model of manhood and the South's idol. General Walker took an active part in the selection of the representative men who were put up as candidates and duly elected to the Legislature that fall.

The franchise had not then been extended to blacks, and as only white men voted at this election the Legislature was chosen on much the same basis as before the war. Meeting December 4, 1865, it continued in session until March 3, 1866.

It found much work to be done and went at it with all possible dispatch. It ratified the Thirteenth Amendment, ordered a constitutional convention, elected judges and state officers, and passed needful revenue laws. Circuit and county courts were reorganized, as well as county and municipal governments, so as to make provision for the changed order and to provide for justice to the freedmen.

There was lacking but one thing more for the complete restoration of the state to its Federal relations, namely: the admission of the Senators and Representatives chosen by its electorate to seats in Congress. They had presented themselves at the opening of the called session of Congress on the first Monday in December and were excluded, along with the Senators and Representatives from the other "Johnson States."

The Radical element was now in control of Congress, and Lincoln's policy of conciliation, which President Johnson had adopted, was not to their liking. A Reconstruction committee was named, southern representatives were denied seats, and there began for the South that unhappy time known as the Reconstruction Period. It was to sow those seeds of bitter sectionalism, which bore fruit for many years in the "solid South," with the practical loss to the nation of one fourth of its citizenry and the eventual loss to the South of political independence of thought or action.

For more than a year, however, the government as constituted by Pierpont under Lincoln's proclamation, continued to act as the Virginia state government, but with such limitations as were imposed upon it by the presence of the military of the United States and the interference of officers in behalf of the Freedmen, spelled with a capital by Congress and the Federal government.

The Virginia Legislature upon reassembling in January '66 passed the Vagrant Act. On the 24th, General Terry, the military commander at Richmond, set aside this measure as to the Freedmen. He based his order on the tendency of employers to combine to lower wages, so as to pauperize the blacks and drive them into vagrancy. It was just the sort of accusation calculated to strengthen prejudice and to arouse a spirit of reprisal in the Congress at Washington and the people of the North, against the people of Virginia and the South generally.

The Fourteenth Amendment was submitted for ratification in June of 1866. It was rejected January 9, 1867. This act sealed the fate of that legislature, and Virginia also was now brought under the Reconstruction Acts of March, 1867, and became Military District No. 1, with General Schofield as commander.

While H. H. Wells was made military governor, General Schofield ordered the election of delegates to a constitutional convention, by those voters designated in the Reconstruction Act, to be held in November 1867 and required the delegates so elected to assemble in Richmond on December 3. These orders were executed under the supervision and control of the military government.

Of the one hundred and five delegates elected, thirty-five were conservative, the rest radical. Of these last, twenty-four were blacks, fourteen were native Virginia whites, thirteen were New

Yorkers, and one each came from Pennsylvania, Vermont, Connecticut, Maryland, England, Ireland, Nova Scotia and elsewhere in Canada.

The fourteen white Virginia Radicals were dubbed "Scalawags," not because they had been Union sympathizers but because, it was believed, they had joined the enemy since the war for political position. Those non-Virginians who had drifted into Virginia as Federal office holders were called "Carpetbaggers." The newly chosen body was nicknamed the "black and tan convention," and Virginians like the Walkers felt themselves insulted and outraged by the power of such a group to frame their state constitution.

A New Yorker, John C. Underwood, was elected as its President, and the constitution adopted is known as the Underwood Constitution. It is a rather remarkable fact that county governments in Virginia years later still operated under the cumbersome plan framed by this convention. It was to those sections pertaining to county government that President Grant called attention as being liable to great abuses when the Underwood Constitution was later submitted to him by a committee of Virginians.

Schofield himself appeared in the convention and urged the delegates to be moderate in the propositions for the disfranchisement and disqualification of those who had participated "in the rebel." But the delegates elected under the Reconstruction Acts and by the electorate created through them were not only radical, but bent upon retaliation.

They would not listen to Schofield but drafted and finally adopted such provisions in regard to suffrage qualifications and the right to hold office as would have put the state government, based on the constitution, permanently in the hands of blacks, "Scalawags," and "carpetbag" adventurers, such as constituted the convention. The opposition to these provisions from all over the state was so universal and emphatic as to intimidate the convention and delay the submission of the constitution to the voters for some months. This opposition crystallized toward the end of the year 1868 in a conference of prominent Virginians assembled at Richmond who appointed a committee to petition Congress and the new President, General Grant, to allow the disqualifying and disfranchising clauses to be voted on separately from the other parts of the proposed constitution.

In January '69, this Commission was permitted to argue its case before both Houses and the President. The impression they made on Grant was such that in his message to Congress April 7th he asked for authority to accede to the petition of the Virginians. That authority being granted him, he issued a proclamation on the 14th of May '68, ordering that the Virginia constitution framed December 3rd 1867 be submitted to the voters for ratification or rejection without the disqualifying clauses which were to be separately submitted. At the election the constitution minus these clauses was ratified while disfranchising provisions were defeated.

Senators and Representatives from Virginia elected under the new constitution again presented themselves for admission to the Congress of the United States. Their claims were sustained by the President who reported to Congress that Virginia had fulfilled all the conditions required for her readmission to the Union, having ratified the Fourteenth and Fifteenth Amendments. After some wrangling the bill was passed and in the last days of January, 1870, Virginia was restored to the Union. The Congressional act admitting her also undertook to control the new legislature chosen by the conservative Republicans by requiring every member to take an oath that he had not been disqualified by the Fourteenth Amendment, or if so, had been relieved by the Congressional act.

It was during these gloomy months of the years of '67 and '68 that General Walker almost despaired of Virginia's future and thought strongly of migrating to the Pacific coast or even to South America. His wife's delicate health and his family of little children made such a move doubly risky. Moreover, General Walker was no quitter and did not wish to leave his native state in the hands of its lowest element. In agony of spirit he wrote to General Lee for advice, receiving from him a reply so calm, moderate and courageous that Walker felt himself put to shame, made new resolves and never again shrank from any public duty his conscience dictated.

General Lee's letter meant, in substance, this: Your country and your state need your services. Virginia never needed her loyal sons so much as she needs them now. It is your privilege to work for her restoration to good government, *within the Union,* and to restore importance in national affairs.

Within the year after his return from Appomattox General Walker had formed a law partnership with Mr. John B. Baskerville of Newbern, one of the oldest, soundest and most learned of the lawyers of southwestern Virginia. A quiet, hard working man, Mr. Baskerville was glad to leave the more aggressive end of the practice to his junior partner, and together they made a strong team. This partnership continued for two years after General Walker had left Newbern to make his home in Wytheville and was never marred by a single personal disagreement, although there were not infrequent arguments on the conduct of a case or the interpretation of a point of law.

Law business was, however, uncertain for several years following the war, and fees difficult of collection. In the hope of adding to his income, General Walker bought a farm a few miles from Newbern and with the help of a brother-in-law, Alpheus Poage, who was now making his home with him, attempted to farm it productively.

Major Poage was an older brother of Mrs. Walker and a veteran of the Mexican as well as the Civil War. Born the son of the wealthy owner of several plantations and many slaves, handsome, gallant, a magnificent horsemen, he had spent his youth in riding from one to another of the plantations, carrying orders to the overseers and making reports to his father, when not visiting about the neighborhood or absent in Mexican campaigns and other adventures. He knew the theory of farming with overseers and slaves but not much of the actual practice, and he found that farming was no longer a gentleman's job. Major Poage tried valorously to plow and hoe and even essayed to split rails, while not infrequently General Walker took a day off from his not overly busy office to help him. But neither made a brilliant success at such efforts, and a few years later General Walker was glad to get rid of the farm.

For helpers about the house there were two white mountain girls whose mothers, Confederate widows, had bound them, through court, to General Walker until their eighteenth year, with contract for board, lodging, suitable clothing and three months schooling each year in return for domestic services. Caroline, the older of the two girls, was about fourteen when she was "bound." I remember her as a strapping, pleased-faced, blond girl of great vigor and cheerfulness. She was a wonderful playmate, and we children used to help with the supper dishes to insure time for a glorious romp with her in the yard before dark.

The girl who came two or three years later, Jinny, was a brunette, good looking and as surly in disposition as Caroline was pleasant.

Caroline stayed out her term and left to get married, carrying with her generous gifts and the affection of the whole family. Jinny was released at sixteen because she became too great a responsibility.

With these two untrained girls, Auntie ran the house, while my mother sewed, knitted, patched and darned as diligently as her health permitted. My father had bought her a small hand-turned "Wheeler and Wilson" sewing machine, one of the first in the country. In February '68 her third son, James Robert, was born, and in June '69 a fourth son, Allen Poage. From this time on, more and more of the care of house and children had to be taken over by my aunt, my mother being confined to bed and couch much of the time.

We children realized but little of the strain, financial and otherwise, our elders were undergoing. I recall many evenings of happy play with Caroline and Jinny, many Sunday afternoon rambles in the woods, many all day picnics, with berrying or nut gathering as their excuse.

The four children of my mother's widowed sister-in-law were always with us on these picnics and hay rides and indeed shared all our pleasures. Their father, Colonel Thomas Poage, had died at his home near Newbern of tuberculosis, the result of wound and exposure, only a few months after "the surrender." He left General Walker executor of his small estate and guardian of his children, and loyally was the trust discharged. Not only did Walker perform wonders of financing in behalf of the children but took the place of a father in guiding, advising and even discreetly disciplining them, when requested to do so by their faithful, hard working little mother. She, by good management, extracted from a small, poor farm a living for her family until they were almost grown, and then sold it for a sufficient sum to buy a modest house in the village and to add something to her limited income. She was but one of many Confederate widows who dedicated their lives to unaccustomed toil and hardship in order to raise and educate their fatherless children.

That we must willingly share whatever we had with our orphaned cousins was early taught us. They spent all their holidays and frequent rainy nights at our house.

Our home-made Christmas trees were equally theirs, those wonderful Christmas trees, so skillfully decorated out of the rag bags in the attic by resourceful Auntie. Balls made of yarn sock ravelings and covered with red, blue and yellow "Morocco" leather, cut from the tops of old boots, for the boys. Dolls made of rags, sticks or china "heads," and gaily dressed in scraps, for the girls. Bags made of old tarleton dresses and filled with home-made candy and nuts from the woods. Strings of popcorn and cranberries. Snow balls of iced cake, dough-nut animals, and ginger bread men. Red apples were also freely used and even tiny bottles of bright red currant wine were hung amid the branches of the tree and added a touch of color and sparkle, while every scrap of tinsel or colored paper that could be found was improvised into gay ornaments. We had also a small supply of colored stick candy from Wall's store, after the first year or so, as a real treat. I do not think our later Christmas trees, when stockings were filled with oranges and "French candy" and the tree hung with real toys and dolls brought from Richmond, ever thrilled us as did the home-made ones of the first few years after the war.

But I have digressed from the main stream of my narrative.

After Congress, through the good offices of President Grant, had allowed Virginia to vote separately on the disfranchising clause of the Underwood Constitution, Virginia Conservatives had met in convention and nominated Colonel R. E. Withers of Lynchburg for Governor of the state, John L. Marye Jr. of Fredericksburg for Lieutenant Governor, and James A. Walker for Attorney General, all Confederate veterans.

It at once became evident that such a ticket would not be acceptable to the other political elements in the state, nor to the Federal government. Hence Withers, Marye and Walker withdrew and joined heartily in the nomination of a New York Democrat, Gilbert C. Walker, once a Federal soldier, now a banker in Norfolk, as Governor, and John H. Lewis, a Virginian but from the first a Union man, for Lieutenant Governor.

General Walker stumped the state for this ticket. Because it fused "conservatives" or Democrats and "true" Republicans, it was safely elected—beating a ticket headed by H. H. Wells, the ex-military Governor, with a black, I. D. Harris, as his running mate.

For nine years Virginia had been separated from participation in the affairs of the Federal government. By this election, she was restored to most of her rights as a component part of the American Union.

TWENTY-SIX

The Practice of Law

The rapid restoration of Virginia to orderly government, prosperity and general good will between 1870 and 1875 was most gratifying to those of her citizens who, a few years before, had despaired of her future. Though Governor Gilbert C. Walker in his first message to the legislature, once more a fairly representative body, raised an issue on the debt question which was afterwards bitterly fought out in Virginia politics, his administration was on the whole conducive to orderly government with a revival of business and industrial development along new lines.

For General Walker, it was a time of increasing involvement in the industrial development of Virginia and rapid growth in his law practice.

In June, 1870, the legislature passed a bill authorizing the formation of the Atlantic, Mississippi and Ohio Railroad by the merger of the Norfolk and Petersburg, the South Side and the Virginia and Tennessee railroads. The next day a salute of 111 guns (one for every vote cast in the House and Senate) was fired, and at night the streets of Richmond were illuminated by burning tar barrels. This merger gave the state a through line of 408 miles from Tidewater to Tennessee and made possible the development of her mineral, timber and agricultural resources.

General William Mahone of Petersburg, who had been chief engineer of the Norfolk and Petersburg line from 1853 to his enlistment in the Confederate army, was nominated for President of the new road by General Walker, one of the stockholders and directors of the Virginia and Tennessee. General Walker became a director of the new A. M. & O. and, under Mahone, active in efforts to put it in condition to adequately serve the territory it traversed. Minus bridges and stations, burned by Federal raiding parties, with broken links here and there, the three roads had been operated in a very spasmodic and unsatisfactory fashion since 1863.

I recall a trip with "Auntie" from Richmond to Newbern, for the date of which my memory does not serve me, when every now and then we had to walk several hundred yards or cross a stream on a foot bridge, in order to take a waiting section of the train on the other side. Usually a wheezy engine, a box car and a coach constituted these relays. There would be a stop now and then also for cord wood piled alongside the road to be loaded in the tender. Once a breakdown occurred, and we had to spend the night in a nearby farm house until another engine could be brought from Lynchburg.

Large deposits of salt near Glade Spring, Virginia, had induced the running of a branch line to Saltville as early as 1856. The Confederacy had depended for its supply of salt on this deposit. Lead had been found in Wythe County in pre-revolutionary times, and there are still ruins of an old Shot Tower at the lead mines near Austinville, used during the Revolution for making shot, by dropping hot lead from its top story.

Copper had very early been located in Carroll County, and iron forges and charcoal furnaces were making "pig" and wrought iron in Wythe and Pulaski Counties before and during the war. These but little developed mineral deposits, the vast tracts of virgin timber and the rich grazing lands of southwestern Virginia were becoming known in other sections, partly through the reports of wandering "carpetbaggers," partly through agents of northern investors seeking bargain lands from land-poor southern owners, and partly by a new policy of advertising the resources of the South in newspaper and magazine articles. Consequently, bonds issued by the A. M. & O. Railroad were easily disposed of outside the state, so that General Mahone and his directors began to rebuild road beds, bridges and "depots" and to buy new rolling stock.

Trade revived. Many blacks returned to work on the farms, either as tenants or hired men. Once more, there was food enough raised in Virginia, as well as some imported luxuries. An orange, however, was a rare treat all through my childhood, and one was often divided among the six of us. Bananas were unknown, and candy existed mainly in the stick variety, with a little "French" for show. Turkeys and partridges, however, in season, were plentiful and cheap, frying sized chickens sold at nine pence (12.5 cents) or a shilling (16 2/3 cents) each, eggs 8 and 10 cents a dozen, and butter at a shilling a pound. Fresh beef was usually sold by the quarter, lamb by the half, and pork by the hog, averaging a few cents a pound. My mother made her own sausage and lard and cured her own hams and middlings. Fresh meat was hung in the ice house, and steaks or roasts cut off as needed.

Many of my father's fees were paid in produce, wood or other commodities. I remember the fun we children had with several wagon loads of shingles, delivered by a client for reroofing the house, and stacked in the back yard. For several weeks we built all manner of edifices with those shingles and peopled them with imaginary folk. It kept us out of worse mischief and in the yard so my father considered some damage to the shingles liberally offset.

The firm of Baskerville and Walker was in active practice by 1870. Mr. Baskerville did the better part of the office work, while his junior partner "rode to the courts" of Carroll, Montgomery and Wythe, as well as doing most of the jury practice in the Pulaski courts. On the first Monday of each month, Carroll court convened, and each first Sunday General Walker, in sunshine, rain or snow, rode or drove over the mountain to Hillsville. We children were always glad when Carroll court came round, for we were sure of finding something good in Papa's saddlepockets on his return home: big moulds of "tree sugar," chinquapins, hickory nuts, chestnuts or else bags of stick candy.

More than once he brought home a two-bushel flour sack full of chestnuts, and there was no restriction on the quantity we could eat. Indeed, my father must have been over-indulgent to his children, and my mother's stricter rule was a very necessary restraint both for our health and our morale.

Once, after hearing us say we'd like to have all the eggs we could eat that coming Easter, my father had a tub full sent from Mr. Wall's store with a note to my mother to let the children have just as many as they wanted. In some disgust my mother decreed that we could have unlimited access to the eggs. The four older children and the two "bound girls" proceeded to cook eggs all imaginable ways and to eat to satisfaction. Most of us were ill by the time father got home that evening, and my mother's wisdom was satisfied. I am afraid that my father was more amused than remorseful, since for weeks afterward he chuckled when we declined eggs. I think it was ten years before I really enjoyed an egg again. There was a similar occurrence a year or two later as to lemonade when lemons first began to be plentiful.

Not only was our father indulgent to his children's material wants, he was also alert to feed their awakening intelligence and to cultivate their taste. Each trip to Richmond or Lynchburg he brought back something to stimulate their interest in the world: a set of Walter Scott's novels for my sister, of Dickens for me, when we were barely twelve and thirteen years old. Which story was to be read first was eagerly discussed and decided on, then first chapters were read aloud with some explanation and hint of what was to come. The next trip it would be volumes of poems: Moore's, Tennyson's, Scott's, Burns's, which would likewise be introduced to us by the reading aloud of his favorite extracts.

He had a rule that we must earn our pocket money. It could be earned by doing chores about the house, or by "saying verses," as we preferred. A cent a verse was the price, and for those of us who had good memories it was quite easy to earn a dime or even a quarter by a few hours of close application.

Again he would return home with a picture, or a picture book, or would announce to my mother that he had ordered some new piece or "set" of furniture for the house. Pictures were rare then, picture books rarer. I prized my set of Dickens more because it had Cruikshank's illustrations.

On one occasion the gift to the household was two chromas—then a viewing process—copies of famous pictures, one of "Titian's Daughter" and the other of "The Jewel Scene" from Faust. This new process of making pictures, my father explained, would soon make pictures cheap, and we would be able to know all the best pictures by accurate colored copies. Then he told us the stories of the two prints and of the artists who had painted the originals. His talk kindled my first desire to study something of the history of art and to visit some of the old world.

It was about this time my father sold his farm and began to devote all his time to law and politics. He was already making a reputation as a well grounded and brilliant lawyer. He loved his profession and studied law books as some men read history, for sheer interest. He practiced assiduously in county and circuit court and soon began winning test cases in the Supreme Court.

In 1872 he argued the case of Mitchell vs. Thornton (21 Gratton) which established the precedent that "land whether its value be great or small could not be taken for public purposes without just compensation to the owner." In a number of other much cited cases in Virginia law practice, General Walker was counsel on the side sustained by the Supreme Court establishing important precedents. Among these were three of the first cases tried under the "Married Woman's Act" passed by the Virginia General Assembly in April, 1877.

General Walker, noted for his clear reasoning and logical presentation, was also a powerful criminal lawyer, fighting several notable cases through the courts, to win finally by a decision of the Supreme Court. It was a working principle of his that a chain of circumstantial evidence is no stronger than its weakest link, and that only when that chain is forged of unbreakable links should a man be found guilty on such evidence. He more rarely prosecuted in a murder trial, preferring to act as counsel for the accused.

Though cases were now plentiful—many unsettled questions having arisen upon the restoration of orderly government—fees were small and paid often, as I have said, in trade. Hence it was a notable occasion when my father came back from Carroll County one "court week" with a roll of greenbacks in his pocket, totaling a thousand dollars, earned, I seem to recall, in the transfer of some large tract of land to "northern capital." I only remember my father's showing the fat roll of money to my mother and to us gaping children, counting it over for us and then locking it up in a desk drawer till he could find a chance to take it to Lynchburg to our nearest bank. How prosperous we felt! How proud of our wonderful father who gathered money from clients as we did berries from the bushes!

Later General Walker became attorney for a number of corporations which were organized in southwest Virginia. The Loddell Carwheel Company, the Pulaski Iron Company, The Ivanhoe Furnace Company and others. Also he was made special counsel for the Clinch Valley branch of the Norfolk and Western road, which the A. M. & O. later became. That road under Mahone's presidency had attempted too rapid rehabilitation, had gone into the hands of a receiver, later been organized largely by Philadelphia capital and renamed the Norfolk and Western.

Let me close my comments about my father's legal career with the following estimation of his as a lawyer, published in the Virginia Law Register soon after his death:

General Walker was a great lawyer. He had few equals and no superior at the Virginia bar...As honest with his clients as a Roman judge he realized in the language of Bacon that "the greatest trust between man and man is the trust of giving counsel." With an energy that knew no bounds, with a capacity for work that knew no limit, with ability of the highest order, he overcame all obstacles, and often snatched victory from defeat.

TWENTY-SEVEN

Starting a School

During the years 1860-70, education continued to be a major problem in Virginia. When my sister became seven years old, Auntie undertook to give her and me daily lessons in the "three R's." Auntie had had no training as a teacher, had only the education of the women of her generation, which in 1830-40 was limited to "belles lettres" and accomplishments. Moreover, Auntie could find but an hour or two a day to devote to us. A school must be started in Newbern, General Walker concluded, for his own and other children.

Getting started required only the hiring of teachers. The teachers who sought the job were widows or sisters of dead Confederate soldiers, and their claims as such were paramount, without regard to their qualifications as teachers. For the first three years of our schooling, therefore, our education was carried on more for the benefit of the ex-Confederacy than for our own.

The Underwood Constitution had provided for "free schools." However, the taxes available were very limited, there were no school houses, and the establishment of a public school system could proceed only slowly.

With others, General Walker agreed to supplement the salary of a teacher or teachers and to rent an unoccupied building of two rooms, one above the other. The Reverend Thomas Kirkpatrick was engaged as a teacher. Pastor of the Presbyterian Church of Newbern and two county churches, he was glad to add something to his meager salary. For seats this school had wooden benches but no desks. The front bench was longer than the others and, placed in front of the stove and of the teacher's table, was known as "class bench." The only time our feet stayed warm was while we were in class.

Mr. Kirkpatrick was a man of brains, logic and eloquence but too profound to be a success as a teacher of young children and too "easy" to discipline them. He usually took a nap in his chair after the lunch hour, when the older boys enjoyed themselves by tormenting the girls and younger boys—threatening worse things in stage whispers if they woke the teacher.

By the next session a larger appropriation was secured, and patrons from the county were induced to send in their children, thus to supplement the school fund. Two teachers of experience were engaged: Mr. Alex Paxton of Rockbridge County and his sister Miss Ruby. The primary grades were separated from the more advanced pupils, and Newbern for the first time in her history had a really efficient school.

Good teacher, organizer and disciplinarian, Mr. Paxton was an inspiration to the whole county. For many, he opened the gates of knowledge. His pupils began to get an insight into the use of maps and the mysteries of algebra, as well as an appreciation of the varied treasures of English literature.

We "trapped" in most of the classes, and to walk from the foot to the head of a long class in spelling, geography or history was a moment of rare triumph. One could only "stand head" for a whole day or in some classes two, then had to "go foot" and climb up again. But one's grades recorded his "head marks."

We studied McGuffey's readers and spellers and Gildersleeve's Latin books. Mr. and Miss Paxton boarded at our house, and Mrs. Paxton used my mother's piano for her music pupils. This piano had been brought from the Poage place near Staunton in a covered wagon to my mother soon after the new home was bought. With it came two huge bound books of old songs, at least a hundred songs in each book. All the familiar old songs were there, and many I have never seen elsewhere: such comics, for instance, as "The Cork Leg" and "The Old Sailor." My mother sang them all, playing her own accompaniment. My sister and I were put to music lessons under Mrs. Paxton, with, alas, but poor returns.

Friday afternoons at school were given over to "Exercises," which consisted mainly of recitations to which patrons were often invited. We dressed in best clothes, especially if we were on the programs, Some of us thoroughly enjoyed this opportunity to strut our brief moment on the school platform, while all took pleasure in the performances of their school mates. For a few there was acute distress in being obliged to recite in public. Most of the selections were from readers, or a book of recitations owned by Mr. Paxton. My father had even then a fair library and was constantly buying books so that we had a wider range of choice than most of the children. I can close my eyes even yet and recall the picture: the principal standing by his desk, the rows of children in their Sunday best, two to a desk, excited, flushed and muttering their pieces under their breath. From the roll Mr. Paxton would call those assigned to that afternoon's recital—usually half the school—as he saw fit.

Ears were strained until a name was called. As if an electric current had been turned on, that pupil would start, stiffen, flush, then rise and make his or her way to the small platform to bow awkwardly or gracefully as he was able and with a gulp begin. A tall young lady of belated education, over-conscious of her height and the schoolgirl length of her skirt, would bend her knees and sway rhythmically to the sing-song emphasis on the last words of

Maud Muller on a summer's day
Raked the meadow, sweet with hay.

Another "reciter" was one of the school's budding orators who in booming tones, with knitted brows and "appropriate" gestures, would make the stove pipe rattle to such selection as "Friends, I come to bury Caesar, not to praise him," or

Lochiel, Lochiel, Beware of the day
When the lowlands shall meet thee in battle array!

Then a timid girl would come trembling to the platform to make several starts, break down on the second verse and retire weeping. The beauty of the school always chose something touching or dramatic: "Curfew shall not ring tonight" or "I am not mad, I am not mad." My own preference was for "The Conquered Banner" or other selections from Father Ryan, Longfellow or Tennyson.

One little girl always brought down the house. She was Dutch in descent and appearance, with two pig tails behind a polished dark head, a very round face, very red cheeks and black snappy eyes. Her costume was usually a striped "linsey" (or woolen), the red green and brown stripes running around skirt, body and sleeves. Her wool stockings were home knitted, her thick leather shoes—her father a cobbler—also home made. Her name called, she started up like a frightened partridge, scurried like one to her place, and as she gave a hasty nod to the audience began rapidly to repeat little verses like:

> *If you your lips would keep from slips*
> *Five things observe with care*
> *Of whom you speak, to whom you speak,*
> *And how, and when—and where.*

With a second quick nod she scurried back, much embarrassed by applause and laughter, for both were allowed within bounds.

Unfortunately, Mr. Paxton got the offer of a position so much more lucrative that he did not return to Newbern after the second year. The next free school teacher was not acceptable to the more ambitious patrons; hence my father engaged a governess for his children, his wards, and the Kirkpatrick children. School was held in one of the big basements or first story rooms of our house. It was comfortable, well lighted, and quiet. This arrangement lasted for two sessions and proved highly satisfactory. When our excellent governess could not return because she was to be married the next fall, my father entered my sister and me at the Augusta Female Seminary (now Mary Baldwin College), Staunton, Virginia, and my two older brothers went back to the struggling public school as "pay pupils" for a couple of years.

The children of my uncle, Thomas Poage, were not the only wards bequeathed my father in the decade following the Civil War. So great was the confidence of his old comrades and his clients in his business integrity and kind heart that again and again he was made administrator of large and small estates and guardian of fatherless children. In no single instance was his faithfulness to his trust questioned. More remarkable still, with two or three exceptions, the score or more of orphaned children for whom he acted as guardian developed into useful citizens.

TWENTY-EIGHT

Lieutenant Governor

In his first message to the Virginia Legislature, Governor Gilbert C. Walker stressed the necessity of the state's settling her debt question, as the first step toward the restoration of her credit and her economic development. He proposed the immediate refunding of her debt of forty-five million dollars, so as to include the unpaid interest accumulated during the war and Reconstruction periods as part of the principal, the whole to bear the same interest as the old bonds. He proposed also that the interest coupons on the whole debt be made receivable for "taxes and other public dues."

The new legislature, without careful inquiry into Virginia's ability to meet such heavy obligations or the effect of making interest coupons receivable for taxes, promptly passed the "Funding Bill" practically as proposed by the Governor. It also set aside a percentage of the state's revenues, as required by the new constitution, for public education.

By the time of its second session, in December 1870, the consequences of the Funding Bill were becoming evident. After setting aside the appropriation for public education it was apparent that there would be insufficient cash from public revenues to pay the operating expenses of government, much less for badly needed public improvements or for reduction of the principal of the debt. More and more taxes were being paid in interest coupons, since holders of the state bonds were glad to sell these at a heavy discount.

To remedy the situation, the legislature hunted up new sources of taxation, increased rates, and passed the poll tax law. But the people were not satisfied, and in the election held that fall, 1871, under the reapportionment act passed by the recent legislature, an entirely new legislature was chosen. General Walker was among its members, representing the county of Pulaski.

This body proved less pliant to the suggestions of the Governor (who, a widely circulated campaign rumor charged, owned a large block of Virginia bonds). It promptly passed an act suspending operation of the Funding Bill. The matter went to the Circuit and then to the Supreme Courts, which ruled in turn that the Funding Act was a valid contract between the state and her bondholders and that interest coupons were receivable for all taxes. As a result, state coffers were filled with coupons, and there was not money enough to pay the state grants to colleges or the salaries of state employees.

In the midst of this financial confusion, James L. Kemper, as the candidate of the "Conservative Party," was elected Governor succeeding Walker. He was a one-armed Confederate soldier, that in itself making him a strong candidate. Facing an empty treasury, Kemper tried unsuccessfully to secure a more favorable debt settlement from the state's bondholders. For the next four years, the state was a stormy battleground of contending opinions about the debt.

General Walker, though opposed to tax receivable coupons and in favor of a refunding measure which would make it possible for the state to meet her obligations, took sides with the Funders as opposed to forcible readjustment. His position was that an honest debt must and should be paid, that the two-thirds assumed by Virginia was a fair share of the indebtedness of ante bellum Virginia, that Virginia had vast undeveloped resources which the establishment of her credit would induce capital to finance, and thus enable her to meet her obligations readily. Native integrity and a proud sense of honor were traits intensively developed in James A. Walker. He applied these traits to his state, declaring that any course which might leave a smirch on the so far unchallenged honor of the Old Dominion could not for a moment be considered. A compromise with the creditors leading to a refunding of the debt on reasonable terms was, he felt sure, the only honorable course.

The debate became hotly contested, one side for forcible readjustment, the other for full payment under the present funding act, with every sort of compromise in between. In every country store or town gathering place, on each court day, at every picnic or camp meeting ground, wherever men congregated, the debate went on. School boys knew the arguments, and women listened to what seemed to many of them more ado than was necessary. Debate became acrimonious, invective and arraignment flew about, church congregations split and neighbors ceased to speak to each other, until the debt question threatened to bring about a state of feud in neighborhoods more disastrous to social amenity and community cooperation than the strain induced by the sorrows and deprivations of war.

The Funders were usually the more substantial elements of communities and did not hesitate to accuse their opponents of trying to draw in the radical and black vote. The readjusters, however, had some leaders of brains and high standing, among them General William Mahone, Harry Riddleberger, Frank S. Blair, John S. Wise, J. P. Funkhouser, and others.

In the gubernatorial campaign of 1877, the Conservative or Democratic party nominated James A. Walker of Pulaski for Lieutenant Governor, running with F. W. M. Holliday of Winchester for Governor. Labeled the "Funders," they pressed the suggestion of a compromise with the bondholders and an honorable readjustment of the debt. The Conservative ticket won by an overwhelming majority.

Nevertheless, the new legislature included a number of outspoken Readjusters. After an opening legislative contest, General Mahone put himself at the head of the forcible readjuster element, who took for their motto "Peaceably if we can, forcibly if we must." Uniting with the Greenback faction, they began a vigorous, determined and bitter campaign.

In the second General Assembly session of the Holliday term, in December, 1878, the fight grew in magnitude and intensity. A compromise bill was passed, to be scoffed at by the forcible readjusters as a "stock jobbers bill." Readjusters held mass meetings all over the state to protest. They carried the election in the fall of 1879 and went to the next meeting of the General Assembly with a good majority.

It was General Walker's duty as Lieutenant Governor to preside over this Readjuster Senate, which had a clear majority of twelve, during a very stormy session. This he did with a courtesy and impartiality acknowledged by the majority as well as the minority. They promptly passed the "Riddleberger Bill," forcibly readjusting the terms on which the debt would be paid and providing that a certain proportion of the taxes must be paid in cash. Governor Holliday immediately vetoed it in terms which angered the militant Readjusters and strengthened their determination. The following

summer their leaders consummated a fusion with the Republican
Party in the state. At their state convention in the summer of 1881,
the Republican Party, now united with the Readjusters, nominated
a full state ticket headed by William E. Cameron.

One of the leaders of the Readjuster Party, an active and able
campaigner, was Frank S. Blair of the Wytheville bar. During the
Cameron campaign, Blair made his famous "Honor won't buy a
breakfast!" speech and gave Walker an opportunity to express
himself about honor.

Seizing the expression, Walker made it the text of a reply to
Blair which is said to be one of the most powerful Philippics ever
voiced on the Virginia hustings. He began by defending honor and
what it meant to nations and to individuals. He reviewed the
history of Virginia and her part in creating America's high ideals
and glorious history. He sketched the character of Washington,
Madison, Marshall, Jefferson, Patrick Henry, Lee and Jackson, and
showed how these great Virginians had put honor not only before
material things but before personal safety and life itself. "Yet, says
Mr. Blair, 'honor won't buy a breakfast!'" He rang the charges on
that phrase and held up to scorn the party, the principles and the
men who would so lower the ideals of the Old Dominion, so cheapen
her statesmanship, so debauch her manhood. It was brilliant,
forceful, bitter—the sort of political speech which was a part of the
hard fought political battles before and for a while after the Civil
War but which now are seldom heard.

The speech added to General Walker's reputation as an orator
and a telling campaigner, but it made for him lasting enemies and
left seeds of revenge which bore unpalatable fruit later on. It
widened too the breach between him and his old comrade and
friend General Mahone.

During Mahone's ascendancy, Walker was out of politics. The
compromise Riddleberger Bill was accepted, and the Funders
surrendered their position on the debt question, which was taken
out of politics into the courts where a final settlement eventually
was reached.

This fusion of the late Conservatives with the Readjusters put
an end to the state party which had sometimes been called by that
name. A section of the Readjuster Party was reunited with the
Democrats, as the Conservatives began to call themselves, while
another group became Republicans. In the convention which
nominated Fitzwater Lee for Governor, the coalition between the

two factions was made apparent by the choice of John E. Massie, next to Mahone the most prominent ex-leader of the Readjusters, for the place of Lieutenant Governor on the state ticket.

Walker had been put forward prominently for Governor; indeed the nomination was offered to him, but he felt obliged to decline an honor he could not in justice to his family accept. With an invalid wife and six children, he could not live and educate the older children on a salary of three thousand a year. He therefore declined in favor of General Lee, with the understanding that the third place on the ticket, that of Attorney General, should be his. That office was in line with his profession and would not necessitate the entire abandonment of a growing practice.

Just how and why he was betrayed, Walker never knew, or if he knew, never disclosed. In a secret caucus, by a small group of those opposed to him, the plot was laid, and not until sprung on the convention floor, did he know it was intended. Rufus A. Ayers was named for third place on the ticket, and before there was a chance for a fight the whole ticket was hurriedly nominated.

Walker felt he had been tricked, deceived, openly insulted, and he was deeply hurt. Nevertheless, he stood loyally by the ticket, working for Lee, Massie and Ayers. The incident marked, however, his disillusionment with machine politics and opened his eyes to the fact that a one-party political system leads to the autocracy of an intrenched few to coalitions regardless of principle, and to political trickery of every kind.

From this time on, he became more and more independent politically and grew further and further away from the methods, policies and theories of the Democratic Party in Virginia. His enemies said it was a revolt instigated by pique, and perhaps there may have been a grain of truth in the charge, for it is certainly true that nothing so quickly opens one's eyes to a lack of confidence compelling attributes in men or parties as treacheries and lies. But aside from his own personal grievance at this time, a break between General Walker and the Virginia political machine was as inevitable, sooner or later, as the evaporation of moisture under the sun's rays. General Walker was not of the stuff that machine politicians are made, nor the sort of man over whom the party whip could be cracked effectively.

TWENTY-NINE

Wytheville

In the late summer of 1879, General Walker sold his home in Newbern and moved to Wytheville, Virginia. Inadequate schools for his four sons and limited social opportunities for his young family induced him to take the step. Too, Wytheville, being the county seat of the adjoining county, was really nearer the center of his extensive law practice in Grayson, Carroll, Wythe, Montgomery and Pulaski counties. It was, and still is, a salubriously located town on a breezy ridge, encompassed by mountains and environed by rolling blue grasslands and purling mountain streams. Its population of about three thousand was made up of substantial, well-to-do folks, many of them descendants of the pioneer settlers, a considerable percent of whom were people of culture and standing.

There was a good school for boys, a full-time pastored Presbyterian church, as well as churches of several other denominations, and a "bar" noted for the most brilliant group of lawyers of any town approaching its size in the state. This last fact was partly due to circumstances at that time and partly to the fact that in Wytheville the Supreme Court held its summer session of six to eight weeks. This brought lawyers from all over the state to Wytheville to mix and compete with the local bar. In addition, Wytheville was a popular summer resort to which, during the hot months, agreeable people from the South and from the coast cities of Virginia repaired, many families returning year after year and constituting a permanent summer colony.

The only house my father found for sale was neither so comfortable nor so spacious as the home in Newbern. Indeed, it would not have been adequate but for two "offices" at the back of a long yard to the left of the house. One of these was large and fitted up as a dormitory served well for the four boys, the smaller office being used as a bedroom for "Uncle Alphe." That left a spare room upstairs for frequent guests. My mother's bedroom was downstairs, while the kitchen was also detached from the house.

In the rear, on an alley, my father built a commodious stable for housing our three riding horses and my mother's driving horse. A man was kept busy grooming, saddling, hitching and unhitching these four animals, working the large garden, on which we depended for our fresh vegetables, and caring for yard and flower garden. The cook never left her kitchen except to go home after supper, so a housemaid served the meals, kept the house in order and waited on my mother.

My mother was a real invalid, with serious physical troubles that today would be largely averted with the skills of the medical profession. My sister too had become almost an invalid by the time we moved to Wytheville, and our household was one which made heavy claims on my father's purse, time and sympathy.

A breakdown had taken me from the Mary Baldwin Seminary in the spring of '77 and kept me in Richmond during that spring and the winter of 1877-78. There, however, Dr. Hunter McGuire's skill succeeded in arresting it. At Wytheville, hence, I was in good health and assumed most of the house management, trying to keep four lively boys in order. This task was not so difficult when their father was in town. But during his absences at court in adjoining counties, there was often a free-for-all fight staged in the dormitory which threatened wreck to furniture as well as bruised bodies and bloody noses, and it took the combined efforts of my uncle, sister, maid and myself to quell.

This was perhaps the busiest period of General Walker's life. His law practice was heavy and varied. Not having a law partner, he employed the first young woman stenographer in any office in the town and, in addition, usually employed a young attorney in the outer office for collections and other routine work. To these young lawyers he was generous with fees and advice, and more than one of them attributed much of their later success to the start General Walker gave them. All became his warm friends and admirers, and some of them later espoused the unpopular political course his convictions led him to take.

General Walker, meanwhile, had become much interested in the mineral development of southwestern Virginia. He became a partner in several large purchases of undeveloped territory, as well as stockholder in companies organized by northern capital. These, too, claimed time and attention. It was his custom, when at home, to return to his office almost every evening after supper and to work there until nearly midnight, turning out briefs, deeds, contracts and the like, usually in his own handwriting, even though they were copied afterwards. One of the young lawyers who shared the outer office said he often stood behind General Walker for ten minutes waiting for his steadily flowing pen to cease, that he might speak to him, without the General knowing he was there.

For diversion, General Walker rode each afternoon for an hour or two before supper or drove with any of us who would accompany him behind our pair of fast trotting bay mares. He insisted, too, that one of the boys must daily drive his mother out in her phaeton, taking her wherever she wanted to go. And the sleek riding horses were brought out each afternoon, saddled, to the front style for my sister's and my afternoon gallop.

I like best to remember him mounted on "Membrino," his handsome black stallion. He was a magnificent horseman, sitting his horse like a Spanish cavalier and riding like a centaur. Membrino was beautiful, worthy of the blue ribbon in any horse show: black and slick as a lump of polished coal, his mane and long tail a rich dark brown, head slender and a little pointed, nostril thin, redlined and dilating sensitively when his master came near. His legs too were dark brown, ending in small black hoofs, his neck arched, ears pointed forward, held in by bit and bridle rein until his mount was on, then prancing and quivering with eagerness to be off. My father was proud of Membrino and delighted in his rides. But family and friends felt he should not attempt, with only one good arm, to manage so dangerous an animal. One day Membrino resented his orders, reared on his hind legs and threw him backward to the ground. He received only bruises, but a few days later he exchanged Membrino for the two bay trotters, with a light high topped buggy to drive them to.

The trotters too became pampered by grooming and feeding and, one afternoon while I was driving with my father, completely wrecked buggy and harness. It was not altogether their fault, for the strap that held them back broke, and the vehicle rolled forward on their legs. They kicked away the dash board, broke down both front wheels, then plunged and reared until one fell, while her mate shivered and snorted with fright by her side.

The accident occurred as we started down a rocky hillside, and my father found his one fit arm lacking in strength to guide the angry mares. Round and round his right arm he wound the reins, steadying the horses as best he could with a disabled arm which had no power save from the shoulder. Faster and faster went the mares, kicking as they ran. "Oh, Papa! Papa! drop the reins and let's jump," I begged. "Sit still!" he thundered. "Sit still, you coward, don't you know jumping's the surest way to kill yourself." So I kept my seat, gripping the sides and shutting my eyes. Suddenly the buggy swerved sharply to the left, and I saw my father had succeeded in guiding the animals into a fence corner, where one of them now reared and fell. We were still perched on top the two hind wheels. Presently, the mares ceased struggling. "You can climb out now," said my father, somewhat sternly, "but no thanks to your lack of courage that you are alive."

I clambered down, quite humiliated, and stood meekly by while my father cut the harness from the still struggling animals while he patted and soothed them into calmness. We then started homeward afoot, my father leading one mare, the other following, until we met friends driving a surry. They picked us up and haltered the mares on behind. The buggy had to be hauled in next day. The bays were afterward so nervous that they too had to be sold, and my father again bought himself a riding horse, almost but not quite so mettled as Membrino, this one being chestnut sorrel in color, a fine "single trotter" and "racker," two gaits my father especially enjoyed.

Entertaining was our next favorite pastime. Frequent were the parties, picnics or week end excursions my sister and I were allowed to offer our friends and the house guests we so often had. General Walker, too, loved to give dinner parties for visiting and town lawyers, and during the session of the Court of Appeals we kept open house. It was during the seven years we lived in the small house on Monroe Street that my sister was married.

The dinners were given here in the dining room, the largest in the house, and each Christmas week a regular banquet was held, to which all "the bar" were invited. Eggnog and hot apple toddy were served from huge bowls in the living room before and during dinner, and by the time the meal was well under way there was apt to be much hilarity and wit. Only men attended these Christmas parties, but I was usually behind a screen near the pantry door seeing that the meal was properly served and enjoyed the stories, anecdotes and repartee that came spontaneously from these bright and ready witted lawyers. My mother, however, disapproved highly of my father's serving drinks and scornfully called his parties "razoos," a word I have heard no one else use and for which I have found no definition.

After about seven years residence on Monroe Street, we moved into the old Crockett Hotel on Main Street in Wytheville, a rambling brick structure with a few stone steps leading from sidewalk to the front doors. This property had to be bought to save a large loan, and an opportunity presenting itself to sell the Monroe Street property, the family was moved into such part of the disused hotel as they could occupy. There we spread ourselves out hilariously, each member of the family fitting up for herself or himself a sort of suite, as individual fancy dictated.

My oldest brother, who expected to be married that fall, reserved a sitting room and bedroom. Frank, the second brother, a medical student at Johns Hopkins, selected two of the rooms over the office wing; he converted one into a laboratory, where he amused himself during vacation with experiments. He was assisted by James, the third brother, a law student at the University of Virginia, with a bedroom adjoining Frank's. The two tried numerous experiments, from cutting up a dead cat or chloroforming a live one, to making all manner of ill smelling mixtures. Allen, the youngest brother, nicknamed "Raggedy" by his dudish older brothers because at the age of sixteen he had no objection to appearing at table in torn trousers or with unwashed hands and disheveled hair, filled up two or three rooms with play junk: tools, lumber, scraps of lead, iron and other stuff to tinker with.

At the other end of the house was a suite of three rooms set apart for my sister and her two children when they chose to visit us. I selected a large room with shaded front balcony far enough away from the boys' quarters to be private and quiet. Downstairs in the main part of the house were "double parlors," a living room where there was always a blazing coal fire in winter, my mother's bedroom, a large dining room, pantry, back porch and kitchen. At the other end, served by a separate entrance, were my father's offices.

My mother loaned a room in that part of the house to the Presbyterian Church, and a student from the Theological Seminary occupied it during the summer months. He served in the pulpit of that church during the absence of the regular pastor, Dr. Preston. This young theolog, James I. Vance, became almost a member of our family.

Each room in our "hotel" was furnished to suit the taste of its occupant, furniture being freely ordered from Lynchburg and "charged to Papa." Open Franklin stoves and grates were used for heating and acetylene gas for lighting. Daily a bountiful dinner and supper were prepared with plenty of extra food and two or three spare places at the long table. My mother, to whom I acted as assistant housekeeper, never knew, when the bell rang, how many guests would troop in. Sometimes my father brought with him one or more clients. More frequently it was Frank or Jim, each of whom had his one group of chums who filled the two or three extra seats at the table. Indeed, no member of the family hesitated to invite company for meals or for more or less indefinite visits.

It was a full, merry and generous life the family lived in the "old Crockett house," with our father always ready to enter into our fun and plans and never complaining of the big bills which piled in, our mother bearing patiently with the noise and confusion. General Walker was proud of his sons, all of whom were over six feet tall by the time they were eighteen, and enjoyed seeing them well dressed and groomed, allowing them almost unlimited credit at clothing stores. He was quite strict, however, as to their conduct and manners.

At about the time his expenses were heaviest, a sale of mineral lands was made by which he cleared a sum of money considered large at that time, about ten thousand dollars in round numbers. He immediately invested one thousand dollars in law books, reinvested a part of the balance in mineral lands and the rest in bank stock in one of the local banks.

This was perhaps the happiest period in my father's life. His oldest son became his partner at law; the second won honors as a medical student; the third was in second year law at the University of Virginia, and my mother enjoyed somewhat better health. He also had two granddaughters who visited frequently.

His semi-adopted children, the Poage family, also followed us to Wytheville and were with us in all our merry makings and holidays, as they had been in Newbern. With the Poages, seven tall youths would gather around the eggnog bowl at Christmas time. It fell to my duty to concoct the eggnog, and I also dispensed it, rationing two punch glasses full to the young men and perhaps a third to my father and his friends. Then the bowl was locked up until evening when another drink all around was served.

I mentioned earlier my father's vow during one of the starving winters in camp that he meant to enjoy in reason all the good things which a lavish creator had provided for man's satisfaction. Hence, not only did he put on his table whatever the local market furnished but kept a standing order in Norfolk for two gallons of shucked Lynnhaven bay oysters each week from November to April, and after that for frying sized chickens by the dozens, with ducks in between. There was no limit to grocery bills, with full liberty to order extras from Lynchburg or Richmond. The conclusion is inevitable that we must have been a very extravagant family, and the wonder is that my father had any money left for investments.

During this period, my oldest brother brought home his bride, a handsome, charming Alabama girl, and my father decreed a big fanfare. He, himself, saw to printing the invitations, which were sent all over the country, and planned the menu. For days, the cook, housemaid, an extra maid and I worked to execute the elaborate bill of fare he ordered.

We baked a dozen huge cakes of different sorts, pickled gallons of oysters, boiled three or four hams and twice that many cured tongues, and made cedar tubs of chicken salad and beaten biscuit. We ordered candied fruits, nuts and fancy candies from Richmond, while Carroll County furnished 150 fat partridges; a hired man picked the partridges for two full days, then helped the cook to draw and halve them.

Bride and groom arrived the day before the reception. Neighbors helped decorate the house and set the dozen small tables arranged in the dining and living rooms. Two extra maids helped to mix ice cream for a dozen freezers which two men turned; we made strawberry, chocolate, tutti-frutti, bisque and fresh lemon, using gallons of the richest fresh cream from our own two and our neighbors' cows, and Jamaica rum for the bisque and tutti-frutti. We also served champagne punch. It was truly a wedding feast as lavish as any I attended. In the roll of host, General Walker was happy, and his enjoyment, ease and gaiety naturally communicated to his guests.

THIRTY

A Lynching Averted

One evening during this period of his life, General Walker was returning home to Wytheville by train from one of his courts when his attention was drawn to a group of rough men who boarded the train at one of the stations. They evidently had some common purpose and seemed to be laboring under an excitement they tried to hide.

Two of them sat behind Walker and talked in low tones. General Walker's ears were keen, and he caught enough of their conversation to piece together their purpose. They were to meet others in Wytheville, go at midnight to the jail, take a certain black man from the jailer and hang him on top of Boyd's Hill.

It was then 10:30 P.M. The black, as General Walker knew, had been brought to the Wytheville jail a few days before, accused of a brutal murder. As he strained his ears to hear the plans of the would-be lynching, General Walker did not look behind him and appeared to be engrossed with his paper. He was not reading, however, but making plans to thwart the conspirators. Their rendezvous in Wytheville and the midnight hour appointed for their descent upon the jail would give him time enough to carry out those plans, if only he could leave the train without being recognized or arousing any suspicion.

When the train blew for Wytheville, Walker sauntered up front, was the first passenger to alight and walked the more than half mile to the jail on the dark side of the street in order not to be seen. The jailer warned, he found his son-in-law and sent him to summon others, while he stopped two or three citizens on the street, asked them to go home for their guns or pistols and to meet him at the jail. Next he found the sheriff and revealed the plan to him. Soon after 11 P.M. the courthouse bell was ordered to be rung clamorously for ten minutes.

Only seven or eight men joined General Walker at the jail, but they were cool, armed and determined. Meantime, the sheriff had secured a team and buggy, and while the guards stood at the front door he got the prisoner out at the back, took him across lots under cover of darkness and into a waiting vehicle, then drove with him by circuitous route to the macadam road and on to Marion.

Stampeded by the clanging of the courthouse bell and the hurrying feet of aroused and questioning citizens, the mob melted away, and no raid ever occurred. By 1 A.M., all the town was asleep, save the few on guard at the jail, and two hours later they, too, were home asleep.

Later, the black was tried, and if my memory is not seriously at fault he was proved to be the wrong man. General Walker's courage had saved a life, circumvented an insult to justice, and prevented a score of men from searing their souls with a terrible crime. Commenting on it in later years, he said, "Mobs were always cowardly." As for his having doing something heroic, he said, "no decent citizen could have done less."

THIRTY-ONE

Tragedies

"The boom" in Virginia started with large purchases of mineral and timber lands by outside capital, followed by the building of iron furnaces at several points and the opening of large lumber operations. Then came the town lot craze, fostered by promoters and speculators. Every village aspired and expected to become a city. Each furnace or saw mill was to be the center of a thriving manufacturing community.

Around Wytheville, town lots were laid off for a mile in every direction. The same was true of Radford, Roanoke, Max Meadows, Basic, Buena Vista, Glasgow and a half dozen other towns. All sorts of development corporations were organized, every one invested all he could raise in cash and discounted his credit to the maximum. Everybody confidently expected to get rich within a few months, and nobody made any money except the very timid and cautious ones who sold on the first rise and dared not reinvest.

Married in 1888 to a "briefless young lawyer," I felt it necessary to sell my riding horse, "Bonnie," as the first step toward beginning life at the bottom of the ladder. The money thus realized I invested in Radford lots. Within a few months I had made a neat profit and decided to forswear speculation. But I could not resist the chance to buy "a small but valuable tract of brown hematite ore bearing land, dirt cheap." The ore may still be there, as a few hundreds of my first speculative profits certainly are.

General Walker scoffed at the lot boom at first, though he believed enthusiastically in Southwest Virginia's prospects as a mineral territory. However, he caught the fever eventually, like so many others. He bought lots and tracts of land in and around Wytheville and nearby towns, as well as in Florence, Alabama, which with the section contiguous to Birmingham was also "on a boom."

My two older brothers, Alex and Frank, were so impressed with the prospect for big industrial expansion in the tri-cities of Florence, Sheffield and Tuscumbia that both decided to locate in Florence. It was a blow to my father to lose as law partner the son he had educated for that position, but the father felt that there might be a brighter future for his son in so promising a section and consented to the move. The partnership my brother relinquished was offered to my husband, while my father insisted that the promise made him before my marriage, that I would never leave home without his consent, must be solemnly adhered to, since as assistant housekeeper I was more than ever needed at home.

Any doubts I may have had as to the advisability of giving up our plan of starting a home of our own were answered a few months later by untoward circumstances which followed one another thick and fast, threatening my father's health and shrouding in gloom the new home he bought and was having done over. The Kent place, made available for purchase by Mr. Kent's decision to move to his country home, was an early American brick house, set in the midst of handsome specimens of Norwegian firs and American aspens with a whole city square of land about it. Already the boom had begun to collapse, and finances were not so easy as they had been, but the opportunity to buy the home my father had always admired, and felt he would like to own, was not to be resisted.

In Florence, my brother Frank met and won a very lovely young woman of an old Alabama family and felt that his growing medical practice justified his getting married in the fall. To the new home he would bring his bride-to-be. But early in June came news that Frank's fiancee had malarial fever, then that she was seriously ill and Frank constantly at her bedside. Her death was nevertheless a shock, for she had been so young and strong and buoyant, so beloved in her native town. Frank, Alex wrote, was inconsolable, broken down too from hours of vigil and anxiety. Alex persuaded Frank to come home for a complete change and rest.

Frank arrived the day after Jimmie, third of the four brothers, had been put to bed with high temperature and a tentative diagnosis of typhoid fever. He had come home for his summer vacation ten days before, thin, tired and complaining of persistent headaches. Extensive excavations had been going on all spring at the University of Virginia in preparation for new pipe lines. Jimmie was not the only student who went home to develop typhoid, because at that time the danger of turning up many yards of old ground, without due precautions as to seepage into sources of drinking water, was not fully understood. Without the opportunity for a single day's rest and with a grim determination no persuasion could shake, Frank constituted himself Jimmie's nurse, having only an untrained boy to help him. Trained nurses were rare then, and in Virginia not to be had outside a few hospitals.

For nine weeks the virulent disease raged, attacking every avenue of the youth's defense. Frank's vigilance, coupled with the professional aid of three physicians who consulted on the case, finally seemed to conquer the disease. One morning Frank came across the hall into my sitting room almost jubilant, but looking distressfully worn, to say that Jimmie really was better. He had overcome each crisis except one, paralysis of the kidneys, and he hoped that would not occur. Within twelve hours it did occur, and valiantly Frank fought for a few hours more, only to admit defeat as Jimmie sank rapidly into a coma from which he never rallied.

The death of the one who was perhaps the favorite of each member of the family, because of his affectionate, loyal nature and ingratiating disposition, was terribly distressing, but almost more so was Frank's utter despair. Twice, he declared, he had put all there was in him of skill, vigilance and devotion into combatting the scourge of fever, and twice all his efforts had proved fruitless; he had lost faith in medical science, in his own profession. Medicine was bunk, pretense, nonsense! Almost too he had lost faith in a God. Certainly he no longer believed in prayer.

He was more reasonable after a few days, and my father finally induced him to promise that he would go to Germany in the fall to study surgery. But first he would go back to Florence to wind up his business and turn his practice over to some other physician. He had been in Florence less than a month when a wire came announcing that both he and Alex had been stricken with typhoid fever. From day to day the news fluctuated. My mother was not strong enough to go to Alabama. It was not possible for me to leave her and my babies, so when the news became alarming, my father went alone. He returned with Frank's body, the second of his four sons to die of typhoid fever within three months.

He left a third so ill that although he recovered Alex was never again in vigorous health. The death of his sons proved almost a fatal blow to General Walker's health. He lost flesh, energy, and cheerfulness, developing a nervous condition evidenced by an unwonted irritability.

That fall, General Walker had an altercation in the court room at Newbern, Virginia, with a younger lawyer, himself of aggressive disposition and drinking at the time. Hot words led to threats, threats to blows. Before the sheriff could interfere, Walker was bent backward over the bar railing receiving a rain of blows in his left side while defending himself as best he could with one fit arm. The blows seemed to have bruised his kidneys, inducing an attack of acute Bright's disease. A stay at Tate Spring, skillful surgical treatment while there, and a vigorous constitution pulled him through, but he never again was so buoyant, so radiant with interest in life, so magnetically cheerful as before.

Until then he had the effect of sunshine on those upon whom he chose to beam, though now and then as a storm cloud to those on whom his displeasure fell. Whenever he came into the house he would begin at the foot of the stairs. "Hello! Hello! Who's here? Who wants a ride? Where are the babies? It's fine out," or "It's disagreeable outside—call Edmund! Let's have a good fire, and a toddy! Come on children, don't tell your mother but I've got something in my pocket for you." However dull the day, the sun seemed to shine out as we heard his voice, and life was more worth the living. Though he never lost altogether the magnetism which gave zest to all friendly association with him, he did lose, as I have said, much of his infectious optimism, and his fun loving nature less often asserted itself. Other troubles, big and little, domestic and business, had to be faced the ensuing year, till there seemed no possibility of surmounting them. It was my father who was the first to brace himself, put them all behind him and again attack life, as it were, with undaunted courage, finally achieving return to full physical vigor and almost to the old interest in and enjoyment of life. On his grandchildren he centered his affection and their idolatrous devotion to him gave him the greatest satisfaction. His knees had to be divided up and apportioned between them, and when knee space gave out there were broad shoulders to be perched upon.

Despite the misfortunes in General Walker's life, Walker Hall, the name his friends had given the new home, was the scene of renewed hospitality. Its spacious back porch shaded by a luxurious grapevine became a regular rendezvous for judges of the court of appeals and visiting and home lawyers. There mint juleps were mixed with meticulous care and sipped with long drawn out appreciation which precluded any intoxicating effect—though they did seem to stimulate conversation and encourage wit.

Social drinking among gentlemen in the eighties and nineties was not infrequently like war in the sixties—that is, given an air of romance and safeguarded by rules of ethics and decency which lent to it a glamour of gracious camaraderie our grosser, more practical age has entirely stripped it of. It is as difficult for one who understood that age to make excuses for its social drinking habits as it is to do justice to old fashioned warfare. If lawful warrant for the conviviality of those days may be found, it would be in the easy sociability and delightful conversation of such men of brains and culture as met and sipped their juleps on the back porch of "Walker Hall," looking as they talked across a deep, gently dipping bluegrass lawn to a gay border of blooming perennials, from which the eye was easily lifted to the graceful ranges of the Alleghenies a few miles distant. The anecdotes were never vulgar, the jokes seldom coarse, but there was rivalry as to who could produce the newest and funniest ones, or could tell the most highly characteristic story "on" one of the judges or lawyers or especially "on the General."

But all the talk was not in light vein. Discussions of public questions, old and new, with their historic analogies and their bearing on the present and future of the South and the United States were frequent. New books and new inventions came in also for their full share of interested comment. Thinking back over these gatherings, I realize that more of my education came from listening to these symposiums of great minds than from my limited schooling.

THIRTY-TWO

Congressman

In the decade following 1882, General Walker had taken no active part in politics, although he frequently was asked to do so. But he kept himself well informed as to the drift of national and state affairs. Watching apprehensively the stronger and stronger grip the state machine was getting in state affairs, and the trend of the Democratic Party toward free trade and other governmental theories he deemed fallacious, he now found himself in 1992 politically adrift, an independent thinker without a party.

Partly through his business affiliations and interests, partly because he foresaw that the new South would and must develop along manufacturing lines, he had become an ardent protectionist. To develop successfully in manufacturing, he thought, the South must have the benefit of that protection which had made New England prosperous. The vital thing for the South and especially southwestern Virginia was protection for her raw products: iron, zinc, wool, lumber, coal. It would soon be needed also for cotton, sugar, citrus fruits and the manufacture of those and other raw products into marketable commodities.

There were already growing imports of ores from Mexico, South America, even China, sent in as ballast in returning vessels. Being mined with cheapest labor, these ores could readily put an end to the development of new mines in Virginia and the South. Free trade might have been consistent policy for the old agricultural South, said General Walker, but for the new, developing, manufacturing South, it was suicidal.

In addition, he became more and more convinced that the South needed to forget, to put the past behind her and to cease to be a cipher in national politics. Out of the idea and habit of a "Solid South," he believed, came more than one unfortunate result: a loss of national influence and prestige; the inevitable growth in each

southern state of a limited, self perpetuating, political oligarchy;
and the gradual loss on the part of the people of any real interest
in government or willingness to face facts as circumstances would
shape them. Walker also believed that a Solid South would retard
the section's economic development and industrial expansion as
well as make for backwardness along educational, civic and cultural
lines. In all of these fears, time has proved him a prophet.

In 1888, General Walker voted for Harrison, but it was
Cleveland's nomination by the Democratic party on a radical free
trade plank in 1892 which finally cut the Gordian knot. He was no
longer in any sense a Democrat; he could not keep quiet while the
South committed economic suicide. Mr. Cleveland was elected, and
Virginia sent a solid Democratic delegation, as usual, to Congress.

Almost immediately, hard times began in southwestern
Virginia. The last vestige of the wave of industrial development
went up in expiring puffs of smoke from closing furnaces, mines
and sawmills. Unfinished hotels were left to fall to pieces, and
again her young men began to "go west" in search of those opportunities their own state might have been so well fitted to offer them.

In the midst of this depression, the handful of Virginia Republicans lost courage, their tentative organization went to pieces, and
in the gubernatorial election of 1883 the Democratic candidate,
Charles T. O'Ferrall, had no Republican opposition, while the
General Assembly was returned almost entirely Democratic. The
machine was now firmly seated in the saddle, booted and spurred
for the enterprise of making Virginia so solid politically that an
opposition party would not again dare to raise its head.

To this end the legislature of 1893-94 enacted the "Walton
Election Law," ostensibly aimed at blocking widespread electoral
fraud but actually a most cunningly devised party measure for
party purpose. Electoral boards, as under the previous law, were to
be entirely partisan, composed of three Democrats. This board was
to appoint three judges of election in each precinct, one of whom
should be of the minority party, but the provision was rendered
invalid by the qualifying clause: "But no election shall be deemed
invalid when citizens appointed as judges shall not belong to
different political parties or who shall not possess the above
qualifications." That left everything in the hands of the electoral
board which also named the registrars for each precinct.

The Walton law further introduced the secret ballot and an
educational qualification for voters which left in the hands of

partisan registrars the right to determine the degree and kind of education necessary for the individual voter. It also made unlawful the previous practice of placing party headings on to ballots, under which candidates of each party were printed or written. Instead, under the new law, the names of candidates must appear under the heading, "For Governor," or "For Congress," and so forth. Innocent as it appeared, this change gave the party in power the opportunity to print ballots of which the poorly educated individual could make neither heads nor tails. Samples of some of these actually used in later elections presently will be shown.

The law further provided that these ballots were to be printed secretly under the supervision of a member of an electoral board, and stamped by him with an official seal. Then the ballots were to be sealed in single packages, one for every precinct, and delivered to the secretary of the Board, he to deliver them before the election to the judges of the several precincts. The sealed packages of ballots were not to be opened until the polls were opened, in the presence of the judges and the clerks. No voter was permitted to see the complicated ballot until he was given one in the polling room. A constable belonging to the majority party was to be named by electoral boards to assist illiterate voters. He was invariably a Democrat and not always an honorable gentleman (as we shall find later.) It is well to say here that electoral boards are named by the circuit judges—thus mixing up the judicial functions of judges with partisan politics in a way that is hardly consistent with an untrammeled judiciary.

The passage of the Walton law was in a sense a challenge to the honesty and courage of Walker, and it completed his severance from the Democratic Party. There was still the nucleus of a Republican Party in the Ninth Virginia District and a tradition of possible victory, from the days when Henry C. Bowen of Tazewell was elected to Congress as a Readjuster-Republican. Walker had opposed the Readjuster movement and the policies of General Mahone. Also, he was at that time an advocate for the free coinage of silver, on parity with its value in gold. It was therefore a decided tribute to their confidence in his high qualities when the Republicans of the Ninth District, assembled in convention in Wytheville, June, 1894, offered him the nomination for Congress on practically his own platform.

Judge H. S. K. Morrison of Scott County was nominated by the Democrats on a platform which contained a strong gold plank. Two

years later, the parties, following their leaders, were to reverse
their positions on the money question. The 1894 campaign was one
of high class debate without the injection of personalities or abuse,
resulting in the election of Walker by a majority of about a
thousand votes, even under the Walton election law. Judge
Morrison promptly sent General Walker a congratulatory telegram,
and they continued to be friends. The result, however, was a
surprise so great as to be a shock to the Virginia machine. "It must
never happen again," was the word passed around. Thereafter until
the time of his death, General Walker was made a target for the
envenomed shafts of the Democratic leaders in Virginia.

There was much rejoicing, of course, among the Republicans,
who poured into Wytheville from all over the district. They united
with Walker's friends in staging a torchlight procession which
ended at "Walker Hall." There, they demanded a speech from the
newly elected Congressman and then responded to it with enthusiasm and general congratulations for Walker and the members of
the newly born Virginia Republican party.

A minor event which marked the day of the election was one
which my children's nursemaid deemed of special importance:
James Alexander Walker Caldwell took his first independent steps
that afternoon, tottering gleefully from nursemaid to housemaid
and back again.

General Walker himself was much gratified by his election,
because he realized that his victory was partly due to the esteem in
which he was held in his section of the state and partly to the
active espousal of his candidacy by a number of personal friends
who still were Democrats. The event was one of great service to
him physically and mentally, lifting the depression which he had
been combatting since the death of his sons and turning his
interests and activities into new and more exhilarating channels.

He began at once to revive his knowledge of parliamentary
procedure, to reread the Constitution of the United States, and to
study the personnel and doings of Congress.

He also studied exhaustively the question of bimetallism, which
he saw would soon become a national issue. In fact, his own
campaign studies and speeches had shaken his confidence in the
feasibility of a double monetary standard. During the last weeks of
the campaign he had, as he laughingly said, trod lightly on the
silver plank he himself had written into his platform. And now as

he thought and read he found himself coming around to a gold standard.

Now and then, he discussed with me his authorities, reasoning and conclusions, using me as a sort of understudy for future audiences. Several times he asked me to read a speech he meant to make before a jury, and he would end with the question: "Now what would be your verdict?"

I responded more than once, "It would have to be against your client, Papa."

"And for why, I would like to know," he would respond. "Then I must 'mend my holts,' for you have just about the gumption of an average juror."

It was interesting to follow this change in my father's views as he gradually convinced himself that anything savoring of fiat money was a dangerous fallacy, on the rock of which most nations had, at one time or another, foundered in a greater or less degree of economic wreckage. Nor was he at all inclined to draw back from the reversal of a pet belief. Rather, he seemed pleased to have discovered that he had been wrong, and to be sure that now he was on the right road.

"Growth means change," he declared. "I hope I'll never be too sure or too old to progress mentally."

THIRTY-THREE

Tribute to Lincoln

Walker's election, and the break which it represented in the solid Democratic congressional representation from Virginia, was by no means palatable to partisan Democrats. Especially did they resent that the break was made by a native Virginian and an ex-Confederate officer of high rank. The press of the state freely applied the epithets "traitor" and "renegade," and some of Walker's clients deserted him.

We in the family noticed an attempt to visit upon us a sort of social ostracism, evident in a cool, resentful attitude on the part of a few of the "leading families." Although the children were not insulted by what they did not understand, they were hurt by the fact that some children no longer came in to play with them. With the adults of the family, the threatened loss of social popularity did not figure very largely, since to my busy father and my well poised mother it seemed a matter of small importance, while I was too much engrossed with other things to care any longer for social leadership. Moreover, there were left so many loyal and devoted friends, made more so by futile attempts to hurt us, that we did not miss the disaffected ones.

But the newspaper attacks on my father and the ugly remarks of old comrades and fellow lawyers did hurt, more than he was willing to admit. They implanted a germ of bitterness in his highly sensitive nature, a bitterness that led to what was perhaps a regrettably aggressive attitude later on.

When the Fifty-fourth Congress met in December of 1894, General Walker was one of hardly a score of Republican Congressmen from the South, including those from the border states. They were regarded by Republicans as well as by Democrats with a degree of suspicion; they had always to face, as it were, a question mark. From the South a Republican? Not a native I suppose? This

last suggestion invariably stung and angered Walker. A born
Virginian and an ex-Confederate who had from conviction espoused
the Republican Party—that was a fact to be proclaimed, to be proud
of. But that he was a Carpetbag or a Scalawag representative he
hotly repudiated.

His position in the South was nevertheless soon established.
Such was his intellect and the impression of power he naturally
made that he could not remain a nonentity anywhere. He was
assigned to the Elections and the River and Harbor Committees
and became a personal friend of Speaker Thomas B. Reed. Two
contested elections from Virginia were before the House, one from
the Fourth District, Thorpe vs. McKenny, and one from the Tenth,
Yost vs. Tucker.

During his first term in Congress, General Walker was invited
by the Middlesex Club of Boston to make an address on the
occasion of Lincoln's birthday. That address so well illustrates the
broad patriotic spirit which animated General Walker and prompted his change of political views that the reading from it will give a
better idea of his position at this time than anything which I could
say about him:

I bring from the people of the South to the people of the
North fraternal greetings. On behalf of Confederate veterans I
extend to the veterans of the Union armies the hand of friendship. I speak with no forked tongue when I assure the Union
soldiers that we rejoice to know that their valor, their suffer-
ings, and their invaluable services rendered to our common
country in the hours of her peril are remembered and rewarded
by a grateful people...

The mists of prejudice and of passion which in the past
obscured reason are being dispelled. The baleful fires of sectionalism are dying out, and the fires of patriotism are again
being lighted in the valleys and on the mountain tops that lie
beneath the Southern cross. The dogma of secession no longer
finds followers in those states where once a whole people believed it was a sacred right...which for four years they maintained with their lives, their fortunes and their sacred honor.
They submitted the question of secession to the arbitrament of
the sword, and they will abide in good faith by the result as
becomes a brave and honorable people...Never again will the
hand of a Southern man be lifted against the life of this Nation

or against the Union of these States. When the people of the
South again go forth to battle they will march beneath the
starry flag to the music of the Union...

I come to proclaim that the solid South will soon be no
more. Maryland, Kentucky and Tennessee have loosened the
chains which bound them to Democratic misrule. West Virginia, the youngest and best beloved daughter of Virginia, has
joined the great Republican column, and the other mother of
States will presently take her place by the side of her child. A
majority of the people of Virginia are Republicans, and if permitted to vote their honest sentiments on the 6th day of next
November, will choose twelve electors who will cast her vote for
the nominee of the St. Louis Convention, whether that man be
Thomas B. Reed of Maine, Levi P. Morton of New York, William McKinley Jr. of Ohio, William B. Allison of Iowa, or a
dark horse from some other orthodox Republican field.

But outrageous partisan registration and election laws,
enacted by Democratic legislatures, with the express design of
rendering frauds and corruption easy and safe and election
machinery exclusively and wholly in the hands of the party
which made the laws, and used by partisan manipulators in
the most unscrupulous manner, bind Republican voters with
iron chains and stifle their voice at the polls. But the day of our
deliverance is at hand. The masses of the people of Virginia, of
all ranks, and of all parties, are honest and true, and detest
fraud and corruption whatever form or shape it may assume.
They have been kept in ignorance of the truth by the party
managers and machine politicians. The light is beginning to
dawn, and now some of the most influential Democratic papers
in the State are denouncing these outrages, and the truth can
no longer be hid. Thousands of honest Democrats, all over the
State, are clamoring for election reform which must come
sooner or later.

Walker then turned to the issue of race, responding to the
allegation by Democrats that the Republican party was the "Negro
party." The Democratic press and leaders, he said, raised the issue
of "Negro rule, Negro equality and mixed schools, until thousands
of white voters...are deterred from expressing their true sentiments
through their ballots." He went on:

Those arguments are losing their power to frighten or to
charm. The tables begin to be turned...In those portions of the
State where colored voters largely outnumber the whites, the
Democrats receive large majorities in every election, while in
the counties where the white voters are in the ascendancy the
Republicans receive a majority of the votes polled.

In 1894, Virginia returned only one Republican to the
House of Representatives, and that in a district where there
are ten white to one colored voter. The Democratic party must
admit one of two things: either they receive the Negro vote
honestly as it was cast at the polls or that it is counted for
them by fraud or corruption or both.

Massachusetts and Virginia are twin sisters of the Revolution and stood shoulder to shoulder in the War for Independence, and though they have been estranged, it is written in
the book of fate that they shall soon be united in the bonds of
one political faith, and stand shoulder to shoulder battling for
the principles of Republicanism. It accords with the eternal
fitness of things that the Commonwealth whose great apostle of
liberty wrote the burning words of the Declaration of Independence, which declares that all men are created free and equal,
should be found in the ranks of that party which was born a foe
to domestic slavery and has always been the champion of
human liberty.

The state which produces nearly two million tons of coal
and three hundred thousand tons of iron, whose mountains are
seamed with mineral wealth and whose valleys are being
lighted with the blaze of struggling infant manufactures should
accept the political creed of that party which has emblazoned
on its banners and written in every platform of its past history,
the proud declarations "Americans for Americans," "Protection
for American Labor, American Manufactures and American
Products against the Pauper Labor and Cheap Productions of
Foreign Lands." Every consideration of self interest and of
patriotism demands that the people of the State of Virginia
should unite their voices with that of the people of Massachusetts, in favor of entrusting the control of the nation in the
hands of the only party which has proved its capacity to create
and maintain a sound national currency, national credit, national faith, and national honor, and at the same time confer
the blessings of peace and prosperity upon the people of every

section of this vast country; the party that enacted and enforced wise and sensible revenue laws which without oppress-
ing the rich man or grinding the face of the poor man, raised
sufficient revenue to defray the current expenses of the government, provided liberal pensions for Union soldiers and paid off
millions of our national debt.

But on this anniversary of the birth of Abraham Lincoln it
is expected that I should talk to you of him. What can a Southern soldier, who followed the battle flags of Lee and Jackson
from Bull Run to Appomattox, say in this presence of the man
whom the people of the South once reviled and hated? In the
memory of the dead past and in the light of the living present
there is impressed on the minds and hearts of the Southern
people two images of Abraham Lincoln. He appears to us in a
dual character—the shadow and the object. The past is the
vanishing shadow; the present is the real, living picture.

No great man was ever more misrepresented or more
misunderstood than was Abraham Lincoln by the Southern
people from 1860 to 1868. It is a curious study to compare the
Lincoln of *then* with the Lincoln of *now*. Then he was portrayed
to us only by the pens of hostile political writers, and by the
eloquent tongues of sectional and partisan orators. Then he
was seen through the passions, the prejudices, and hatreds
engendered by inter-necine war, across rivers of human blood
that flowed between the North and the South, over the graves
of tens of thousands of our brethren and kindred slain in battle, and standing amid the desolation of our fields and the
ruins of our homes. Then we believed he was our bitterest foe,
and we hated him. Then he was described as a man of low
birth and low instincts...an uneducated man, ignorant of the
usages and customs of polite society, and we ridiculed him. He
was painted as awkward, ungainly, and grotesque in person,
and we dubbed him the ape. He was the hero of innumerable
shady anecdotes, and we wrote him down a vulgarian. The
unveiled face of the false prophet was not more hideous than
were the features of Abraham Lincoln to the people of the
South, while yet his true character was concealed from our
vision by the prejudices and ignorances of that time.

But the day came when that veil was torn asunder, when
the Lincoln of *then* was revealed to us in his true character and
the Lincoln of *now* stood before us. The first glimpse of the true

image of this man came to us when we received the accounts of
the Hampton Roads Conference, at which it was said that Mr.
Lincoln wrote "Union; Abolition of Slavery," and handing the
paper to the Confederate Commissioners, said "Write what you
please under it."

And when his tragic end came there went up a cry of regret
and sorrow all over the South land. A sense of impending
danger seemed to take possession of us all, and we felt that his
corpse would be laid at our door and that his blood would be
made to cry out from the ground against us. It was a gloomy
day way up in the mountains of Virginia, where we were without railroads, without telegraphic communications, without
mails or post offices, without civil or military law, when a
Confederate soldier returning from prison brought to us, more
than a week after the occurrence, the first news of Mr. Lincoln's assassination.

No particulars were given, but somehow by some unseen
intelligence it was impressed upon our hearts that the Southern people had lost a powerful friend in the death of the man
they once despised, reviled and hated. From that day to this,
history has continued to reveal the truth to us, as his biogra-
phers have laid bare the life and character of this wonderful
man. From hour to hour his greatness and goodness have
grown upon us, and his image has been lifted up before our
eyes till the Lincoln of *now* stands revealed to us in his true
character as a patriot, as a statesman and a philanthropist
worthy to occupy a niche in the temple of fame as exalted as
the greatest of the sons of earth. To his resplendent fame as a
man there is added a martyr's crown radiant with more than a
hero's glory and typical of more than a saint's reward.

We can now see and understand that beneath his rugged
breast beat a heart as kind and true as ever animated mortal
man and that he was one who loved his fellow men, even his
enemies. We can now see that he bore no malice to the Southern people, but in the discharge of his official duties imposed on
him by the American people, struggled bravely and successfully
to accomplish the great task which his destiny had set before
him—the task of preserving this country from the untold evils
of disunion; the task of striking the shackles from millions of
slaves, and handing down to posterity "an indestructible Union
composed of indestructible States," "distinct as the billows yet

one as the ocean." We hail Washington as the "Father of his country," "First in war, first in peace, and first in the hearts of his countrymen." We hail Abraham Lincoln as the preserver of this Union founded by Washington, as the restorer of a united nation whose foundations are laid deep in the hearts, the affections, and the patriotism of the American people, South as well as North.

May this great fabric erected at such cost of blood and treasure endure in splendor so long as the names of George Washington and Abraham Lincoln shall be remembered and revered by the sons of liberty. May wise and conservative counsels guide and keep us in the path of peace and moderation, guarding the honor and the destiny of the nation at all hazards and against all foes, domestic and foreign, but avoiding the Quixotic ideas of modern statesmanship which would make this government the protector and guardian of all the oppressed nations of earth.

The patriotism which would extend the ill-defined terms of the Monroe Doctrine until it makes this nation assume the ridiculous attitude of a second knight of La Mancha, seeking to redress the wrongs of every Republic on the American continent, is abnormal and unhealthy. The nation which undertakes to act such a part should have well filled coffers, a powerful navy, and secure harbor defenses. Mr. Cleveland, in his Venezuelan message, declaring for war with England one day, and filing a petition in bankruptcy for the United States the next, gives to the world a specimen of vacillating for the country under his leadership. It has been well and wittily said that "It is a misfortune for this country that Mr. Cleveland's last term was not his first." The only hope for the future of this country lies in the return of the Republican party to power. It takes no prophet to foretell that on the 4th of March 1897 a Republican President will be inaugurated amid the loud acclaims of a gratified and happy people.

Mr. President, allow me in conclusion to thank the members of the Club for the honor they have done me and for the pleasure they have given me. I return to my Southern home full of kind recollections of my visit to your city feeling that in the future we should know no North, no South, no East, no West, but should remember only that we are an united people with one country, one flag, and one government.

THIRTY-FOUR

Re-Elected

During his first term in Congress, General Walker lived very modestly and quietly in a boarding house on Capitol Hill and worked very hard. His speech on Lincoln's birthday before the Middlesex Club of Boston brought increased attention to him. Quoted extensively in northern as well as in southern papers (though it brought down fresh maledictions on his head from the latter), it helped to extinguish the still slumbering embers of sectional misunderstanding and dislike, to pave the way for that burst of national enthusiasm which flared up a short time later in the sinking of the Maine and the refusal of Spain to make apologies and amends for doing so.

General Walker had an efficient secretary in Mr. S. E. Godell of Marion, Virginia, but even with his assistance each day's demands were all he could manage. Patronage claims were necessarily heavy even on a Republican congressman under a Democratic president, especially when there were rival claimants for every crossroads post office in the state. This part of his political duties was most distasteful to him. With a decided gift for statesmanship, he was never a good politician in the usual acceptation of the term, and never learned to pull wires for himself or his friends or to barter and compromise for exchange of place and power. Nor would he ever consent to act as a lobbyist for any corporation or group. It was inevitable at a time when machine politics was supreme in both parties that, as a politician, General Walker would sooner or later be victimized by his own as well as the opposing party.

Financial claims became now somewhat pressing, his boom obligations having left him with a considerable debt. Hence it was a matter for serious consideration as to whether or not General Walker would be a candidate for a second term. In justice to his family and his creditors, he felt he should decline. Moreover, being again a candidate meant throwing down the gauntlet to those within his own party who were not friendly to him, as well as to the Democratic Party entrenched behind a barbed wire election law.

Elected a delegate to the St. Louis Convention as an outspoken Reed man, he was again in opposition to the Virginia Republican machine which was pledged to Mark Hanna. Mr. Hanna's candidate, McKinley, was nominated, and Walker therefore was not on the machine bandwagon. Understanding his combative temperament and his disposition never to quit under fire, I am not at all sure that this was not one of the factors which finally induced him to allow his name to go before the Ninth District Convention which met early in July and nominated him by acclamation.

A few days later the Democrats nominated Samuel W. Williams, also a member of the Wytheville bar. Williams was, of course, nominated on the William Jennings Bryan platform and was personally an ardent "free silver" man.

There was glee in the Democratic camp, for Walker had made his previous campaign as a bimetallist. Either he must reverse himself or go against the strong gold plank in the McKinley platform. Moreover, there was no reason he should receive any enthusiastic support from Hanna, McKinley's campaign manager, since he had been a Reed man, and since the Virginia Republican machine, in close touch with Mr. Hanna, was luke warm, if not antagonistic, to Walker.

The Democrats did not reckon sufficiently, however, on Walker's frankness and boldness. He was able to respond to the charge that he had changed his view on the money question simply by pointing out that the Democrats of the Ninth District had likewise reversed themselves. Only they had changed from the right viewpoint to the wrong one, while he had discovered his error and gladly deserted it for the truth; he had abandoned specious reasoning for logic and common sense. As for this untenable "sixteen to one" promulgation, calling for the free and unlimited coinage of silver at the sixteen to one ratio with gold, which was so eloquently embroidered by Mr. Bryan as a specific for all present and future economic ills, it was no more and no less than the old, old fallacy that a single government could manufacture fiat money. Under its working, the United States would actually establish its coinage on a silver basis, her dollars would be worth just what Mexican dollars were worth, with good prospect, at the present rate of silver production, of a still further debasement of her coinage under a full and free coinage of silver act until business men would need wheelbarrows in which to trundle about their loose change.

But it was around the tariff issue that General Walker concentrated his arguments. Until the presidential election in 1892, he said in one of his campaign speeches, "prosperity reigned throughout the country; there was employment for everybody willing to work, at remunerative wages. No tramps, enforced to idleness, stalked about the country...Business of every kind was in a flourishing condition...Such were the fruits of Republican rule for thirty years."

But in 1892, he said, the Democrats misled the people into believing that "free trade would open the markets of the world to all American products and enhance the prices of all that we raised and produced while making cheap all we bought. They prophesied of the good times that were sure to follow."

Instead, he argued:

Let us look at some of the results of three short years of Democratic rule and free trade. It has failed to raise revenue sufficient to defray the annual expenses of the government; has created a deficit in the Treasury of sixty millions annually, thereby creating the necessity of bonding 262 millions of dollars and increasing the interest bearing debt of the government by that sum, and taxing the people to pay the principal and interest of this increase...It has reduced the value of American livestock 758 million dollars. It has reduced the sales of American cattle abroad from 1892 to 1895 105,257 head, valued at eight million dollars. The highest value of sheep in the United States was in 1892; the lowest in 1896...From 1892 to 1896 our foreign trade declined more than 300 millions, and our export of breadstuffs decreased 114 millions. Our credit too is impaired...

It is estimated that our imports of cheap goods manufactured in Europe, in 1895, would have given employment to one half a million of wage earners for a whole year...

It was a scathing arraignment of the Democratic party, citing "blunders and crimes against the people" so overwhelming that the Party "in 1894 was repudiated in nearly every state in the union where the voice of the people was not stifled by fraud and corruption." Reorganizing "with all the odds and ends of parties in the United States who were opposed to the principles of the Republican party," he said, the Democrats set forth a "declaration of principles in their platform which contains more heresies, more dangerous doctrines than were ever set forth in the same space, in any document ever published."

The speech naturally increased partisan bitterness against Walker, as did his appeal to the young men to strike off the shackles of prejudice and remain at home to develop the rich and varied resources of their own state rather than banish themselves from home and loved ones to go west and make their fortunes. Virginia needed only a free and progressive government to make her the most prosperous of all the states, he argued. His firm belief in this statement gave force to his utterance of it and carried conviction with it. It was the younger men who rallied to his banner, and in the coming generation he saw the realization of his hope—namely, a free, progressive and prosperous South.

Walker's opponent, Judge Williams, was an accustomed speaker and something of an orator. He too made an active campaign. Pendleton notes that it was

one of the most thorough and hotly contested campaigns ever witnessed in this section of Virginia. The respective merits of gold and silver, for use as standard money, were debated in every town, hamlet and neighborhood. Though warmly and vigorously conducted by both parties, it was free from the partisan bitterness and vices that prevailed in the subsequent campaigns in the Ninth District. James A. Walker was elected, receiving 16,077 against 14,900 for Samuel W. Williams. And this in spite of the now smooth working of the Walton election law.

It is a pleasure to record that the campaign did not bring about strained relations between the large Williams family, our neighbors, and Mrs. Williams, a woman of sterling character and exceptional common sense, congratulated my mother as Judge Williams did my father. Mrs. Williams frankly averred that she did not like General Walker's politics, but she did like the General and all his family and hoped there would be no severance of neighborly relation. There was none, and as long as Mrs. Williams and the Judge lived, we counted them among our friends.

This was the last time Walker's candidacy was met in a spirit of fairness and good sportsmanship. Already the man had been chosen who would stop at nothing to defeat Walker two years hence, a machine man whom his own party had already arraigned for political trickery. He and all the manipulators of party tricks in the state presently put their heads together in a predetermined plan to make sure of "getting Walker next time."

To "get Walker" became a sort of slogan among the more ruthless Democrats in the Ninth, and as we shall presently see it was understood that if they could not "get" him in one way, they would in another.

THIRTY-FIVE

Yost vs. Tucker

Early in the short session of the Fifty-fifth Congress, the House Elections Committee, of which Walker was a member, brought in a report in a contested election in Virginia's Fourth (Southside) District. The Committee report recommended in favor of the contestant and against the seated Congressman. Having administered this rebuke to the Virginia election laws, the committee was inclined to let another case, in which Walker had much interest, drag.

The other case was that of Jacob Yost, a Republican, vs. Henry St. George Tucker, a Democrat, in the Tenth District, which then covered the Shenandoah Valley. Walker and Yost's attorneys did not see how a verdict favorable to the contestant in the Fourth District could possibly presage anything but a similar verdict in the Tenth, which seemed to them the stronger case of the two. Politics, however, is a queer game with many angles, as more and more General Walker was finding out. He never fully realized, in truth, how much at a disadvantage is one who plays the game in the open, with conviction and patriotism as his primary motives.

In the matter of the Yost case, several factors worked against Yost's and Walker's interests. The Republican party had already a sufficient majority in the House of Representatives. Tucker, a charming Virginia gentleman, was popular with his colleagues, and he had already been drawing his salary for the better part of the congressional term when the case came up for review. To seat Yost meant two salaries for the same position. Moreover, the theory of no interference with southern affairs was gaining ground, and it was accepted as an axiom that the best and most representative people in the South were Democrats. They were good fellows, too, and as a rule were satisfied to let the Republican Party run the nation if only they were let alone to run the South.

Certain practical politicians from the North talked to General
Walker along this line, favoring the idea, "Oh, let the South alone!
As long as she keeps quiet, we don't need her anyhow." To Walker
that point of view was even more antagonistic than that of the
members who said, "Tucker is a good fellow. He's talked to me
about his case. I'd hate to hurt his feelings. Besides, why should
Virginia draw the salary of an extra congressman?"

Added to these currents was another more subtle and more
dangerous: the secret opposition of the Virginia federal office
holding group. This inside ring did not want Yost seated. He had
opposed Mahone, had been a leader of the independent Republican
movement, and was a man of brains, of courage and of honesty. He
was thus one of the pioneers of that group which had grown slowly
and painfully in the South of Republicans from conviction, with an
earnest desire to build up a representative Republican Party in the
South, primarily for the good of the South.

The development below the Mason-Dixon Line of a respectable
Republican party strong enough to elect candidates to Congress
was, however, not the desire of the small ring which controlled
federal patronage; strong, independent Republican congressmen
threatened their supremacy. Moreover, as long as the party
consisted of a leaderless minority in each community, the patronage
group could call an executive committee meeting or even a state
convention and with a few previously arranged motions from the
floor put across any measures they chose.

These various influences proved strong enough for the committee, with Walker dissenting, to bring in a report favorable to
Tucker. On January 21, 1897, Walker laid before the House a
minority report favoring Yost. In that report, he arraigned the
Walton Act, which the General Assembly recently had enacted as
a supposed reform measure, spoke of the personal relationships
which Tucker had built up with his colleagues, and presented the
question before the House as one of monumental importance to the
Republican party in the South:

...We hear of [congressmen's] personal relations with the
contestee [Tucker] and their reluctance to vote against him. I
fully appreciate all this, and I join with them in respect and in
kindly sentiments for Mr. Tucker. He is worthy of the high
regard in which he is held by members and by the people of his
district.

But the question for the House to decide is not one of personal friendship or personal regard. Sentiment has no place in a contested election case. It resolves itself into the simple legal inquiry: Is he entitled to hold the seat he now occupies in this House?...If the contestant [Yost] was fairly and honestly elected, then the gallant Republicans of the Tenth Virginia District who contended and won against such fearful odds, against unfair and iniquitous election laws, against partisan and unscrupulous election methods, against corrupt election officers, look to the Republicans of this House for that justice which is denied them elsewhere.

The Republican Party in the South points proudly to its thirty-six representatives on the floor of this House, hailing from ten southern states, who have "come up through great tribulation."...They are living pledges that the solid South is no more, that the fires of sectionalism have died out, and that the fires of patriotism have been rekindled...

Republicans of the North, to you the Republicans of the South look for justice! They ask no more; they demand no less. Each mail from Virginia brings messages from all parts of the State urging and begging me to appeal to this House for justice. The Republicans of Virginia feel that the cause of the contestant is their cause, and that their most sacred rights and their dearest privileges are imperiled by the majority report. They say, and they feel, that if this battle is lost it will be the death knell of all their hopes for honest elections, the triumph of fraud and corruption over manhood suffrage.

The Republican party is today great and powerful, and on the fourth of March next will again have control of every branch of this government—"a consummation most devoutly to be wished..." Virginia is naturally a Republican state, and all we ask is an open field and a fair fight; an honest ballot and a fair count. The national Republican party has no more devoted followers than the Republicans of the South, who have burned their bridges and will never turn back. They ask justice for one man, but they ask it in the name of two hundred thousand Virginia Republican voters...

The vote in the House resulted in the acceptance of the committee report by a small majority, many voting against their convictions, as they afterwards told Walker, because of their practice of voting to sustain the majority report of committees as well as because of a personal friendship for and pledge to Mr. Tucker.

THIRTY-SIX

McKinley's Inaugural

In February of that year, 1897, I paid my first visit to my father in Washington. It was a great experience for me to meet the interesting friends he had made, to sit in the galleries of House and Senate, to listen to the proceedings of those august bodies, to visit my father's committee rooms (Congressmen had no private offices in those days) and to go with him to the army and navy reception at the White House.

My father was a most ardent admirer of Mrs. Cleveland, to whose graciousness and charm everyone was glad to pay tribute. He loved to tell a personal incident illustrative of this. One spring afternoon when hastening from one department to another he decided to take a short cut across the White House ground. It led him by the east portico where, to his surprise, stood Mrs. Cleveland, alone, gazing meditatively across the lawn. Subconsciously his eye was held by her attractive person, and realizing a possible though unintentional rudeness, he lifted his hat in spontaneous homage and apology. Instantly, Mrs. Cleveland returned the salutation with a gracious bow, a friendly smile and a manner which, he affirmed, said as plain as words, "It is a beautiful day and a beautiful world, isn't it? Why shouldn't we all be friends."

I well remember Mrs. Cleveland's graciousness that night of the last of her big receptions and how young and charming she looked against the background of elaborate floral decorations in the East Room. Mr. Cleveland, like most of our presidents under similar circumstances, looked bored and anxious to get the affair over with as soon as possible. And no one blames them.

The biggest thrill I got out of Washington during this, my first stay of any length, was the newly completed public library. It was only two blocks from our boarding house, and I spent morning after morning there, guide book in hand, studying the plan, the decorative scheme and each detail of it. It filled me with pride that our capital had added another really beautiful and dignified building to its permanent possessions, one too with so much of inspiration, of call to the ideals of America, in the coordinated vision of its architects and artists. Especially was I thrilled by the plan and ornament of the rotunda, beautiful in its soaring yet intimate proportions. I thought the vision of its builders spoke eloquently and plainly to all discerning beholders: a noble sermon of duty and a grand symphony of praise all in one.

Another pleasure I found in my visits to the library was in hunting up material for a speech my father had promised to make at a banquet in Detroit on Washington's birthday given by the Michigan Club. General Walker's subject was "Virginia, the Mother of Washington." With considerable elimination and some dressing up, he used, to my great pride, not only the facts but the outline I suggested for his speech.

He was a very busy man at that time but found opportunity to show me the most interesting places in and around Washington. I remained to the McKinley inaugural, in which my father was to take part. Astride a handsome mettled horse which had been loaned him for the occasion, he rode at the head of the Southern line in the parade, followed by the Stonewall Brigade Band of Staunton, which played "Dixie" during the march, and the VMI cadets of Lexington.

The McKinley ball was probably the most brilliant of all the colorful inaugural balls that have been held in Washington, as it was one of the last. It was held in the old Pension Office Building, the entire floor being cleared of partitions, desks, etc., to make a setting for it. Through the center of the long room thus made, fountains were constructed at intervals, each banked with a profusion of blooming spring plants, their pots concealed by moss and ferns. Tens of thousands of crocuses, daffodils, hyacinths, tulips, freesias, cyclamens, violets and lilies of the valley bloomed under the mist of spraying fountains amid slopes of artificial verdure. The effect was enchanting. The air was filled with spring fragrance, while birds in gilded cages here and there added to the illusion of spring. The sides of the barn-like building were covered with gold colored bunting against which the American flag was picked out in red white and blue electric globes. From the ceiling, yellow bunting was draped, caught in place by small electric flag designs. Huge ferns and palms banked the lower side walls, at their feet mounds of spring flowers.

Alcoves on the gallery at either side of the building had been turned into boxes and allotted to cabinet members, diplomats, senators, congressmen and others. Filled with gorgeous evening gowns, dotted with black spots of men in swallow tails, the scene was brilliant as well as beautiful. The Marine Band broke into jubilation—"See the Conquering Hero Comes"—and the presidential party entered at one end of the room, a procession of dignitaries and ballroom officials falling into step behind them. Mrs. McKinley, lame and frail but attractive in appearance and manner, was supported by her husband on one side and by an aide in uniform on the other. The president's mother and brother followed, and then a procession of diplomats, dignitaries, officers and distinguished personalities. Among them I remember Mrs. Hearst of California, wearing a gorgeous costume of lilac brocaded satin with short train and low bodice, outlined around neck, sleeves, skirt and trail with hundreds of small lilac ostrich feathers, tiara and necklace of resplendent diamonds, with buckles of diamonds on lilac satin slippers. My! thought I, the cost of that costume would educate all three of my children and then some!

I recall watching one other person on the floor of that ball room with some pride and satisfaction. It was pretty Edith Bolling of my own town of Wytheville, recently married to Mr. Norman Galt of Washington. She was simply dressed in white, and my father and I voted her the prettiest woman on the floor. Mr. Galt was, I believe, one of the floor managers for the ball, and they were among the first couples to lead off in the opening dance, after the parade was over and the McKinleys were seated in their box. The Bollings were neighbors of ours in Wytheville, in fact lived directly across the street when we occupied the "old Crockett house." They were a large and charming family and were known as the handsome Bollings. They lived quietly, were the best of neighbors, and as famed for their good breeding as their good looks. My mother and Mrs. Bolling were continually exchanging trays and baskets, samples of their housewifely skills, while my father and Judge Bolling were warm friends and associates in a number of cases. Judge Bolling supported my father politically, as did one of his sons. The young people of the two families were likewise intimately associated, so it was natural my father and I should take pride in

Edith's outstanding good looks in this assemblage of the nation's wealth, fashion and beauty.

THIRTY-SEVEN

Letters Home

Two of General Walker's letters from Washington that spring of '97 show some of his personality: one his love of home and his devotion to his grandchildren, the other to indicate that he realized the efforts to discredit him within his own party. The first, dated April 25, 1897, is addressed to a granddaughter:

My dear Little Fairy:
I received your nice sweet little letter this morning and answer at once. I am more distressed than you are that I have been unable to go home and have the great pleasure of spending a few days with you. I had set Easter Sunday as the day to be there, but business was so urgent that I could not leave. Then I was all ready to be with you today but Speaker Reed appointed me on the committee of congressmen to attend the Grant ceremonies at New York on Tuesday the 27th and I have again to give up my visit. The committee will leave this city at 10 a.m. tomorrow, and I will go with them if I feel well enough. I have been quite much out of sorts for a day or two and lie down in my room most of the time. You needn't be uneasy for it is nothing serious. You don't know how badly I want to see youall, and enjoy a few days quite under the shade of our trees.
I am getting tired of Washington with its noise and turmoil and long for the cool yard and the quiet of home. I think Washington is a beautiful city now and its wide streets as hard and smooth as a floor and swept as clean. The trees are all in leaf now and hundreds of parks scattered all over the city are green with grass and bright with flowers. The little children here seem to have a nice time and hundreds of them ride on bicycles and go whizzing along on the smooth level streets.

I saw the Easter egg rolling on Easter Monday. The White
House, as the President's House is called, has a great big lawn
in rear of it—twenty times as large as our yard—and it is a
custom to open it to the public on Easter Monday, or rather to
children and their parents and nurses. I passed through last
Monday, and it was just full of children of all sorts, rich and
poor, white and black. Everyone had a lot of colored Easter
eggs and they were rolling them down the slopes and romping
over the clean nice grass. They took lunches and some were
eating their lunches. The children were dressed nicely in gay
colors, and it was a beautiful sight...

I am glad Aunt Maggie's house is almost completed and
that she will soon have a nice snug little home of her own. Tell
her I will have her wallpaper shipped tomorrow. Mr. Will Kent
has just called in to see me and says it is almost as warm in
Wytheville as it is here. It is very warm here, and I write with
all my windows open and the door too. I just looked out the
window and saw five little negro boys go by on bicycles. A great
many colored people ride on bicycles in this city.

Now, I have written you a long letter and hope you will
answer it very soon. Don't trouble yourself to think what you
will write but just scratch down anything. Give my best love to
Mother and Father and to Sarah and the boy, and to Aunt
Maggie and all her children, and accept the *very very* best love
of
                    "Papa."

The second letter, dated May 8th, was one of his weekly letters
to me. The reference to his interviews with the President—to his
"not being disturbed, etc." and to the appointment of J--- B--- all
have reference to the plot of the patronage group, no longer under
cover, to minimize his political influence, to make federal appoint-
ments in his own district without consulting him and if possible to
get rid of him politically.

Your welcome letter is just to hand. Don't be uneasy about
my health for I am not at all seriously ill. Only bilious and
dauncey. Am feeling much better today and have just finished
a hearty dinner. The office seekers are not worrying me nearly
as much as they did, as they have all left except one or two. I

mean all from my district. There is always a new swarm on hand, but they don't worry me worth talking about.

I had a long interview with the President all by myself yesterday afternoon and one today in company with four others. I also had an interview with the Atty. General yesterday and one today. I am getting along very nicely with the President and am not disturbed by anything that had happened. As to J--- B---'s appointment, I never heard of it until yesterday afternoon about 3 o'clock. Thereby hangs a tale which will be unfolded later. Don't mention this, but the sequel will be seen in about three months if not sooner.

As to the heavy expense I am at, I am somewhat troubled about it. My salary for the next two years will be about $600 per month. I can get along in Washington, say six months each year, for $100 per month, say $50 per month the year round. Taxes, insurance and interest will make $1500 more per year. Household expenses per month $150.00 This makes a balance sheet:

Receipts	per year		$7200
Expenses in Washington	"	$600	
Taxes Ins & Int	"	$1500	
Household Expenses	"	$1800	
M-----	"	$720	$4620
			$2580

Leaving say $2500 a year to pay on my debts. Of course if I am to have a whole lot of extras to pay I will not be able to do it. As to the little I spent to have you visit me in Washington it was well spent and I hope you will come again next winter.

Now about my coming home, I can't leave here now, and I am not certain when I can. I have to watch things closely, and I am to meet the Executive Committee next week one day. Don't be uneasy about me for I am feeling quite well now. I am hungry to see you all but the pleasure will be more appreciated when it comes. I am almost beside myself to see the children, and have a romp with them on the grass. Tell them I think of them every time I see a nice little child on the streets.

I must close as it is late and I am tired. Love to all
   Yours affectionately,
   J. A. Walker

Though entirely personal, these last paragraphs are interesting to illustrate the difference between the cost of living in 1897 and now. Think of a Congressman's expenses in Washington totalling one hundred dollars per month and of the possibility of running a comfortable home at a cost of $150 per month.

THIRTY-EIGHT

California

That summer of '97 General Walker went with the River and Harbor Committee to California. It was almost the only real holiday I remember his taking. A considerable appropriation had been made the previous spring by the committee for the improvement of Pacific coast harbors. How that appropriation should be apportioned was now a vexing question, and it had been agreed that the committee should settle the matter after a tour of investigation. Transcontinental railways offered free hauling for special coaches and special conductors for the party. The larger cities along the way and on the coast sent invitations for the party to be their guests at banquets, luncheons or sightseeing tours. Therefore the cost to each member of the committee would be comparatively small and each was invited to take his wife or some member of his family with him. My father had promptly written me to make my plans to accompany him, which I did. Attached to the congressional coach was a second, under the direction of Congressman Dovener of West Virginia (who was also a member of the River and Harbor Committee) filled with citizens from Wheeling, West Virginia, a service of silver, glass and china—the last two manufactured in West Virginia.

The two groups made up a party of about seventy which proved to be a jolly and congenial crowd of sightseers. Mr. Cannon, "Uncle Joe," was one of the jolliest, while Mr. Dovener and his wife, acting as semi-official host and hostess, concerned themselves constantly for the comfort of the party. We had efficient directors furnished by the railroad and delightful meals in our own special dining car, served us at a flat rate per meal, agreed upon beforehand.

From the time we crossed the Mississippi we received hospitable courtesies at every stop. Whether we had only a few hours between trains for a drive over some thriving western city or our itinerary

called for a rest of twenty-four hours at some hotel, chambers of
commerce sent committees to meet our train, speeches of greeting
were made, keys of cities presented, ladies and gentlemen waited
to drive us around, excursions to nearby points of interest were
conducted and in the evening there was a banquet or else private
dinners for different groups.

My father and I were everywhere welcomed by ex-Virginians (as
were residents of other states by western emigrants from their
particular states) offering us more hospitality than our time allowed
us to accept. Among these were some who knew all about us or
were distantly related. In other words, the vast West made itself
the party's host extending a lavish hospitality which shamed
anything the East knows how to do. For instance, while we were
absent from our cars on some sightseeing excursion, a committee
would pass through, to leave in each seat baskets of luscious fruit,
great bunches of roses or mixed flowers, sometimes bottles of
California grape juice or wine, occasionally a small souvenir gift of
some kind. Always these offerings were accompanied with illustrat-
ed leaflets advertising the West, booklets of California or bunches
of postcards—thus combining attractive advertising with gracious
hospitality.

It was a great delight to me to see my father enjoying himself
so thoroughly, during the whole month of this trip. He was erect,
handsome and always well groomed, the toast of the party, even
more popular than "Uncle Joe." Each lady declared she was proud
to enter a room with him. Beside a personal magnetism, General
Walker had polished manners and a spontaneous geniality. These
characteristics, combined with a sense of fun, a quick wit and
conversational gifts, made him socially irresistible whenever he
found time to relax and make himself agreeable. When he left the
party at Memphis—it having been routed eastward through Mexico
and Texas—for a straight shoot home via Chattanooga, there were
resolutions of regret at parting and a vote recorded that General
Walker was the most popular member of the party.

THIRTY-NINE

War With Spain

The second session of the Fifty-fifth Congress found General Walker in his place, busy with the routine of Congress and committee meetings and still overwhelmed by all manner of demands from a large constituency too conveniently close to Washington. On February 17, 1898, he introduced an amendment to the Bankruptcy Bill (Bill S1035, to establish a uniform system of bankruptcy throughout the United States) which was later incorporated in the original bill, modifying considerably its harsher provisions. As a clear-headed lawyer he had sensed injustice in some provisions of the bill which his forceful speech on the proposed amendment made plain.

The smooth and even tenor of national affairs with returning prosperity under the Dingley tariff act was suddenly given a serious jolt by the sinking of "The Maine." This apparent affront to the United States was heightened by a letter from the Spanish ambassador, de Lome, which had been made public within the week, speaking most disrespectfully of President McKinley and impertinently critical of the politics of the United States. In addition to such immediate irritants to the pride of the country, there was the long standing agitation against Spanish misrule in Cuba and that country's reiterated appeals to the United States for intervention. These circumstances so wrought upon the sympathies and the national spirit of the people that there was a widespread demand for an immediate declaration of war against Spain.

President McKinley showed admirable calmness and self restraint, responding to the demand for war by appointing a commission to examine into the cause of The Maine disaster. The commission, after due investigation, reported that the cause was not from within as Spain had claimed, but plainly was an exterior explosion which most probably was the result of a well laid plan.

Public opinion could no longer be held in leash. The demand for war became clamorous, and in March Congress resolved itself into a sort of Council of War.

Mr. Cannon led the debate, yielding again and again from two to three minutes to representatives from different states—among them General Walker of Virginia, who spoke as follows:

Mr. Speaker, I would be untrue to the constituency I have the honor to represent on this floor if I failed to voice their unanimous approval of the bill before the House. They are opposed to war if peace can be maintained with honor. They have supped full of the horrors of war and they instinctively shrink from a renewal of its cruelties and its sorrows, but they prefer the honor of their country and of its flag to their personal wishes and private interests. As a Virginian and as a Confederate soldier I am glad and proud to know that in this crisis of our country's history a noble Virginia gentleman—an old Confederate soldier, one of my comrades in arms, bearing an honored name, known and respected in every part of this country, North as well as South—is upholding the honor and dignity of the United States in a foreign land [applause] with a courage, patriotism, and fidelity which challenge the admiration of this whole nation. I point to Fitzhugh Lee as a typical Virginian, a typical Confederate soldier, who truly and faithfully represents the people of Virginia of all parties and all classes. If war shall come (which God forbid,) let this country keep its eye on Fitz Lee and the men of the South, for they will be heard from on every battlefield where the Stars and Stripes wave in the faces of the enemy.

Still, the president continued negotiations with Spain hoping and striving for peace, but making meantime no plans to meet the contingency of war, should war come. On April 11, he sent in a message to Congress reviewing "negotiations with Spain and their unsatisfactory termination." I have a letter from my father written at 10:30 A.M. April 11, '98, which gives a fair idea of the mind of the country and its determination to force President McKinley into war. This is an extract from it:

It will be an hour and a half before the House is called to order, and I am in my seat because my clerk, Mr. Goodel, is not on duty today, having asked permission to hear the proceedings in the body, and to do so he had to be in the gallery by nine o'clock. The galleries are now packed as full as they can hold and have been for an hour and every available loafing place in the corridors and passages is swarming with people, mostly women, who are too late to get seats in the gallery.

The President's message will be sent in this morning, and the question of war or no war will be virtually settled today. I'm afraid the policy of the President as outlined by the papers today will not meet the approval of the Congress in either House. The intimation this A.M. is that he will favor "armed intervention in the affairs of Cuba" at the *discretion* of the Executive. This means further delay and leaves the question of war as the will of the President, and I don't believe Congress will consent to further delay.

I am for peace, but I believe the time has come for the representatives of the people to act, and express the wishes of the people. The country should be relieved of the suspense and the policy of this nation should be definitely settled. The President has had time enough to decide upon and adopt a fixed policy, and if he had failed to do so, then the Legislative branch of the government, having power to so declare war or not to do so, should take the responsibility. The decision will be for war, I feel sure.

Mag Eddins has just been in and took a seat beside me. I introduced her to several members among whom was one from Maine and one from Vermont. We had a good laugh at her rebel talk. She sends much love to you and quarrels with me all the time for being a Republican.

I must close now as the bustle is too much for me. A dozen people have talked to me since I began. Love to all.

Yours affectionately,
J. A. Walker

War was not declared until April 25th. Still it found the country in a state of shameful unpreparedness, as war has always found the United States, causing delay, confusion, waste of money and worst of all wanton waste of the young lives of the nation. On March 9, Congress had placed an appropriation of fifty million dollars in the hands of the president to be used as he saw fit for national defense. Volunteers by the thousands responded from the South as well as other sections of the country to the call for additional troops, and dozens of late Confederate officers offered their services to their country.

General Walker was one of these, receiving from the president
a most appreciative letter in reply, accepting his services condition-
ally. His age and his disability naturally placed him on the reserve
list which, though recognized as inevitable, proved a genuine
disappointment to Walker. For like his own war horses he used to
tell of, which at the first gun of an impending battle began to
prance and snort and pull upon the bit, so Walker felt in a
declaration of war by his country "a call to arms" he could hardly
resist. His attitude of unfading interest in military matters is
reflected in a second letter from him that spring, written on May
30:

Dear Will:
    This is Decoration Day, and I am all alone in my committee
room, having a nice quiet day! I have been kept from going
home for two weeks now by visitors. I told you of Colonel W. B.
Preston's visit week before last, and now an old friend, Colonel
Harrison, is here, and I can't leave him. He is stopping with me
at the Normandie. Is here trying to sell his coal property. The
colonel has gone over to Arlington today with Paul Haxlin. Mr.
Goodel and wife have gone down the river on an excursion to
Colonial Beach. I had my outing yesterday, went over to
Groveton Saturday afternoon with two other gentlemen and
visited the battlefield of Second Manassas on yesterday. We
walked all over Jackson's line (at least five miles), and I was
greatly interested. Had no trouble in locating all the positions
of my regiment, finding the ground very little changed. It is
nearly thirty-six years since that battle was fought, will be on
the twenty-ninth of next August. I am very proud of the way I
stood the long tramps over rough ground and through woods
and fields, for I did not feel fatigued by the walk and am fresh
and vigorous today as ever.
    We have no news here. Congress is doing nothing and may
not adjourn for a month. We are waiting on the sluggish movements of the Senate. I don't think I told you of my trip up to
Culpeper Court House last Wednesday to attend memorial day
there. Went up at eleven A.M. and returned at 9:30 P.M. Had a
very pleasant day. Saw my old servant Henry Jackson and met
a number of my old soldiers. Saw Mrs. Burdett who sent love to
you all. I am glad the boy enjoyed my letter. As he appreciates
my efforts as a correspondent so highly, I ought to write to him

more frequently. Tell him I am awaiting a reply to my letter; he owes me one. With best love to all, I am

Yours affectionately,

J. A. Walker

FORTY

Opposition

In 1897, it was openly said that a year hence the Democrats meant to defeat Walker for Congress, if it took all the resources at the command of the Democratic state machine to do so. It was rumored too that certain trades had been arranged between the patronage group of "old line Republicans" and the Democratic leaders by which the Democrats would be given a free hand in defeating Walker, if no opposition would be made by their congressmen to federal appointees named by the Republican patronage group. As part of the plan for defeating Walker, Democratic papers began to print editorials suggesting that General Walker was not so popular with his party as he had been, that Mr. Hanna was not his friend, and that therefore the administration was indifferent to him, to say the least.

General Walker's family and intimate friends, noting these ominous signs of a coming political storm, suggested to him that it was not his duty to allow himself to be sacrificed. They advised him to make a statement to the effect that he would not again be a candidate for Congress in the Ninth District. But this suggestion seemed to General Walker to savor too much of fear and cowardice to be considered. He had never turned his back on his enemies and he would not begin now. True, he could not afford to stay in politics, in fact was threatened with financial ruin if he continued to run for Congress, practically at his own cost. But even that was preferable to an acknowledgement of defeat before the race was made.

Especially did he intend to stand and fight as long as he lived for a Republican Party in Virginia that was based on honest belief in the principles of the national Republican Party. There were many, especially among the younger men, who were Republicans by conviction; to abandon these—to leave them leaderless—and turn the party over to a group who were Republicans for patronage only,

ready at all times to trade the party for federal offices, this he could
never do, cost him what it might.

The attempt to build up a Republican Party in any one of the
southern states since the Civil War had been a thankless and
difficult task, attended by misconception abroad, misrepresentation
and persecution at home, as already our narrative has shown. It
had been made doubly difficult by two factions within the party, in
nearly all of the southern states, based on the same difference in
purpose. First was a faction which honestly believed that a two
party system was essential as the guarantee of political independence and good government for the South and that Republican
policies were best for that section, as for the whole country. The
second faction thought that it was hopeless to expect any change in
the political bias of the South for years to come, and meantime,
since they were Republicans, that it was the part of wisdom to
gather in the perquisites by keeping up a form of organization—not
so aggressive as to bring down upon their heads the maledictions
and persecutions of their neighbors. This second faction was always
opposed to putting up candidates and only became active just before
national conventions, when delegates could be traded for hopes or
promises of future patronage.

Pursuant to this, their usual policy, the state committee refused
to call a convention to nominate a candidate for governor in 1897.
The chairman of the party, Colonel William Lamb, took issue
against the committee's decision and issued a call for a convention
at Lynchburg October 5, 1897. It was attended by representative
Republicans from all parts of the state to the number of about eight
hundred, and a full state ticket was chosen.

The ticket was headed by P. H. (Pat) McCaull, a young man
who had been raised in Newbern, Virginia, and a warm friend of
Walker. This ticket called itself "Independent Republicans." Though
the office-holding faction declared neutrality, they used their
influence against the Independent Republicans ticket.

In the meantime, General Walker accepted the nomination for
Congress in the Ninth Virginia District for the third time, and he
soon found the office-holding faction was working against him, too.

Both before and during the gubernatorial campaign, Walker
considered himself actively engaged in a life and death struggle for
the perpetuity of Republican principles in that stronghold of
Republicanism in Virginia, the Ninth District.

Even the district Republican chairman, H. E. McCoy, it was afterward proven, had lent himself to secret plottings against the candidates nominated by his party. An Ohio man, shrewd in business as in politics, McCoy was accused of trading first with the Democrats and then with the office-holding group. He refused to allow known Republican counties to nominate candidates for the General Assembly and did all he could to defeat the ticket put out by the Independent Republicans. The fight Walker now made against these odds was aggressive, bold, spectacular, arresting the attention of the nation, alarming the state machine and compelling the admiration even of his foes.

Knowing how heavy were the odds against him, he had accepted the nomination on one condition: namely, that if he were "counted out," as the phrase ran in Virginia, it would be understood that the Post Office vacancy in Wytheville should be filled by a member of his family whose support he had assumed, a responsibility he could no longer meet, if defeated.

FORTY-ONE

Defeat

The more honest Democrats in Virginia deplored the fact that the election laws gave open countenance to fraudulent practices, and the higher type of newspapers from time to time condemned the General Assembly for enacting those laws. In December, 1897, Governor O'Ferrall advocated the emblem ballot and asked that the form of the ballot be published in the newspapers and posted at every polling place on the day of the election. In the same Assembly, a populist member introduced a bill allowing the illiterate voter to select the election judge he wished to prepare his ballot.

"This would mean of course," commented the Richmond correspondent of the *Lynchburg News* about the latter bill, "that the Negro would be told to call on the Republican for such aid." The patron of the bill, the newspaper said, "seems to be satisfied with less than Governor O'Ferrall. His demands in the way of election reforms are far more moderate than Governor O'Ferrall's. It is hardly probable that the recommendations of either of these gentlemen will have much weight with the Democratic caucus when that body comes to consider the important question of changing a law which has given it the largest representation in the Legislature it ever had and elected by forty thousand, a Governor who is now dissatisfied with the operations of the present plan."

In a different spirit spoke the *Richmond Times* and with a far broader conception of what the growing power of a partisan machine was doing to emasculate the citizenry of the state and limit participation in her government. In 1894, it had published this warning:

In addition these causes of apathy which affect Democrats in all parts of the Union, the Virginia Democrats have the special cause of apathy that our State politics of the past few

years has developed. The people have seen an era of ring rule
and machine politics gradually grow up in the State under the
corrupting influence of money used in elections and cheating at
the polls, which has utterly disgusted and disheartened the
strong and active elements of the party. When they see their
party's authorities stuff ballot-boxes with false ballots, every
citizen asks himself: "Why should I vote? My vote will have no
influence upon the result. After all the voting is over, the
managers of the machine will put such and as many ballots
into the boxes as will be necessary to make the result of the
election what they desire it should be, and I had, therefore, just
as well have not voted as to have voted."

Now, in 1898, it had this to say:

The Times found out nearly four years ago to its amaze-
ment, that the public service in Virginia was falling into disre-
pute to an alarming degree and it raised its voice in solemn
warning to the people against what it said was coming on
them. Its warnings were unheeded and its counsels were
scoffed at. But even the most incredulous are now beginning to
see that *The Times* was justified in what it said and that something must be done to arrest the course of public decadence or
Virginia will become as badly debauched as some of her northern sisters have become.

The effectual measure for cutting the cancer out of the body
politic is to bring fraudulent elections to an end. That is the
fruitful source of all corruption. That is the noxious spring from
which all the poisoned waters flow. The man in office by fraudulent elections bends all his energies to corrupt everything that
he may stay in office by fraudulent elections. That is the point
to be attacked.

Futile, as the *Lynchburg News* had prophesied, proved all plans
for reform. The arraignment of more than one high-minded
Governor, the protests of many frank editorials and honest
Democrats and the repeated denouncements of Republican plat-
forms and speakers would be required to wrench from the machine
such slow and gradual reforms as have lifted Virginia's election
laws from the mire and stench of every conceivable dishonesty,
trickery, swap and corruption, to a plane where there is the

possibility of an honest count for those voters of both parties who can manage to run the gauntlet of still partisan registrars, three years of paid up poll taxes, inadequate voting facilities, secret ballots and such prejudice as yet adheres to the individual who espouses the minority party.

But we are back in the summer of 1898 when prejudice was rampant, when politics meant trickery, and when men averred that women could not risk the knowledge of, much less the participation in, "practical politics." The platform on which General Walker was nominated said: "We arraign the Democratic machine and the Democratic leaders in Virginia for corruption and fraud and for the most offensive partisanship. We denounce the election laws and election methods in the state as a disgrace to the state and a stigma of her people." It also endorsed the administration of President McKinley for having "caused our flag to be respected and feared throughout the world."

General Walker who had much to do with drafting this platform practically wrote this resolution:

We congratulate the people of the whole country that sectionalism is dead; that dead issues have been buried; that it has remained for a Republican executive to rise high above party politics; that a Federal-soldier-President, by conferring high rank in the army of the United States on such true and tried Confederate soldiers as Fitzhugh Lee, Wheeler, Fosser, Oats, Butler and others and by appointing hundreds of Southern men, irrespective of party, to positions in the army and navy, has shown his confidence in the loyalty and patriotism of American citizens of all sections and of all parties and has done more to unite the blue and the gray and bring together the people of our whole country than all other causes combined since 1865.

Ten days previous to the nomination, again by acclamation, of General Walker for re-election to Congress, Judge William F. Rhea had accepted nomination by the Democrats. As a lobbyist, Judge Rhea had been accused of crooked practices in connection with the contest between Fitzhugh Lee and Thomas L. Martin for election to the U.S. Senate, and an investigation had been ordered which was later hushed up. That Judge Rhea would take every possible advantage of the Walton law and the Virginia election machinery no one for a moment doubted. Their platform came out again for the free and unlimited coinage of both silver and gold at the existing ratio of sixteen to one, "without the aid and consent of any other nation;" for law tariff; and for the repeal of the ten per cent tax on state banks.

So great was the interest that a series of joint debates were arranged between the two candidates. The first of these was held September 8 at Lebanon, Russell County. The courtroom was packed with men only, about equally divided between the two parties. The discussion was opened by Judge Rhea with a virulent personal attack on General Walker's record—as a Democrat, as a silver man and now as a turncoat and a truckler in Congress to the enemies of his state and the South.

General Walker replied with dignity to the personal charges and with forceful presentation of the issues. He then turned his logic and sarcasm against Virginia's dishonest election laws and methods and ended his speech thus:

> If you will consent for the Republicans in each county in the district to select Republican judges of election for the precincts in the counties and will further consent for the Republican judges to mark the ballots of Republican voters when requested to do so, and I do not beat you two thousand votes in the district, I will agree to not accept the seat in Congress.

In Rhea's rejoinder he made no response to this challenge but continued his attack on Walker and the Republican party, appealing to prejudice against the Negroes and the Yankees, advocating free trade, free silver and the further solidification of the South against the machinations of the enemy. In closing, Walker put up to Rhea a second challenge: "Are you willing for the Republicans of the several counties of the Ninth Congressional District to select the Republicans who shall act as judges at the precincts in their counties and are you willing for the Republican judges of election to mark the ballots of Republican voters when requested to mark them?"

"That," answered Rhea, "is a matter for the electoral boards; I have nothing to do with it."

"I repeat the question," said Walker, again stating it.

Rhea rose, glared at Walker, and in effect answered, "The Democratic Party made the law, and I am in favor of Democrats administering it."

The audience was wrought up to fever heat by this time. Calls, cries, shouts, hisses came from the crowd, and only the presence of the sheriff who was on the platform prevented possibly a personal encounter between the rival candidates angrily facing each other.

There were three more joint debates—one at Gate City, one at Pulaski, and one at Marion. "The one at Pulaski," says Pendleton, "was so fierce and strong that the candidates were at times on the verge of violent encounter. Believing that it was the purpose of the Democrats to provoke General Walker to some act of violence so that they might kill him or do great bodily harm, his Republican friends insisted that there should be no more joint discussions." Both campaign managers had already reached that same conclusion. The letter sent me by my father October 22 from Mendota, Virginia, shows how keenly alive he was to the frauds which were being planned and how unafraid of the verdict of the people if it could be fairly counted.

Mendota
Saturday, 10:30 A.M.
October 22nd 1898

Dear Will:

I am here safe and sound. Will go to Big Stone Gap this P.M. and to Wise tomorrow. It is useless to give you an account of my journeying for the past week. You have seen accounts of the joint discussion at Marion Monday. From Democratic newspapers it appears I was used up again, but between us, I got the better of the discussion and my friends were highly pleased. In fact, they were jubilant. I spoke in Rye Valley Tuesday afternoon and had a good audience in spite of the rain. At night I spoke at Holston Mills to a fine audience. Wednesday at Sinclairs Bottom to a good crowd and at night at Chilhowie to a large and enthusiastic audience. Thursday at Olympia in the afternoon to a fair audience, and at night at Chatham Hill to a fine audience. Yesterday, Friday I spoke at Wallace's to a splendid audience, but as it was after four P.M. when I got through and pouring rain, I did not attempt to drive across the mountains ten miles to my appointment at Phelps. So I stayed all night in Bristol and came here on train this

morning. It is a gloomy, rainy day, and I do not suppose I will
have an audience, unless it fairs off by noon.

I spoke at three P.M. I am well and hearty and do not feel
the least fatigued. Now as to the outlook, I must say that it is
all right so far as the people are concerned, but each day fur-
nishes fresh evidence of the intention of the Rheaites to do all
manner of dirty work. You see they have brought out a Negro
candidate at last, but the Negroes will not vote for him and it
is not expected, however they will try to count them for him all
the same. You have also seen the letters published in the
Bristol News of yesterday. They too were intended to be secret
but some one gave them away. We have also gotten hold of the
names of the candidates for Congress to be printed on the
tickets in this district. There are four—viz: Rhea, Walker,
Watkins and Harris, the last two Negroes. Harris is a Pocahontas Negro whom the Democrats have hired to run, but who
Watkins is I have no idea. He is, I believe, a stoolpigeon,
brought out in order to confuse the voter in marking his ballot,
because his name when printed looks like mine: **WALKER :
WATKINS**.

The Democratic organization in Virginia is as corrupt as it
can be. I give you below my estimate as to the vote for me, and
the vote for Rhea, barring stupendous frauds:

Counties	Rhea	Walker
Craig	250	
Giles	425	
Bland	75	
Pulaski		200
Wythe		50
Smyth		100
Washington and Bristol		300
Scott		100
Lee	100	
Russell	100	
Wise		200
Dickenson	50	
Buchanan		50
Tazewell		600
	1000	1600

I will be home Sunday, the 30th, if no accident
befalls. Love to all the family.
Yours affectionately,
J. A. Walker

The official returns gave Rhea a majority of 744 votes. Tazewell
did even better for Walker than he had hoped, having a population
of fearless, intelligent citizens who could not be cheated. Rhea's own
county, Washington, the same sort of people as in Tazewell, were
unable to cut down Walker's majority to less than 384. But Scott
County, with a mountain population, many of whom were illiterate
though strongly Republican, gave Rhea a majority of 204.

Realizing that there had been glaring frauds, Walker immediately gave notice of a contest and began in his customary bold and
energetic fashion to collect evidence of fraud and collusion. Finding
that not even yet was Walker's courage daunted, Democratic papers
increased the virulence of their attacks on him. Frequently old
friends became cool and resentful in their attitude, and there was
a distinct atmosphere of disapproval of Walker's "stubborn disloyal-
ty to his native state" whenever he encountered groups of Democrats, old Confederates or fellow attorneys, either in business or
social mingling.

Meantime, Rhea and his backers plotted to play upon Walker's
well known aggressive, sensitive temperament and thus to make
him the apparent agent of his own destruction. As soon as the
taking of evidence began, a systematic course of side comments,
impertinent questions, sarcasm, taunts and all manner of attempts
to provoke Walker began. Now and again the defense was so
abusive of Walker's witnesses that he had to interpose with sharp
reproof and warning. On one such occasion Rhea drew a pistol, and
Walker, who was not armed, dared him to lay it down and fight it
out man to man, declaring he was able to whip Rhea with his one
good arm.

This incident was afterwards denied by Judge Rhea but
sustained by the witness in question, as well as by others who were
present. It is necessary to relate these regrettable and unpleasant
occurrences in order to elucidate the tragic event which happened
a few weeks later.

FORTY-TWO

Courtroom Shooting

One afternoon early in March, 1899, my father came to my room and handed me two letters. "Read them," he said.

One was from an acquaintance in Bristol, Virginia, urging General Walker to have someone else than he take the deposition in his contest case, set for the latter part of that week in Bristol. The acquaintance had been confidentially informed that a plot was brewing to get rid of Walker and that under cover of a general scrimmage growing out of the depositions Walker was to be shot. He begged Walker to stay away from Bristol and to turn over further taking of depositions to someone else.

The second letter was an anonymous one warning Walker not to go to Bristol, for he would be killed if he did. The plot to shoot him was laid, even to naming the man who was to use the gun. But if he would go, the warning said, by all means go armed. The writer was a Democrat, had voted for Rhea but was unwilling to see a brave man and an ex-Confederate killed because his politics were wrong. He hoped Walker would heed the warning, but whether he did or not the writer had cleared his own skirts.

"You won't go, of course, Papa?" I asserted, phrasing my assertion as a question.

"Won't go?" in tones surprised and indignant. "Of course I shall go. But I'll buy a pistol and keep it handy."

"Please don't go," I urged. "Any of your friends will take your place, and I believe there is some truth in what these letters suggest. Why risk your life? The contest isn't worth it."

"No, but my self-respect is. The writer of one of those letters I don't know very well, and he offers no proof. The other is anonymous, hence was written by a coward. Do you think I am to be frightened by such letters or put on the run by the threats of my enemies? Once they succeed in making me afraid to face them they have me at their mercy. No, I shall go to Bristol, act just as if these letters had never been received, and if attacked shall defend myself as best I can. We won't discuss the matter further."

The next day, Friday, General Walker went to Bristol. Naturally, I was anxious and nervous, but I did not tell my mother my fears.

Between five and six o'clock Sunday morning the door bell rang peremptorily.

"It is a telegram saying Papa has been shot," I said, as my husband threw on his dressing gown to hurry downstairs.

The wire read about like this:

General Walker badly wounded. No immediate danger. Come at once.

My husband caught the next train, and I followed that afternoon.

In a small, poorly ventilated room in one of Bristol's old hotels, on a bed that sagged uncomfortably in the middle, I found my father in a semi-coma. He seemed to me to be in a more serious condition than the telegram had indicated. He roused himself with an effort when I spoke to him, smiled, said that he was glad I had come, and that he'd be all right again in a few days. Then he dropped back into a stupor, which I knew later was partly the effect of great weakness and partly of sedatives.

His physician came presently and explained, in the hall, that the first bullet had severed an artery in the right breast, just under the collar bone, while the second had entered his right shoulder. The lucky formation of clotted blood was now closing the severed artery, from which there had been great danger of his bleeding to death, and if the patient could be kept very quiet for several days there was a good chance for his recovery. But it was imperative that he be kept very still. I was to watch closely, keep the room quiet and well ventilated, soothe him when he waked, but with as little talk as possible, and when he grew restless give him the sedative. Above all, he must not be allowed to excite himself or to toss his arms about. Visitors were best excluded for several days. He would have to be fed in a recumbent position as far as possible and water and medicine taken through a tube.

The facts of the shooting were told me next day by R. M. Calfee, my father's devoted friend and secretary, who was taking down the deposition the evening it occurred. These facts were later sworn to by Mr. Calfee in the courtroom, confirmed by A. R. Hickman, a friend of my father's who was present, and sustained by other evidence brought out in the trial.

Walker was acting as his own counsel. W. S. Hamilton was serving as counsel for Rhea. Hamilton was very drunk, grew maudlin, offensive and persisted in trying to browbeat Walker's witnesses. Walker showed irritation, warned Hamilton he must conduct his questioning more courteously and finally refused to go on with the depositions unless Mr. Rhea would secure some other counsel in place of that "damned drunkard and bully Hamilton." Hamilton, with an oath, started to rise from his chair, drew a knife from somewhere about his person, and lunged toward Walker declaring, "I'll cut your damned throat."

In an instant Walker drew the small derringer pistol he had borrowed and was carrying in his hip pocket and fired at Hamilton, who fell back in his chair. A second report rang out, this time from the group around Rhea, then a third. The pistol was seen in the hands of Rhea's secretary, George E. Davis. As the smoke cleared, Walker's friends caught him as he staggered, tore open his shirt and tried to staunch the blood from the wound in his breast. They then supported him between them to the street and the hotel, a short distance away, before calling a physician, named Dr. Vance.

Next day, Mr. Rhea's friends made a statement to the *Bristol Tribune* in which it was said that General Walker shot Hamilton and "took to flight with his friends R. M. Calfee and A. R. Hickman following in quick pursuit," a statement nullified by the one which came after: "During the great commotion and confusion that followed, two shots were fired by an unknown person and General Walker was wounded in the right shoulder and breast, both shots taking effect." If "in flight," he could hardly have received wounds in the breast and shoulder nor have fled very far with a severed artery spilling his life blood.

The newspaper interview went on to say that "The only other pistol that was seen in the room was in the hands of A. R. Hickman. Report and rumor has it that A. R. Hickman was the person who fired the shots that took effect in General Walker's shoulder." It added, however, "There is another rumor to the effect that George E. Davis did the shooting which inflicted the wounds on General Walker. So far as could be learned no one saw Davis with any pistol and Davis positively denies having any pistol or that he did any shooting."

It may be well to state here that it was afterwards proved that
Davis did fire the pistol which wounded Walker. He was tried in
the Bristol courts before a carefully chosen jury and acquitted on
the ground that in the confusion and excitement of a scrimmage, it
was difficult to fix blame and that no premeditation was shown.
General Walker did not prosecute.

For two weeks, Walker's condition remained critical and for still
another week he could not be taken home. During all this time
Bristol was seething with excitement, with partisan charges and
counter-charges, with rumors and whisperings. General Walker's
friends from all over the district came to see and watch over him.
They were still hearing threats that Walker would not be allowed
to leave Bristol alive, and night after night his friends watched his
room, one usually sitting in the hall just outside his door and
another at the foot of the steps in the lobby. Major Silas Walker
came from Mt. Meridian to take his turn with the watchers, and
among the score or more of stalwart Ninth District Republicans
who shared time as his guards were Mr. C. Lincoln of Marion, Mr.
Thomas Muncey of Bland, Messrs. Barnes and Gillespie of Tazewell, Judge McBroom and other prominent southwest Virginians.

One day, soon after the tragedy, my father was sleeping quietly,
and the volunteer guards for the day, my uncle and Mr. Calfee,
were at dinner. I was to go down later, when Mr. Calfee would take
my place. Suddenly there was a loud rap on the door. I opened it
cautiously and slipped into the hall, to face a huge policeman
waving a paper and affecting the look and manner of a stern
upholder of the law.

"I must serve this summons on General Walker in person," he
said.

"But he's asleep."

"Then I must wake him. The summons is important and must
be served immediately."

"But I have orders to keep him very quiet and dare not wake
him," I said. "Why can you not serve it later? And please speak
lower. General Walker must not be excited. His life depends on
keeping him quiet."

"This summons must be served before he leaves Bristol," the
policeman said. "We have no guarantee his friends will not spirit
him away. You must let me pass, madam." He reached around me
for the door knob.

Keeping between him and the door, I blazed at him in tones that were low but desperate: "If you enter my father's room, it will be over my dead body."

With a single contemptuous look which said plainer than words, "Who can contend against a woman and a fool at the same time?" he turned and tramped down the hall to the stairway. I watched him go, then slipped back into my father's room to find him sleeping so soundly that I dared allow myself the relief of a good cry.

I was still at it when Mr. Calfee came to relieve my watch. My account of the occurrence aroused red hot indignation among my father's friends and was one of the instigating causes of the still closer watch kept over him by his friends, until the day a dozen or more of them put him on the train which took him home.

He was yet weak from loss of blood, and his right hand was useless from paralysis of certain muscles, due to the second wound he had received in his shoulder. This made him practically helpless, as his left arm already was of little service because of his war wound. To have to be constantly waited upon, partly dressed by a body servant, his food cut up, books he read propped before him and all his letters and notes dictated, was most exceedingly irksome to a person of General Walker's independent, proud nature.

Characteristic too was the fight he made to regain the use of arm and hand. Persistently he exercised it, though every use of it was painful, making it serve him more and more each day. One of his exercises was to go through the motions of writing with a small broomstick—he could not close his fingers on anything smaller— hour after hour, while he read from a book propped on a table by his side, the pages of which he turned awkwardly with his left hand. A huge pen handle—as big as a small cane with a large pen in it—was given him, and by practice with this he learned in a few weeks to write legibly. After several months he got back entirely the use of his right arm, but his accustomed vigor did not return, and he aged rapidly, for the first time looking his sixty-eight years.

He had been arraigned, meanwhile, before a Bristol grand jury for malicious assault on W. S. Hamilton, and on July 3, 1899, the case came to trial.

Half a dozen of the most noted lawyers in that section of Virginia volunteered their services to assist the counsel employed by General Walker. Mr. Daniel Trigg of Abingdon and Captain J. H. Wood of Bristol, two prominent Democrats, were among them.

A change of venue had been denied Walker's counsel, and on the opening of the court a demand was made for a jury from another county. There was a determined effort made by the judge to refuse this demand, but the pressure of public opinion was so great he finally yielded. A jury was secured from Montgomery County, composed as it turned out of seven Democrats and two Populists.

Again, General Walker's friends rallied to his side. From all over the district they came, vigorous, upstanding men, the stronger in their Republican convictions by the fight they had constantly to make in order to keep them and ready to do anything necessary to prove their allegiance to their leader.

Each morning a procession of fine looking men, bred in the mountains of Virginia and as unafraid as they were stalwart, lined up in twos behind General Walker and marched with him to the courtroom. Some days there were twenty of them, some days not so many, for they came and went as their business allowed. But first and last, probably, a hundred of the most substantial men of that section of the state testified thus their loyalty to General Walker.

The judge sitting in the case was a strongly partisan Democrat and a personal friend of Judge Rhea. Again and again he ruled out testimony which would have proved a conspiracy to provoke Walker into some act of rashness and then to assassinate him.

Finally the defense got a witness on the stand who reluctantly, under oath, testified to a conversation with Hamilton, himself, in which Hamilton had freely revealed the plot to him. The witness testified that he had warned Hamilton not to do it, and afterwards had related the conversation to certain friends of Hamilton's.

For five days the jury heard evidence, interspersed with many a hot argument between opposing counsel as to the admission or exclusion of this or that testimony. The tension in the courtroom and town increased from day to day, and in order to bring the trial to an end as soon as possible it was decided to hold night sessions. Late Friday afternoon, the commonwealth concluded its rebuttal evidence. That night the instructions to the jury were argued. All day Saturday the lawyers argued the case, though each was limited as to time. Tenser and tenser became the suppressed excitement in the courtroom. I kept my self-control only by keeping watch on my father, who never for a moment lost cheerfulness and confidence and who now and then gave me a reassuring smile.

Argument was concluded at eight o'clock Saturday evening and the case given to the jury. Now and then I stole a glance at the clock while friends crowded around reassuring my father. There was hardly any occasion to do so, for in twenty-five minutes time the jury room door opened and the jury filed back into the bar.

"Not guilty," the foreman answered to the judge's question.

Spontaneous applause swelled from the courtroom, which the judge sternly rebuked.

In a few dignified words, General Walker thanked the jury, then was so pressed upon by congratulating friends that he was forced to hold an informal reception. Later, after he had returned to the hotel lobby, it resolved itself into a spontaneous ovation of speeches, cheers, and some tears. "I would rather have such manifestations of friendship and esteem as is being shown General Walker tonight," commented Mr. Trigg, Walker's leading counsel, "than to have a seat in Congress."

For the rest of the summer General Walker was practically an invalid, though he did not admit it. Intending to resume actively the practice of law, he had built a six-room law office on a lot on Main Street which he had owned since the boom. The three lower rooms he planned to use for his own firm, renting the upper floor.

Meantime, he worked hard on his contest of the election results, in collaboration with his attorneys Dudley & Michener of Washington. The evidence showed that all sorts of fraud had been used to give Rhea a majority in the Ninth district, such as doctoring poll books, the interchange of ballots by means of "sack coat pocket trick," the use of ballots impossible of proper marking by one who did not read rapidly and easily; by the confusion resulting from the printing of the name of the supposed candidate Watkins on the ballots; by voting dead men and men who had moved out of the state, through the use of disguised repeaters; and by various other means. Among the prearranged plans for fraud certain instructions from Democratic leaders to constables were discovered. These "instructions" said in effect, When an illiterate voter asks you to mark his ballot, say: "Of course I will, and you can trust me to mark it right for you." Naturally every good Democrat knows the *right* way for a ballot to be marked in this election, which lets you out of any fraud on the voter.

The contestee's brief attempted to prove that Walker was very unpopular in his district and that leading Republicans were opposed to him, giving the names of several who were either disappointed office seekers or machine Republicans.

Congress adjourned without a report from that section of the Elections Committee which was hearing the case of Walker vs. Rhea. It was rumored that the committee was divided, that there would be a minority report, and that federal patronage had been promised to those "prominent Republicans" who had gone over to Rhea during the election and given testimony in the contest to the effect that Walker had become unpopular in his own party. In each instance these were men who had a grudge against Walker, either because they had not been recommended by him to some office they had sought or for other personal reasons.

Finally, more than a year later, on January 30, 1901, the committee made its report. The majority report was to the effect that though gross irregularities and frauds had been proven, they were hardly enough to account for the majority of over seven hundred votes given the contestee by the official count. The minority report strongly advocated seating Walker and denounced Virginia election laws and practices.

General Walker surprised everyone by the philosophical way he accepted the verdict of Congress. Within a few days he ceased to refer to it and turned his entire attention to other matters. He had long discounted the result, knowing the forces of treachery working against him.

FORTY-THREE

Last Battles

General Walker was now making the fight of his life. It was a fight calling for more courage than storming Culp's Hill in face of the enemy's well posted artillery, or in leading the last offensive movement of the remnant of the Army of Northern Virginia in the grey dawn of a raw spring morning against Federal redoubts and big guns at Petersburg.

For this last conflict was a daily trial of his spirit, a daily strain upon his resolution to fight on and either to snatch final victory from repeated defeats, or to die fighting. It was a struggle against physical weakness and nerve depletion following two severe wounds; it was a battle against financial demands heavier than his resources could be stretched to meet; it was a daily encounter of the spirit with an atmosphere of coolness and dislike among certain of his fellow lawyers, judges before whom he must argue his cases, and some of his neighbors who did not admire his political course and were glad to believe the whispers being circulated as to his overbearing manner, his high temper, and his growing unpopularity with "leaders" of his own party. Besides all this he was going through personal experiences, well calculated to embitter him and break his spirit.

One who knew and understood him therefore watched in anxious admiration his fresh attack on life's difficulties each morning, when he would start the day with cheerful, optimistic spirit, and with an aching heart as he came home in the evening exhausted physically, quiet and bitter of mood. But this was not always the case, for his fighting mood included all the diversion his spirit allowed. The hospitality for which "Walker Hall" was famous was to an extent resumed, and as soon as he was strong enough he bought a riding horse, named it "Wild Bill" and rode almost daily, frequently giving his young grandchildren a turn on the pommel of his saddle.

On June 19th, McKinley and Roosevelt were nominated at Philadelphia on a construction platform endorsing protective tariff, a gold standard, the annexation of the Hawaiian Islands, the Peace Conference at the Hague, an Isthmus Canal and the extension of rural free delivery. It so pleased Walker and the Republicans of the Ninth District that the leaders were able to persuade him to allow his name to go before the district convention once more. The renomination of W. F. Rhea by the Democrats settled the matter, and on August first Walker was nominated again as the Republican candidate for Congress with enthusiasm at Wise Court House by the largest district Republican convention ever assembled—about two thousand persons being jammed into the courtroom.

Three months of a political contest followed, still bitterer than the previous one between Rhea and Walker. There were however no public debates between the two candidates. Walker and his friends stressed the appeal made by the presidential candidate and the platform of the Republican Party and exposed some of the frauds which had been committed in the previous election in the Ninth District.

As naturally follows where there is a jealously guarded one-party system, with all the officials, all the newspapers and a large proportion of the representative people on one side, there was but little chance of getting these facts before the people except those already Republicans. For a Democrat to attend a Republican speaking or meeting was branded as disloyal and discreditable. For a newspaper to publish Republican statements—except as paid advertisements, at regular rates—was to risk a loss of business, with criticism and odium thrown in. Therefore Walker could only hope to strengthen and consolidate Republicans, and an occasional convert was truly an achievement. Though Republican by a narrow margin, the Ninth District, being a mountainous section with a considerable percent of scattered and illiterate vote, offered an inviting field for political trickery as well as a subtle form of bribery. In this election the main reliance of the managers of Rhea's campaign was in the ballots used.

In several of the counties, those most likely to give Walker a majority, these ballots were so involved and confusing as to make the proper marking of them possible for the well educated only and difficult even for them in the time allowed. Republican newspapers in Virginia published copies of the Scott County ballot for President of the United States and Congress, showing long lists of names and identifying information about some forty candidates and electors, all of it run together without punctuation or proper capitalization in more than one hundred lines of type, a ballot that the voter was allowed two and a half minutes to mark. A newspaper in Pearisburg, Virginia (a Democratic newspaper supporting Rhea), said: "If what the Republican newspapers in the state have been publishing recently is really a true copy of the ballot used in Scott County, we unqualifiedly condemn its use at the polls as an outrage, despicable and indefensible."

Again General Walker was counted out as a matter of course, and again within a few days he gave notice of a contest. This time he meant to base his contest on the ballots alone, leaving out all other instances of fraud, which were numerous. "We must keep up the fight," he said. "at whatever personal cost, till we secure honest election laws and political freedom for the citizens of Virginia. It is unthinkable that the Mother of States and statesmen should throw away her proud heritage and become the political property of an office-holding oligarchy."

Among the evidences of these frauds was the surprising fact that McKinley and Roosevelt rolled up a majority of 1,504 in the Ninth District while Walker was counted out by a majority of 1,751 votes. "Walker's unpopularity," said the Democrats—in face of the three weeks' demonstration and Mr. Trigg's tribute at the Bristol trial, and the largely enthusiastic convention which had nominated him in the last campaign.

Walker quickly got over the loss. During the summer of 1901, he seemed to be again enjoying a measure of serenity and satisfaction in life, delighting especially in the shade of his porches, the charm of lawn and flowers, the development of his grandchildren, and in gathering about him, after his life long habit, small groups of old friends to sip a mint julep, tell anecdotes and exchange reminiscences.

It was on such an occasion, the afternoon of June 22nd, 1901, that he formally presented to his grandson namesake, James A. Caldwell, who had been born and had lived in his home, one of his most prized possessions, his sword, the one he had captured from a Federal colonel at Winchester in the first battle in which he led the Stonewall Brigade. Little James had begged to be given the

sword many times, and Walker presented him with the coveted
trophy at the home, along with a brief speech.

In telling his grandson about the sword, he also gave one of his
last accounts of his fighting in the Civil War, and like his lifetime
the story was filled with action. It was only fitting that he told of
his first adventure as commander of his beloved Stonewall Brigade.
He told his grandson, according to a published report of the
presentation from the *South West Virginia Enterprise:*

My dear Boy: I present to you the sword carried by me in
the Civil War. It was once the sword of Colonel Wilson of the
123rd Ohio Volunteer Infantry and was presented to him by
the officers of his regiment, as will appear from the inscription
on it, and fell into my hands in the manner I will now relate.

In June, 1863, the Army of Northern Virginia commanded
by General Robert E. Lee broke up its camp near Fredericksburg, Virginia, and began its famous Gettysburg campaign. The
Second Corps of the army commanded by Lieutenant General
Richard S. Ewell was in advance and when near Winchester
encountered the Federal troops commanded by Major General
R. H. Milroy. After some considerable skirmishing which lasted
an entire day, General Milroy retired into his fortifications and
fought behind his breastworks. Late in the afternoon of the
second day, he was assaulted, and his strongest works were
carried by our troops. During the night, General Milroy, abandoning his artillery and his baggage and destroying his stores,
attempted to retreat by the main turnpike road leading from
Winchester across the Potomac River.

General Ewell, anticipating this movement, ordered Johnson's division early in the night to make a forced march by a
circuitous route around by Jordan's Springs and striking the
turnpike at or near Stevenson Depot cut off Milroy's retreat.
The Stonewall Brigade, which I then had the honor to command, formed a part of Johnson's division and on that march
was the rear brigade of the column. We marched all night at a
lively gait, and just at dawn as the head of the brigade was
passing Jordan's Springs, about mile from the turnpike on
which the enemy was retreating, we heard the sharp report of
musket shots fired in quick succession. These shots came from
the leading brigade of Johnson's division which struck the head

of Milroy's column as it reached Stevenson, and the fight began.

Both sides formed rapidly in the line of battle and in a short time the roar of cannon and the crash of musketry informed my men that the battle had begun. At the familiar sound the men of the Stonewall Brigade closed up the ranks and at the word of command moved forward at "double quick." We were soon in line of battle on the right of the division and advancing through a dense fog encountered the enemy and drove him back for half a mile when he hoisted a white flag in token of surrender.

I at once rode forward with my staff and met Colonel Eley of Connecticut who surrendered his command. We captured over eight hundred prisoners with their arms and accoutrements and six regimental flags. Among the officers captured was Colonel Wilson of the 123rd Ohio, who surrendered this sword to me.

It was then new and bright and was a beautiful weapon. It is now rusty and shows marks of hard usage. I carried it for two eventful years in sunshine and storm, in victory and defeat. I wore it in the battles of Gettysburg, Mine Run, Payne's Farm, Bristoe Station, Wilderness, Spottsylvania Court House, Hare's Hill, Petersburg, Farmville, Sayler's Creek and in many more combats and skirmishes. I marched hundreds of miles with it buckled around me and slept on the ground many nights with it lying by my side. It was buckled around me on the morning of the twelfth of May, 1864, at the Bloody Angle at Spottsylvania Court House when I received the Minie ball in my left arm which rendered necessary the resection of the elbow joint. It was in my hand on the ninth of April, 1865, at Appomattox, where my command (Early's division) was driving Sheridan's cavalry before it, when the white flag was raised by order of General Lee, and the Civil War was over.

This was more than thirty-six years ago and the old sword has lain ever since idle, neglected, and almost forgotten. I am now sixty-eight years old, and can never again draw it in defense of my country or the cause of my people. Therefore, my dear boy, I resign it to your care and keeping because you bear my name, and because I believe you will grow up to be a brave and good man, worthy to wear the sword once worn by your grandfather as commander of the immortal Stonewall Brigade.

Lay it carefully away and preserve it, but I charge you to remember that war is a dreadful evil, and that your voice and your influence be ever for peace. But if the time shall ever come in your history when peace can no longer be preserved with honor, then be "no laggard in the fray," but draw your sword in defense of right and justice; wield it like a brave knight and true, until peace is restored, and then return it to its scabbard untarnished and unstained by word or by deed unbecoming a Christian hero. God bless you my boy, and spare you to a useful and happy life!

FORTY-FOUR

The Sun Sets

News of the shooting of President McKinley on September 6th at Buffalo by an anarchist threw the country into wild excitement. Bulletins from the president's bedside grew steadily more discouraging until September fourteenth when announcement of his death was flashed on the wires. "Possibly he was not a great statesman," says William Stan Meyers in his history of the Republican party, "but assuredly he was a great politician, using that much abused word, only in the best sense of the term. His death came at the height of his power and success and he left behind him a record of great achievement. With him may be said to have ended the last vestiges of real civil war politics. A new era dawned and with it had come a man to lead the people in a new direction, but with the hand of a master."

Though he had admired President McKinley, General Walker had never felt that McKinley understood the South, especially that he did not realize the true inwardness of the struggle being made to found in the South a representative Republican Party as the basis of a two-party system and the restoration of the South to her lawful share in the government of a reunited country. In Theodore Roosevelt he believed the new South would find a new interpreter, for Roosevelt was national rather than sectarian in spirit and had spent months in Kentucky and weeks in Abingdon, near Wytheville, gathering material for his "Winning of the West." He understood the problems of the South and liked her people. And although Walker may not have put the idea in concrete form even in his own mind, he must have realized, as others did, that between Theodore Roosevelt and himself there was a marked kinship of spirit. I know he felt that he would be understood by this great leader of his party, that the integrity of his purpose recognized, his course vindicated.

That premonition was verified when early in October before
Roosevelt had been a month in the White House Walker received
from him a gracious letter, requesting him to come to Washington
to confer on southern affairs as soon as a date could be arranged in
November, and suggesting that he would be glad to have General
Walker lunch with him. The letter greatly pleased my father who
immediately ordered from his Richmond tailor a Prince Albert suit
of black broadcloth.

Grapes were ripe at Walker Hall, grapes in variety and
abundance, especially big and luscious bunches this fall. A huge
platter of them, freshly gathered, was on the table in the sitting
room that afternoon, a few days after he had received the President's letter, when General Walker came home from his office.

Sitting down by the table with an exclamation of admiration for
their rich beauty and flavor, he ate very heartily of the grapes
before mounting his horse for his usual canter. That night he had
an attack of diarrhea, but next morning he went to his office. He
came home early in the afternoon and went to bed.

Next morning, we took the matter into our own hands and sent
for his physician, Dr. C. W. Gleaves. The bowel trouble did not yield
to treatment, and within a few days flux developed. Two other
physicians were called in consultation. Son, brother and sister were
telegraphed for, his condition admittedly being very grave, though
the predetermining cause was yet deemed obscure.

"If General Walker had the vigor which was his two years ago,
before he was wounded," said one of the physicians, "he would pull
through, but his vitality is low, he has been living on his nerve. I
am frankly apprehensive."

Meantime, the sick man chafed at his weakness. He could not
realize that he must be lifted up, turned over, by Edmund, the
family hostler and gardener for some years, who was devoted to the
general. At the end of two weeks, General Walker was delirious and
sinking rapidly. One of his physicians was almost constantly at his
bedside, but they allowed only one member of the family at a time
in his room. He called often for the children in his delirium,
especially for "the boy," asking frequently why they didn't come in
to see him.

I happened to be alone by his bedside late in the afternoon of
October nineteenth when he woke from a stupor, reached feebly for
my hand and fixing deep set eyes on my face spoke quite naturally
and with a strength and firmness of tone which surprised me.

"Will," he said, "help me to get up. I'm tired lying here."

"You are not strong enough, Papa. You've been so ill."

"Yes, I know, but I'll be stronger once I get up from this bed. It saps all my strength and will."

"Dr. Gleaves will be here in a few moments, Papa. I'll ask him to help me take you up."

"The sun is setting, daughter. I can't wait. Once more I want to stand by the window there and watch the sun set. Help me to get up, Will. I want to stand on my feet again, and die like a man, and a soldier."

Sobbing and desperate, I leaned over to put my arms under his shoulders to see if I could at least lift him up a little on his pillows and satisfy him. But even as I did, his eyes closed, his body relaxed, and he sank into unconsciousness. He did not speak again.

As I sat by his bed holding his hand through the night, while family and physicians sat or stood around, two or three times I whispered in his ear: "Papa, do you know me, Papa? Is it all right?" The faintest pressure of his hand would answer, and an effort at a smile would tremble about his lips. Thus he went to sleep in that hour of early dawn when so often the dread sister of the three fates clips the thin worn thread of mortal life.

A few days before his going he had told me he knew he must die and he wanted me to know he was not afraid.

"Nor am I afraid for you, dear Papa," I said. "Are you not a child of the Covenant? Have not countless prayers gone up for you, and are not you yourself a believer in Christ Jesus?"

"Yes," he answered simply, "but you must have lots of faith, daughter. I haven't been much of a Christian—professing or otherwise."

He was dressed in the suit in which he had intended to have lunch with President Roosevelt and lay for two days on a couch-like casket embowered in flowers, in the front parlor at Walker Hall. Hundreds of townsmen and friends from all over the district passed by his bier to drop a tear or a sigh. There were scores of blacks who stopped on their way in or out of the room to relate to some member of the family how the general had helped them when they were in trouble, or how he had sent them food when they were sick, or a load of wood in a bitter winter. There were many old Confederates who had nothing but good to say of him now—tales of his gallantry, comradeship, generosity to needy ex-Confederates, and members of the bar who said that one of the ablest lawyers in the

state was gone. One neighbor who had fought him politically
stopped now by his silent form and said involuntarily, "He looks
like a statesman taking his rest, or a gallant warrior in repose. He
reminds me of Valentine's statue of Lee."

One of the most cherished tributes came from an officer of the
Stonewall Brigade, Major Leathers of Louisville, Kentucky, who
wrote he did not believe "the famous Stonewall Brigade ever had a
more able commander than General James A. Walker."

Stonewall Jackson, Major Leathers wrote, as the first commander and founder of the Brigade, was "one of the greatest names upon
the pages of American history" and "his genius as a great soldier
naturally overshadows the other names connected with that
Brigade." Then he wrote:

All the commanders of the Stonewall Brigade were great
soldiers but I say none greater than your lamented and distinguished father. The supreme test of a commanding general is
the confidence the men he commands repose in him, their
belief in his ability, their confidence in his courage, his inspiring presence as a leader in battle—these are the tests by which
a soldier—a common soldier—the boys in the trenches—weigh
their commander. General Walker had all these qualities in a
degree equal to any general who commanded the Stonewall
Brigade, or any other brigade, and well he vindicated, on all
occasions, this confidence of his men.

There were two elements combined in making the later
reputation of the Stonewall Brigade as the most daring and
dependable brigade in the Army of Northern Virginia. The
Brigade had in General Walker a leader, and General Walker
had men to lead who would follow him anywhere. Moreover, he
always led and never followed. His magnificent appearance in
battle was an inspiring picture. A superb horseman, a man of
magnificent physique and handsome appearance, he was an
ideal commander.

One of the soldiers of the Duke of Wellington said at the
Battle of Waterloo, "The Duke is worth a thousand men, simply
to look at him," and so I believe it may have been said of General James A. Walker. His superb and courageous bearing on
the field of battle, his splendid conduct in trying times, was
worth a thousand men just to see.

This is a simple tribute from one who served in an humble capacity in the Second Regiment of the old Stonewall Brigade, one who, when he looks back over the past and recalls the brave deeds of that splendid body of men and its superb commanders, can recall none who holds a deeper place in his love and affectionate regard than his dear old commander, General James A. Walker.

The Tazewell *Republican* ends thus its account of the funeral:

On Tuesday afternoon the funeral service of the old Confederate hero was held in the Presbyterian Church at Wytheville, conducted by the pastor, Rev. Hall.

The Confederate veterans of the William Terry Camp followed immediately behind the pallbearers. The procession was said to be the largest ever seen in Wytheville. When it came to Main Street from the church the pupils of the public school—four hundred in number—stood with heads uncovered on each side of the street while the procession passed. All the stores and business houses in the town were closed for two hours in honor of the distinguished dead.

The burial took place at the East End Cemetery, and the body of the gallant old soldier now lies beside his two sons, James and Frank.

Bibliographic Note

Though I have given my authorities, here and there, throughout this narrative, I have not always done so. Hence I wish to make this special acknowledgment of the sources to which I am indebted for my historic facts and the connecting links which fasten together the original material in my possession:

Confederate Military History, especially *Volume III,* by Major Jed Hotchkiss

McCabe's *Life of Lee*

From Manassas to Appomattox by Longstreet

Life of Jackson by Dabney

Life of Jefferson Davis by Mrs. Davis

Four Years with General Lee by Walter H. Taylor

The War Between the States by Alexander Stephens

Official Records of the Rebellion published by the U.S. Government

Destruction and Reconstruction by Richard Taylor

The Army of Virginia by George H. Gordon

Twenty Years in Congress by James G. Blaine

John Sherman's *Recollections*

Meet General Grant by Woodward

Political History of South-West Virginia by Pendleton

History of the Republican Party by William Stair Myers

Index